THE RISE AND FALL OF
CAPTAIN
METHANE

Autobiography of a Maverick

DAWingo
5-14-2018

THE RISE AND FALL OF
CAPTAIN
METHANE

Dorcey Alan Wingo

author of Wind Loggers

Outskirts Press, Inc.
Denver, Colorado

The Rise and Fall of Captain Methane
Autobiography of a Maverick
All Rights Reserved.
Copyright © 2010 Dorcey Alan Wingo
v7.0 r2.0

Cover Photo © 2010 JupiterImages Corporation. All rights reserved - used with permission.

Outskirts Press, Inc.
http://www.outskirtspress.com

ISBN PB: 978-1-4327-4828-9
ISBN HB: 978-1-4327-4518-9

Outskirts Press and the "OP" logo are trademarks belonging to Outskirts Press, Inc.

PRINTED IN THE UNITED STATES OF AMERICA

Stories previously published:

"Bad Boys" – Vietnam Helicopter Pilots Association Website – Spring 2007
"El Papazzo" – _HelicopterMonthly.Com_ – November 2006
"Flying the Panamints" – The Panamint Breeze – June 2007
"If You Can't Stand the Heat" – Autorotate Magazine - April 2007
"Lorena Bites the Loader" – _HelicopterMonthly.com_ – Aug/Sep 2006
"My Purple Heart" – _HelicopterMonthly.com_ – June 2006
"Philthy Phil" – _HelicopterMonthly.com_ - October, 2006
"The Beam or the Bike" – Vertical – Aug/Sep 2007
"The Velcro Lizard" – The Panamint Breeze – March, 2007
"Lightning Fire at Flooter Rock" – Autorotate Magazine - January 2008

Contents

Introduction xi

Section I: The Sundown Kid **1**
A Shoeshine Boy and the Methane Connection 3
Leaving Home...25
The Tape 29
A Hole in the Wall 33
Section II: From Jungle Warrior to Burger Flipper **41**
Bad Boys 43
My Purple Heart 49
The Elephant Brander 53
Burger Flipper Redux 57
Section III: La Torre de Paz **67**
Adventures Recalled 69
Back in the Saddle 71
New Horizons 77
Puerto Amelia 87
If You Can't Stand the Heat... 91
Cargo We'd Rather Not Haul 97
El Papazzo and La Torre de Paz...101
Wildlife in the Jungle 107
Losing One's Load 111
Giving Notice 117
Going Against the Flow 121

Section IV: South of the Border **133**

El Gringo Wingo de Chilpancingo.....................................135

The Forbidden Fruit of Tierra Blanca 145

Como Se Llama Creek 157

Section V: A Southern California Operation **163**

Flying the Panamints..165

The Beam or the Bike?...169

Stringing the Center Phase 173

Section VI: See Hollywood from the Air **181**

On Camera, Off Camera 183

The Twilight Zone 197

A Movie Pilot Drops By...235

Section VII: All in a Day's Work **241**

A Little Help from "Hose B" 243

Comes a Lineman 247

Picking Up the Pieces..251

Lightning Fire at Flooter Rock 255

Section VIII: So You Want to Be a Heli-Logger?.........................**261**

The Velcro Lizard...263

Too Close to the Trough..267

Hook Riders Anonymous...271

Within Reach of the Hose..281

More Collective Pitch, Scotty! 285

Neener Nena, Tough as Nails 289

On Getting Fired..297

The Line 307

Lorena Bites the Loader...313

Section IX: Old Friends, Pain, and Closure **319**

In Memoriam..321

Flash Sikorsky 323

Philthy Phil 335

On Losing Face...347

Pedo Heights 359

Photo and Illustration Credits

Title	Photographer/Artist	Date	Page
The Author on his Yamaha	Blanche Wingo	1965	23
The Author in Vietnam	Warren Finch	1969	56
Sun Oil H&P Heli-rig No. 9	Dick Izold	1975	109
Vertical Magazine cartoon	Chris Rohrmoser	2007	171
UH-1H Accident Scene	Kelly Cannon	1997	283
The Wilkins on their Harley	Brian Wilkins	2004	296
UH-1H Accident Scene	US Forest Service	2004	315

Introduction

It all started with "America the Beautiful."

It was a beautiful California summer morning and we were airborne, somewhere above the rugged San Jacinto Mountains east of Hemet, and southwest of Palm Springs. There had been some storm activity in the area and the cumulus clouds provided a wonderful contrast against the brilliant blue skies and the rugged rocky terrain several thousand feet below us.

I was in the right front seat of a venerable Hughes [MD] 500D and Dorcey Wingo was at the controls just a few feet to my left. The 500D is not the most comfortable ship in the world, but veteran mountain pilots swear by them, and the view from the front seat is extraordinary. Add an old stick like Dorcey Wingo in the driver's seat and it's quite a ride.

Now, I'm not a pilot, but I've done enough helicopter work in my career as a TV news cameraman to know the difference between cyclic and collective, and I noticed the cyclic being pulled back ever so lightly. We were slowly climbing. Just ahead were two very compact and separate clouds, separated by what appeared to be a space of a few hundred feet.

"Gosh, but it would be great to fly right between those clouds," I thought.

Hmmm…. banking slightly to the right. I wouldn't dare suggest it, lest I be accused of a rotary-wing version of backseat driving, but it appeared Mr. Wingo and I were on the same page.

My soundman partner – Tom Morris – was seated directly behind Wingo. I couldn't see him but I knew he sensed that things were going to get interesting. Next to him, veteran Los Angeles reporter Bob Banfield was reading the paper, oblivious to it all (try reading anything – in flight over the mountains – in the backseat of a 500 and you'll understand Mr. Banfield has, among other talents, a cast-iron stomach.)

We seemed to be on course to fly over the tops of these almost dream-like clouds, when, as if on cue, the cyclic moved a few millimeters, the helicopter banked slightly to the left and started a steep bank between the clouds.

If a Disney imagineer had been sitting in my place, it was the kind of moment that would have inspired a new thrill ride for the Magic Kingdom. Spielberg would have incorporated the same kind of scene into an Indiana Jones chase sequence.

The exhilarating moment was matched only by the sheer beauty of the scene. The term "Kodak moment" hadn't been invented yet, but "E-tickets" at Disneyland were the only things that could bring you close to what I felt in the front seat. And even Hertz could not put you near this driver's seat.

I was speechless.

Then it sort of happened……naturally.

"Oh beautiful, for spacious skies, for amber waves of grain.." came over our David Clark headsets. The guy couldn't sing and the whine of the Allison engine didn't add much to the fidelity, and there was a distinctive Oklahoma twang to the "waaaves of graaaain…."

It was perfect music for the moment, provided at no extra charge by the pilot.

For more than two decades since that flight, I've shared many moments with Dorcey Wingo, and my flight time with him is just a fraction of the hours that he has logged.

Somewhere in perhaps a hundred filing cabinets there are page upon page containing maintenance logs, Hobbs meter readings, countless notations of takeoffs and landings, all containing the initials DAW for authenticity. And on a bookshelf in Rialto, there is a collection of logbooks with the Wingo signature, noting hours flown, places visited, and jobs accomplished.

Logbooks and Hobbs meters tell you a lot about where flights started and ended, but there's very little official record of what really happened.

As I learned that morning coming over the San Jacintos, it's those minutes in between start and stop times that are priceless – the gift to modern civilization from the Wright Brothers and Igor Sikorsky.

There are thousands, maybe millions of books and articles about flying. Most will bore the reader to tears. Thankfully, a few pilots came along who stayed awake in English class and later, noticed more about the flying life than just the mechanics of flight. Ernest K. Gann, Len Morgan, Gordon Baxter, John Nance and a few others became the poet laureates of aviation journalism, regaling us in books and magazines about the loneliness of night flying, the challenge of flying airliners when the industry was young, machismo, getting the wits scared out of you, and almost as an afterthought, the sheer beauty that happens when men who defy gravity pause for a moment to take it all in.

Add Dorcey Wingo to the list of aviators who see the big picture. In his writing, Mr. Wingo tells frightening tales of life in the air and on the ground: war, peace, near misses, hapless co-workers, awful living conditions, lousy food, cheating bosses, exotic locales, and the sheer beauty of flying, and getting paid for it.

And yes, there are stories of death – many of them. This is fun work, but it is also dangerous, and many of the subjects of his tales are not around to see Mr. Wingo's work in print.

If this were the 1800's and there were no helicopters, I am certain Dorcey Wingo and a few of his helicopter pilot brethren would be cowpokes, riding the range, cheating death, staying one step ahead of the bankers, ex-girlfriends, the law, and who-knows-who-else.

At night, sitting around the fire in the middle of nowhere, with the horses rested and a bottle of cheap whiskey at the ready, Wingo would be the storyteller.

So don't read this book and say "Jeez, this guy missed his calling, he should have been a writer."

Thankfully, Dorcey is a writer, a great one. And a career of flying helicopters happened to provide him with an endless supply of material!

Watch out for the tail rotor. Don't slam the door. Keep seat belts fastened and enjoy the flight.....

And the occasional singing.

David R. Busse
Diamond Bar, CA

Section I:
The Sundown Kid

A Shoeshine Boy and the Methane Connection

My friends call me "Dorce," as in "horse." Either that or "Dorky Bingo," which should be said with a smile. A man doesn't have much control over what his mother names him or what his friends nickname him, nor his skin color or the DNA that defines him so precisely. With the possible exception of plastic surgery, he's stuck with his looks, for better or worse. That's just the way it is. You play the cards you're dealt, amigo. The rest is up to the grace of God, gravity, and luck.

The youngest of four children, I grew up in a southern-fried, Christian family. Blanche Beulah Burch and James Beauford Wingo (everybody called him "J.B.") headed the household; both came from large Oklahoma farming families, Christians all. On the poor side, mostly—but hardworking and proud. And every Sunday morning, Sunday evening, and Wednesday evening, we marched off to church. It was simply impossible to overdose on the Church of Christ!

If you dropped in on the congregation, you'd notice right off that they sang from traditional songbooks, but without an organ or piano accompaniment. "Music comes from the heart," we heard frequently. The Church adhered to the scriptures that pointed to the early separation from Catholicism. And that goes double for "no dancing!" All that rubbin' up and down, up close, leads to sin! There'd be no sinnin' 'round Blanche and J.B. [Does the movie *Footloose* come to mind?]

Blanche's parents came to settle their family of twelve in tiny Springer, Oklahoma, near the turn of the twentieth century. These gentle souls lived in the time of the "great" Oklahoma Dust Bowl, which would un-gentle and ruin many good families before it was finally over. In speaking of those days, with the grandchildren gathered on the front porch, Grandma Burch spoke haltingly…softly…*proudly,* and she always gave credit "to the good Lord Jesus" for seeing them through the terrible times.

J.B.'s father died of *consumption* soon after The Great War[1] ended; at least that's what we were told as children. Migrating west from the Carolinas, Grandpa Wingo's dream was to have a dairy herd. Within a dozen years, out of money and faced with a failing farm, he just gave up one day. Inexplicably, he took one last walk out to the woodshed, where he had left his rifle.

It was there that he shot himself in the chest. Narrowly missing his heart, the wound was nonetheless mortal. Six long agonizing days later, he left his grieving widow with nine children to raise. Blanche shocked me with this revelation when I was over forty years old, on the way to visit J.B.'s grave near Hennepin. Nobody keeps a secret like Blanche.

After Grandpa's suicide, J.B. fell under the charge of his older siblings. Corporal punishment was the rule of the day, and according to oral history, Dad used to get a whipping every morning "because he'd need one before the day was over," his siblings insisted. They did things their way, with little outside interference.

No stranger to hard work and sacrifice, J.B. knew what pickin' cotton and dairy farmin' was all about, from the bottom up. Despite the hardships, he managed to pay his way through college, working at a dairy *"for seventeen cents an hour,"* a wage we kids heard plenty about over the years.

J.B. rode a Harley-Davidson before he and Blanche got hitched. I saw what looked like a Service Cycle once in an old black and white photo from 1930. A college writing club decorated his macho machine as a float in a local parade, virtually hidden under an enlarged, eloquent black feather quill (sponsored by *The Pen and Quill Club*, the inscription read). Dad looked quite striking as he posed for the photo, one of the few of J.B. with hair. No smile, though. He wasn't exactly a *smiler,* I'd discover soon enough.

---

1   World War One

In 1931, Dad graduated from Texas State Teachers College with a degree in Industrial Arts. Mother's credentials were in Elementary Education; a born teacher if ever there was one. Blanche married J.B. soon after, and began teaching right away in Springer's single-room schoolhouse. Some of her younger sisters and brothers were among her first students.

In a time of reflection, my mother would characterize her marriage to J.B. as one of "economic necessity," a term that dismissed the very idea of romance, but may have typified the prevailing paranoia of college graduates in the Depression-stressed America of the early 1930s.

Dad initially worked as a labor manager in the CCC movement, one of President FDR's *New Deal* programs to put people to work. He was in charge of uniformed platoons of young American men who otherwise would have been on welfare. J.B. helped to keep 'em busy clearing roads, building bridges, and conserving the nation's natural resources.

I recall seeing Dad's old extreme-wide-angle, official CCC photos of the time, scores of men seated and standing stiffly for formal photos. Hardly anyone ever smiled in these photos, especially Dad, I noticed. Serious stuff, being a leader.

Before long, my father was pulling Blanche around in a small trailer; her teaching skills were put aside while baby sons James Warren and Jon Lance came into the world. Joy arrived during WWII, my big sister. We learned from Blanche, in a rare weak moment, that James and Jon were *planned*. My sister and I—well, we *happened*.

Cue my month-premature birth in Duncan, Oklahoma, November of 1946: Mom was horrified when the nurse brought me for my first meal, after weighing, measuring, and cleaning me up. Blanche insisted there had been a mix-up and sent me back: I was too lizard-like and pitiful to be her child, premature or not. Dad finally appeared and was sent to fetch *her baby*. He dutifully returned with my wrinkly-assed whining self, and the rest is family history.

In moments of reflection, I debate whether an unplanned child or two, in hard times, is enough to push people over the edge. It looked that way to me, as I was raised under the firm belief in corporal punishment. As a young kid, I was forced to select which belt I was going to *get it* with. My brothers and sister, too. We all got a taste of terror.

Dad's hands were disturbing to look at. Rough as a professional cornhusker's, they could delicately guide a virgin piece of cherry wood through a band saw, perfectly duplicating a French curve. But as a young carpenter, he had smashed three fingertips so badly the nails never grew back. It was an Old Carpenter's Lament, *"Don't look at your finger when you swing the hammer!"* But Dad had a lot of hammerin' to do to keep us in the pink; he dealt with the pain.

"Grin and bear it," he'd say. "'Cause there's always some *honyocker*[2] waitin' to take your place." It made him tough, and he expected us to appreciate that pain won't kill you—and it shouldn't slow a grown man down. Just part of life. And being the figure of a man he perceived himself to be, he required a ton of respect. We had to call our elders "Sir" and "Ma'am," starting at home. That was one lesson that didn't hurt at all.

We skipped from Longmont, Colorado (then just a tiny settlement) to Plainview, Texas before moving on to tiny Sundown, Texas, in 1953. "Population 1292," the sign said, but everyone knew there were fewer, and slowly shrinking. One blinking red light marked the intersection of Highways 301 and 303, which headed toward Whiteface, Levelland, and the big city of Lubbock, forty-eight miles away. Buddy Holly country!

Sundown city limit—circa 2003.

Something we noticed right off, there were *tons* of Air Force planes in our local sky, courtesy of nearby Reese Air Force Base. Before the town came to be, the Air Force used Sundown as a practice bombing range! Along with the family dog, "Timmy," my buddies and I dug up practice bombs around the teacher's quarters. We kept the bombs a secret from the adults, who would just blow the whistle and ruin all our fun. It was way

2   Old Montana mining term for a transient, chicken thief, etc.

out here in the middle of nowhere that I started looking to the sky, and dreaming about becoming a pilot.

Once an oil boomtown, the Sundown Independent School District had built a fine brick school, grades one through twelve. Big on athletics, they flocked to a football stadium across the street from our cottage with the intimidating name "Slaughter Field."

Both Mom and Dad signed on as Sundown schoolteachers for a little over $300 per month. We lived where all the teachers lived, on "Teacher's Row," a short walk from the schoolhouse.

Two small bedrooms weren't enough for our family of six, plus our faithful collie-shepherd, and a cat or two. No problem for a family raised in trailers, however! Dad just pulled our boxy forty-foot trailer up alongside the cottage and *presto!* We're home!

My brothers got the trailer all to themselves, while Joy and I shared a bedroom for what seemed like forever. Eventually, the district added single bedrooms to the cottages to keep their teachers happy. Few educators wanted to teach in Sundown, but at the time, it paid well.

I was happy to be in school. My first-grade teacher, Mrs. Mooney, was already Blanche's friend. Mom would visit me—on occasion—from her nearby fourth-grade class. She doted on her little first grader, calling me "Dar-cey Dar-lin'" loud enough for the whole world to hear, her Okie nasal twang making it all the worse. I took more ribbing about my new nickname than you'd ever believe. It was no bowl of cherries being a "Dorcey" in a world of Butches, Dubbs, Dougs, Johns, Jimmies, and Joes.

Then there was the double jeopardy. The school district supported corporal punishment as well. So if we got a paddling in school (I'm raising my hand, here[3]) we'd get it again when we got home, "for embarrassing the family."

Early in life I learned that my father would come *unglued* if I answered him with a simple question like, "What do you *mean*?" He would start shaking like a pressure cooker full of beans about to blow up! Then he'd show his teeth, making a fearsome, seething face, and come at me. "You don't understand!" he would growl, correcting my impertinent phraseology, shaking me hard, and leaving me in an emotional heap.

3   Unauthorized playing in the snow during recess. Guilty as charged.

Mom almost never took part in the *discipline*. Sometimes, witness to the violence and wailing, she would cry. But the Good Book was clear, "spare the rod and spoil the child," so she let J.B. handle the violent side of parenting. I was surprised to learn later in bible study the accompanying biblical passage, "Fathers make not thy children to hate thee." Because that's where I ended up, almost to the bitter end.

Living on the South Plains of Texas demands that you tolerate tornadoes and "Northers." In those days, weather forecasting was laughable compared to the meteorological technology of the 21st century, but we all became believers when the city's *twister* siren sounded its mournful wailing.

Having no storm cellar, we'd leave our dry cottage in pajamas and robes to dash through the shrieking wind and pelting hail for Miss English's root cellar. There we would huddle in the dank, earthy-smelling hole, feeling safe but intimidated by fury unlimited above us.

Miraculously, no twisters hit Sundown during that span, but the tortuous process of listening for a siren and running through lightning flashes in the dark scared a few years off all of us.

The first time I saw a Norther, I thought it was **The End**! A massive black and red wall of dirt, hundreds of feet high, came upon us from the north in broad daylight. It seemed to approach in slow motion, but all too soon it would come crashing down on our little town, blinding anyone caught out in the open. After a good hard blow, it would take days to rid the house of that red Hockley County dust. Looking back, I don't miss the tornadoes or the Northers, not one iota.

Somewhere in the midst of all the storms and strife, I managed to land a shoeshine job at one of the two barbershops in town, "Tommy's." Mr. Ivy had come to town a few years back, bringing with him a wife and daughter. He was stricken by polio as a child, leaving his right leg weak and withered. Withered or not, Tommy would strap on a heavy leg brace in the morning and cut hair all day long if he had to—which wasn't all that often.

The little barbershop had the standard barber's spinning red and blue spiral hanging outside its window. Tommy's shop featured two big orange upholstered chairs, but in tiny Sundown, he really only needed one. Like most barbershops of the day, there was an old-fashioned shoeshine stand in the back of the shop.

Tommy provided all the shoe polish and stuff. I had to compete for the job with another ten-year-old who could shine 'em 'bout like me, but he couldn't *pop* his shine rag as loud as I could—so I got the job! I collected a quarter for shining a pair of shoes, plus one whole dollar for mopping the barbershop floor come Saturday evening.

When times were slow (and they frequently were) Tommy would crank up the volume knob on the big old Motorola AM radio standing against the north wall. Why, as flat as it was for miles around, we'd get country music from Lubbock like nobody's business! Tommy Ivy and the Shoeshine Kid heard it from *Hank* and *Gene*, *Woody* and *Charlie*, *Loretta* and *Patsy* all day long. I wasn't always happy with that, but the tuner knobs did not move for the shoeshine boy.

Tommy loved to horseplay, too. He'd sneak up and grab me and park my lightweight butt horizontally on the customer's chairs. Then he'd sit on my middle until I farted. He'd laugh like a kid when he mashed one out. He sometimes had to bounce a couple of times to get something going. Entertainment came cheap in Hockley County Texas, folks—which is *dry. Booze* leads to *sin!* And shoeshine boys grow up with enlarged colons, rippling with muscles[4] and an abundance of gas. (Little did I know, one day they would call me *Captain Methane!*)

On a rare day off from school and Tommy's, I would get permission to go shootin'. I'd whistle for Timmy to come a-runnin' for one of our famous long hikes—usually taking my single-shot BB rifle along. Not knowing any better, I plinked at the usual targets: English sparrows, old bottles, beer cans, and large black flying wasps. Timmy liked to pounce on horned toads and lizards, and there were lots of 'em. We heartlessly wiped out a herd of 'em in the 1950s. Back then, I thought it was no big deal to shoot 'em dead!

When I discovered some fancy hard liquor bottles tossed into the bushes around the schoolyard, I began wondering where a drinker could buy <u>whiskey in Hock</u>ley County. When I asked Barber Tommy, he kinda looked

---

4   To this end I hide my secret ability around noisy machinery: helicopters, motorcycle races, bowling alleys, etc.

the other way, ducked his head down to my eye level, and said with a wry look in his eye, "This might be a one-horse-town, but there's more than one *bootlegger* around!"

The best thing about Tommy's Barbershop stood only six feet from my shoeshine stand: our very own (leased) old-style 5¢ Coca-Cola machine, loaded to the gills with short, thick green bottles full of ice-cold "belly wash," as J.B. called it...and two large, clear glass jars on top of the machine, loaded with Planter's Roasted Peanuts—a nickel a bag. Yummy!

I'd wait for our first customer to roll on in to Tommy's, and if he halfway smiled at me, I'd talk him to *death* until he finally agreed to a shoeshine. Or a boot shine—fifty cents, please—and I'd get 'em seated in the box, center their shoes on the iron boot rests, and commence to do my thing.

First I'd buff 'em down real good with the starter brush, then comes the sole dressing dye, applied carefully with a truly ancient toothbrush. Wipe that down good with a black rag, two or three light coats of this or that color of Kiwi or Shinola shoe wax, my clean shine rag a'poppin' to ol' Charlie Pride and gettin' nothin' on them white sox, neither. "Yes, sir," I'd say, "and how does that look, sir?" holding out my right hand. Tips were okay with me, too, but tips were rare in Sundown.

With my newfound wealth, I'd stride right on over to that big red *thing of beauty* and drop my nickel in the slot and crank the lever down hard to the right, releasing the bottom-most Coke bottle into the opening. Using the machine's gooey bottle cap opener, I'd slowly pry off the cap to avoid triggering a rush of carbon dioxide bubbles. Then I'd carefully take a sip or two before pouring half the peanuts into the foaming cold Coke. Looking back on it, there's little wonder I had so much gas in those days!

Dad learned from Tommy once that I left one Saturday afternoon early without mopping the floor. (Tired from being sat on all day?) And before I knew what hit me, there my father was. I thought he was going to kill me. He got right in my face and yelled, "Never shirk your duties! Never!" Dad felt obliged, somehow, to terrify me over a dollar. *My* dollar, no less!

In a couple of years I had shined enough shoes to pay cash for a nice, new, full-sized Western Flyer bicycle with twin "D" cell headlights, with the help of Mom's "good grades bonus," that is—one dollar for each "A" on our report cards. The bonus kept me motivated, making almost straight A's through seventh grade. She figured I'd go to college and be another teacher. I wasn't so sure 'bout college, but I sure loved that Western Flyer!

I'd ride my new bike as often as I could, day or night. I'd get permission to take off, and I'd burn rubber. A trick we bored small-town kids employed to liven things up was to clamp stiff pieces of cardboard onto the front and rear bicycle forks. The spokes would strike the cardstock and make loud flapping noises as we pedaled down the sidewalks and back streets! We imagined that we were riding Harleys, right out of a *Hell's Angels* movie!

(We also learned that all this nonsense was *hell* on bicycle spokes, as our thundering wheels were soon wobbling side to side! We were quickly reduced to something resembling a parade of bicycling clowns, until we learned to "true" the spokes ourselves.)

In the summer, I'd ride to Sundown's lone municipal swimming pool and dive and swim until I resembled my former wrinkled baby-self. In the evenings, I'd chase the DDT wagon around town, riding in its foggy wake, diggin' the way my twin light beams cut through the dangerous oily mist. (Come to think of it, it might not be a good idea to donate my liver, once I'm done with it!)

Things at home were not so carefree. By age twelve, the traditional goodnight kiss and hug for Dad were a thing of the past. At bedtime, with selective contempt in my heart, Mom would get her kiss. But I would avert eye contact with Dad and silently make my way around his outstretched recliner, never knowing when he would make his move.

More than once, he followed me back to my room and closed the door behind him. He would proceed to stick his face in mine and start growling. He would launch into another lecture about this and that and go *on* and *on*, but I was beyond listening by then. I just waited it out, hating every moment.

By that stage in my development, I loathed his face, his bald head, his coffee and tobacco breath, his very *self*. Nothing I could ever do would make him happy. As James and Jon grew up and went off to college, his focus narrowed to Joy and me. The *accidents*.

I saw my very first live helicopter in Sundown, and I remember it all too well. It was Armed Forces Day, and our elementary class was allowed to view a real live H-21 landing on the practice football field!

The big helicopter was supposed to land and shut down, but our faithful dog Timmy had other ideas! As the loud, strange *flying banana* approached, Timmy ran the half-mile straight from our cottage. Before the pilots could put the rubber tires down on the grassy field, Timmy—transmogrifying into *the Hound From Hell*—arrived and began jumping high into the air, trying to bite the frustrated crew chief positioned in the open doorway!

My little collie-shepherd jumped again and again, biting at the tires as the pilot made several attempts to land, and much to my embarrassment, the tandem-rotor Piasecki slowly climbed back into the blue Texas sky and flew back to Lubbock. We came *that close* to getting a royal tour of a real live helicopter, and *that* had to happen! Of course, I was singled out as the culprit, seeing as how it was my dog. *"Darcey-Darlin', Darcey-Darlin'"* came the chant, ad nauseum.

Sundown's lone drugstore carried a few plastic airplanes and jet fighter model kits, and I eventually assembled most of them. You'd find an F-102 here and a Rockwell Shrike there in my room, a JN4 *Jenny* biplane yonder. Then one day a Hiller OH-23 model helicopter appeared on the top shelf. My eyeballs almost popped out! I couldn't wait to glue it together, which I did in Dad's woodshop at the high school that afternoon.

Carefully pressing the cool, clear plastic bubble onto the cabin floor, I could finally appreciate where the pilot and a lucky passenger would sit and enjoy a magic carpet ride! This little plaything began fueling my fantasies; my life almost seemed pointless until that day, when Stanley Hiller's technology and my imagination came to the rescue.

1959 turned out to be Dad's last year of teaching. His blood pressure was alleged to be the problem, but it was also no secret that he was *fed up* with high school students and wanted to start a small business in New Mexico. Adding to the stew, there was a rumor that something had happened in the woodshop. It started with a prank, pulled off by one of the football jocks.

After woodshop class one spring afternoon, some goofball squirted a whole bottle of Elmer's glue into Dad's office door skeleton keyhole. They filled the keyhole up with glue, taped it shut, and left quietly.

The next morning, J.B. Wingo was *not* impressed. Dad wasn't a hair over five feet and nine inches tall and of medium build, but he wasn't intimidated by "a bunch of young *honyockers*," neither!

It must've run his blood pressure right off the scale, because he called all the jocks together and—after they failed to provide him with the culprit's identity—he lined 'em up. Yessir, Dad lined up the Sundown Texas Class A "Roughnecks" football team (and a few geeks, too, probably) and swatted every one of 'em with his bad-ass woodshop paddle. It was a stout hardwood maple affair; a two-hander with holes drilled in the honyocker end of things. I was already familiar with that paddle. Class dismissed!

This activity made a certain twelve-year-old underclassman (last name Wingo) in the tiny town of Sundown wish he was *invisible* when the word got out. Bullies from eighth grade and up were soon lining up to take out their wrath on *my* skinny little butt. And that was the end of Dad's teaching career, one way or another.

So, after finishing up my seventh year of school, we loaded up our new 1960 Dodge Dart station wagon and pulled the heck *out* of Sundown. The forty-foot trailer we moved in with was liquidated; a relic of our past. Las Cruces, New Mexico, lay on the horizon, a long day's drive west over the high plains and colorful living deserts.

We almost lost Dad the same night we moved to Las Cruces. Unbeknownst to him, he ruptured an old hernia while moving in the furniture. Going to bed that night, he endured a lot of pain until early the next morning, when his suffering woke everyone up.

Dad had become delirious, whereupon Jon and Mom got up and hauled him off to the hospital's emergency room. The ER promptly wheeled him in. The surgeon on duty reported that his patient had gangrene, and "almost didn't make it."

Our father was home a week later, pale and shaky, but with a new outlook on life. Dad believed that the Lord had saved him, and he got more religious. (He was still mean to *me*, but *he* was goin' to heaven!)

Mom would resume her teaching of elementary children at a school in Las Cruces that fall. Meanwhile, she and Dad signed a six-month lease on a small grocery store with a residence on north Main Street. In comparison, our new home was roomy, built attached to the store. We all helped run the small grocery/deli business from morning to evening, slicing meats and ringing up sales.

The owner of the trailer court and the deli was alleged to be a multi-millionaire who worked six days a week and dressed like a migrant worker. He was an interesting fellow, always busy; his dilapidated work truck looked like it rolled right out of a Steinbeck novel. He had no interest in running the store, but he regularly had his hand out for the lease money it created.

James had just finished his degree in theology at Abilene Christian College and married Dolly. My oldest brother was soon a practicing preacher for a small Church of Christ somewhere in the vast interior of Texas. Dolly gave him two babies, then, during hard times, she left. Ran off with the local dentist and took the kids, too, we heard. Afterward, Mom harped on the fact that the Burches didn't get *divorced*; it wasn't the *Christian* thing to do. I think Mom was hurt worse than James over his break-up, a family first.

Jon's a genius, it turns out. He got Mom's keen wit. "Juan," as he was also known, was a perfectionist who, before he went off to college, broke his little brother's heart by setting fire to his prized soapbox derby racer, the *other* thing that his little brother had fallen in love with. He did so *for my safety* he told Mother afterward. *Aaargghh!*

Jon Lance Wingo would spit-shine his leather ROTC boots until they gleamed like a mirror. In his free time he would painstakingly assemble beautiful balsa wood fabric-winged model planes and sailboats—which I could "never-ever" touch! In these days, we were six long years apart. Living in close proximity to Jon would take quite a while to master.

Jon had a couple of years in at Texas A & M[5] and was packing to rejoin us in Las Cruces. There he'd attend New Mexico State, another A & M

5   College of Agriculture and Mechanical Arts created by the Morrill Act of 1862.

university. Big on ROTC, Jon was determined to earn a commission and become an Air Force jet pilot! The Cold War was coming of age and Ho Chi Minh was on the rise.

Turns out, our little grocery store was a loser. The competition in town was keen. Around Las Cruces, a new style of convenience store was pulling in the shoppers: the local *Pic Quik* chain. Looking over the books, it was clear that the folks would have to give the store up.

After a long search, we said good-bye to city life and moved a whopping seven miles south of town. The folks bought a small, three-bedroom house on one acre near the Rio Grande. It came with a healthy stand of peach trees, and a great view of the Organ Mountains, thirty miles or so off to the east.

All around our little acre was Robert M. Mayfield's spread, over a thousand acres of tall cotton and alfalfa, flat and green. Irrigated by the Rio Grande, this was some of the richest farming country to be had. The Mayfields had a big ranch house about a half mile to the south by a private dirt road.

In many ways, the little place was marvelous. Along with the peach and cherry trees, there was a plethora of hawks, hummingbirds, mockingbirds, dove, quail, rabbits, and roadrunners.

I noted with great displeasure that there was a weeping willow growing near the pump shed. A willow switch was the weapon of choice for an angry father. We had grown up listening to the threat: "If I have to stop this car, I'm going to find a *willow* and cut off a big ol' *switch!*" And now this.

Joy and I were both quite crestfallen with the move way out to *the sticks*, a terrible situation for a couple of would-be sociable teenagers in a one-car family. Joy was a Las Cruces High School junior by then, well over a serious blood platelet disease and becoming quite pretty and curvaceous.

Jon soon bought a sharp-lookin' 1958 Chevrolet Biscayne by working at the county cotton gin. After school hours, he'd weigh the cotton trailers arriving and departing the busy gin. This was accomplished from inside a comfortable office, his engineering homework papers scattered here and there. A nice setup for a working college student.

My relationship with J.B. deteriorated as soon as we got unpacked, it seems. He had me doing more chores than I could imagine. I'd already learned to hate gardening in Sundown, and now J.B. was plowing up a whole half acre for corn, beans, peas, radishes, squash, okra, green beans, and watermelons. And fifty fruit trees!

My youth was a seething thing. There were times I thought I'd never survive it. I picked up the cigarette habit by age fifteen. In the face of authority, I became a rebel, and rebellion was repaid with whippings, and whippings led to beatings with green willow branches.

The folks were on to me about cigarettes, so I had to lie about smoking all the time, leading to more screaming and discipline. My siblings turned a blind eye to the violence, but it really played with Timmy's brain. Our poor confused dog ran around in circles, tail tucked and barking nervously during the beatings, not knowing who to protect or who to bite.

One school day morning after breakfast, J.B. said something that triggered my anger while I was washing the breakfast dishes. So sick of his abuse, I imagined my hands around his neck. I clenched the glass tumbler I was washing so hard that it shattered, cutting both of my hands.

I was in the tiny hallway bathroom washing the blood off when the old man came in swinging. He swore loudly at me for breaking the glass while he swung like a man possessed. The green willow branch broke three times before he beat me down to the wet linoleum floor. Then he threw the last piece at me and stormed out. Blanche appeared belatedly from her bedroom, pleading for her husband to stop.

It was war from then on. As the welts on my back bled into my shirt, I decided that that was the last time the old man would lay a hand on me. I endured a keen, seething hatred as J.B. drove me to school that same morning, thirty minutes later. I'd be arriving twenty minutes late. During the thirty-minute drive, not a word was exchanged, as he drove and I stared straight ahead. Alternately, I clenched my fists and my jaws, painfully realizing that I was capable of patricide.

When the dusty station wagon arrived curbside at Alameda Junior High, I got out in a fury, opened the Dodge Dart's passenger door as wide as it would go, and slammed it with all my might. The window didn't shatter, to my surprise, but the whole car shook. I stood there and waited for J.B. to climb out, my legs spread, ready to knock him down with a flying tackle. I wanted to smash his smeared-up bifocals into his snarling face, my heavy history book at the ready.

From where I stood, I couldn't see his face, but I so wanted him to try something, right here in front of the old school house. J.B. didn't say a word, and never touched his door handle. He drove slowly away.

Thereafter, I avoided the man whenever I could. The best way to do that was to jump on the old Puch moped that I picked up for $75 from some kid in town. He'd gotten into trouble and had to sell it; his mom made me a good offer. I had to plead for a week before the old man finally gave in, and before long, I had the wind in my hair and I was frequently *gone*. The little motorized bicycle got over sixty miles per gallon, and I drove it everywhere.

Bobby Mayfield[6] and I were about the same age, and we used to race around on the moped, taking turns to see who could lap our latest race course the fastest: from a standing start at Mayfield's tack shed, we'd tear off down the dirt farm road, the tiny two-stroke engine screaming like a chainsaw going nuclear.

Climbing up on the river levee, we'd duck down, putting our chins right over the handle bar to speed south along the Rio Grande levee road, the moped's two-stroke engine wound out like she would explode at any second, then braking hard at the last possible instant to turn left and drop down off the levee, pedaling hard as we accelerated eastbound on the downwind leg: a washboard road leading to Mrs. Lee's place.[7]

Emerging from billowing clouds of that fine Mesilla Valley river-bottom farm dirt, we'd dodge several big dusty potholes and swing north at the irrigation canal bridge, tearing on back to the tack shed. Bobby always beat me, I recall, 'cause he pedaled harder.

Bobby also had access to the horse herd, a 1950 International pickup, and a black '56 Ford pickup, which I got to drive on occasion. I learned real quick that the life of a rich kid was way different from how I was brought up!

6   Robert M. Mayfield's only son
7   Descended from Confederate General Robert E. Lee

When Bobby offered me my first taste of Mogan David blackberry wine that fateful New Year's Eve, 1962, I thought it was some kind of heavenly nectar. I sneaked another glass a little later while Bobby was involved talking on the phone to the young ladies who liked to call. The whole house started acting silly shortly after that, and before you could holler borrácho,[8] I was pickled like a cucumber.

Bobby was accustomed to me being a gentleman in his house, so he couldn't possibly imagine that I was secretly draining his father's bottle of wine. You can understand his disbelief after he heard the *crash*. While he ran to see what the heck, I had already wandered outside, stumbled around, and broken the waterlines off the maid's swamp cooler!

Maria was alone inside the one-room cottage, dressed in her nightgown. After I collided with her plumbing, she blew my cover, screaming Borrácho! Borrácho! a few times beyond what I thought was really necessary, as I thrashed around outside her window in the cold mud—tangled up in brittle copper water lines, frigid water spraying everywhere.

'Bout then the floodlights came on, which was very impressive out there in the middle of the starlit Mesilla Valley, so I wandered off into the dark to get a better look at all them pretty stars, and ZAP-ZAP-ZAP my star-gazing-while-drunk led me straight into the Mayfield's electric fence. I discovered that I could hang on to it and take it, jolt after jolt. J.B. can hurt a lot worse than this, I rationalized.

Suddenly Bobby was outside standing over me, and looking none too happy. He had something in his hands. He then reared back and dumped not one, but *two* large mop buckets of cold water on me as I fell back from the pulsing wires. Bobby was good enough to stand me up and point me in the direction of my distant abode, where a New Year's Party awaited a certain fifteen-year-old baby of the clan.

Bobby may have been secretly hoping that I'd fall in the deep irrigation ditch that took off north through the darkness toward the Wingos' one-acre *spread* and maybe break my stupid neck; the ditches were dry this time of the year.

It was scary-dark out, but my pickled green eyes soon adjusted to the starlight and—relying on my Indian instinct—I jogged quietly between the

8   Drunk guy!

dried Johnson grass clumps on one side of the irrigation bank and the starlight glinting off the barbed wire fence on t'other; *The Way of the Warrior*, by way of Mogan David.

As things became easier to see, I remember running a bit; getting the most out of being drunk for the first time, since I was *screwed*, anyway. Timmy heard me shuffling up the dirt road from the west pasture and barked his friendly "I know you" bark, trotting happily up to me as I stumbled the last hundred feet or so to the backyard.

Taking a break, I flopped down on the cold ground. Timmy licked my face as I giggled and squirmed under his tickling tongue. All this nonsense just delayed going into the house, which was half full of guests from the church, anyhow.

Darned if Bobby Mayfield wasn't back in my blurry field of view again! He had retraced my steps in the dark to make sure I made it home. He was bein' real nice, talking to me—but not mentioning anything about my throwing a valuable hand-carved alabaster sculpture inside the Mayfields' refined music room so hard that it shattered against the south wall, making a big-assed divot in the plastered adobe, next to a fine painting. As if I'd remember that.

Bobby finally suggested I sneak inside the house before I got discovered missing; maybe he could pass me off as having food poisoning from the tacos we ate or something. That excuse for my condition held up pretty well for about five seconds; then Blanche knew something was *up*.

I was sitting there on my bed trying my best to explain my condition to Mom when suddenly I jumped up and ran down the hall to the bathroom—flinging open the door with my left hand. All them tacos and that incriminating wine and Lord knows what else launched themselves outta my neck, straight into the bathroom's twin, red-hot electrical wall-heater elements. The jig was up.

Blanche got on the phone the next morning and really blasted the innocent Mayfields for "allowing a child to drink alcohol in their house."[9] Bobby and I had a very strained relationship after that, and I was grounded for-freakin'-ever.

That particular phone call didn't go over very well with our well-to-do

9   They weren't home at the time, but Blanche wasn't interested in the facts.

neighbors. Mr. Mayfield soon shipped his only son off to the distant New Mexico Military Institute in Roswell, where Robert quickly disappeared from my life—such as it was.

The abuse continued, refueled by my stupid *borracho* trick at the Mayfields. At that time in my life, I didn't have the courage to go over and apologize. Before he left for good, Bobby met me out by the blacktop on the levee road in his brand-new Oldsmobile and suggested I just let it be. He drove off smelling like a barbershop to his formal date in town while I walked back home alone, never to see Bobby G. Mayfield again.

I never heard Dad apologize for anything, either. His disciplinary tactics were simply not challenged. J.B. was the judge, the jury, and the executioner. How we kept from tearing each other to shreds, I'm not sure, but two years later, I almost blew it. It was shortly after Timmy died.

My old hunting dog stumbled into me one evening as I sat in the dark out back of the house, in the open doorway of Dad's makeshift furniture refinishing shop. I was talking to sultry Sheri Suggs on the telephone; the tone of our conversation went better with moonlight. Timmy ambled feebly past the big cling peach tree and bumped right into me. His weathered old nose brushed my bare arm; it felt cracked and dry. His coat was matted and dusty; the old dog bounced off me like a cold, hairy skeleton.

Ol' Timmy kept his head pointed straight ahead and wandered off into the far corner of the shop, collapsing thereabouts among the mahogany scraps. I heard him let out his last breath as Dad burst upon the scene with his blinding, big-assed flashlight, destroying my romantic interlude and bedeviling Timmy's transition to *Spirit Dog*.

I buried Timmy the next day, wrapped up in a white towel. I dug his grave deep, covering his body with large flat rocks to discourage any coyotes or wild dogs. Pounding a white wooden cross into the ground near where his body lay buried, I said my best prayer for an old friend. I had decided on the gravesite: overlooking the Rio Grande, where we used to chase rabbits together. I walked away from the deed with a lump in my throat big enough to stall the giant cotton pickers tilling Mr. Mayfield's withered fields.

Now I had to go it alone without my faithful Timmy for the first time since I could remember. The way things were going, I would have to maintain a healthy distance between my father and me. Marching band, Explorer Scouts, and the junior play were some of the excuses I came up with to keep a distance between the Old Man and me. I had advanced in Explorers to a Star Scout by then, but like the band, I wasn't there to compete for Eagle Scout or first chair. I just needed a little refuge from the storm.

My Explorer Scout buddies gathered on Saturdays in the summer to make homemade ice cream. We had financed a two-week excursion to the Seattle World's Fair in 1962 and were raising more cash for another summer trip to Washington DC, selling Christmas wreaths, tickets to enchilada dinners, and big buckets of homemade, hand-cranked ice cream.

But my activities with the Scouts conflicted with Dad's needs for his seventeen-year-old son's hands. His "Ace Furniture Shop" had lots of newly arrived furniture to strip, and the half-acre garden had many a row to hoe.

As far as paying for my labor? He'd throw his arms up in the air and wail, "You'll get *no inheritance* from *me* if I have to *pay you!*" After working for *seventeen cents an hour*, Dad threw a nickel around like the proverbial manhole cover.

On that trip to Seattle, I took with me a whole twenty dollars. The rest of the guys had at least sixty bucks for spending money, which made the Sundown Kid the designated *poor boy*. Twenty dollars was what Dad felt like paying me to strip and steel-wool the lacquer and varnish off of several old tables and chairs over a three-week period.

Reading the label on the caustic stripper, I was already high on the toxic vapors:

Danger. Avoid breathing *volatile fumes.* **Avoid** *contact with eyes and skin.* **Avoid** *prolonged exposure. Work in well-ventilated area, etc.* The watery stuff splattered easily. I was sick of getting burned by the acid-laced crap and its caustic mineral spirits wash. My fingers were cracked to the point that steel wool stuck to them like Velcro after I scrubbed the finish off a heavy table's ball-in-claw.

The long, hot days of summer along the Rio Grande were frequently lacking in the category of breezes, and the mercury in the shed often rose above 100° F. I spent most of the day crouched by the big floor fan, scraping wide bands of ugly old paint and varnish with a metal scraper, steel wool, and a toothbrush—listening to "Butch Boogerweed" on KGRT, the local (AM) rock and roll radio station.

Dad always seemed to have the next few days planned out for me, too. There were row upon row of green beans to pick, snap, and wash up for canning. Six rows of corn needed to be picked and shucked. The irrigation from last week had left the soil weed-filled, cracked, and hard-panned; it needed to be cultivated. A snarling, old-fashioned eight-horse rototiller awaited me for a long waltz through the rows of young fruit trees, exposing Johnson grass roots, something the old man also wanted pulled up by hand. No shortage of chores to be done around J.B.'s outfit.

It was around noon on an especially hot Saturday—that terrible day in July when I nearly lost it; I was seventeen. My moped was broken down, making my escapes all the more difficult. J.B. had me doing double-duty between the garden and the furniture shop. Miles away, my buddies churned cold, sweet homemade ice cream in the shade of Mike Sandell's front porch.

Thinking about what I was missing, I squatted in the shade, taking a breather from hand-cultivating with the fork-spade, when Dad wandered out of the house with his bent-up, sweat-stained straw hat on crooked, glaring through his dirty bifocals in my direction.

Knowing his perpetually critical disposition, I didn't want to hear any of his *guff* but damned if he didn't start in on me, calling me a *loafer*. I glared at him, and he threatened a right-handed swipe at me! Then he thought the better of it, I guess, but that was all I needed.

I got to my feet quickly, grabbed the muddy four-tined spade fork I'd been laboring with. I held the fork close to me, the steam building up under my eyes—threatening to blow my head clean off in a blind rage. J.B. acted like he didn't notice and turned around, walking back down the dirt path toward the house.

My dark brown hands gripped that thick wooden handle, and man, I was shaking! Gripping the antique tightly, I shook with a consuming red-hot murderous contempt as J.B. increased the distance between us. I so wanted to sprint after him, to chase him down and run my father through with the dirt-caked, polished steel tines—front or back didn't matter to me. I'd hit him with all my strength, and drive those cold iron spikes...

Thank God that I didn't. Maybe it was the sum total of all the God-fearin' sermons I had to sit through over the years, bolstered by the honorable codes of all my years with the Scouts, the Way of the Warrior, and the sobering realization that I'd never become a pilot with a murder rap.

And poor Blanche. Mom would never forgive me. I came so close that day. I ended the day's work right there and then, in dirt-strewn tears, once Dad reached the safety of the back door.

Dad knew he was losing control of me, and he made the mistake of jumping me one evening a few weeks later. My rebel mouth pushed him over the edge somehow, and he jumped me in the living room in front of Blanche and my sister.

I was kinda surprised that he would try to wrestle me down, and I had the upper hand soon enough. It was a shameful moment to overpower the old man that night. I got no pleasure from it. When Dad quit struggling, I loosened my grip, stood slowly, and helped him to his feet. His chest was heaving from the exertion; he said nothing. That was the last of that.

Leaving Home

My junior and senior years of high school were spent growing up under the threat of global thermo-nuclear war. Nikita Khruschev was a loathsome figure of a man on TV. His snarling promise, "We will bury you!" convinced me to start digging a bomb shelter in the backyard, wondering if I could *duck and cover* before the inevitable blinding flash seared my flesh.

The walls of my sandy shelter sloughed in when I got down to four feet, and Rio Grande water began to seep in. That's when I parked the shovel and J.B. started using the sizeable hole as a compost pit.

I sold my tired but trusty old moped to a *bracero's*[10] son one sunny day for twenty-five dollars and applied the cash toward a new Honda 150 twin-piston motorcycle down the highway in old El Paso. This buoyed my attitude considerably, having a lot more power and four gears to speed me on my way.

1964 was a very upsetting year. We were all still suffering over John Kennedy's horrible assassination in Dallas. Then Barry Goldwater lost the election to LBJ. A foreign country named *Vietnam* was appearing in the news more and more. And Cassius Clay knocked out big ol' Sonny Liston, just like he said he would.

---

10   Common term for a Mexican farm laborer of that era for one who uses his arms, or *brazos*.

On a personal level, my passionate junior year romance came and went. It was becoming apparent that some people *enjoy* breaking your heart. I hadn't *truly* learned that yet, but since I insisted on going back for more, another heartbreak was inevitable.

Jon became a second lieutenant in the Air Force and learned to fly jets, and Joy moved into a large old two-story house in Mesilla Park with a long-haired hippie art student from New Mexico State. They drove to Ciudad Juarez, Mexico, one night and got hitched. Mom was crushed.

I moved out from under my parents' roof not long after graduating from Las Cruces High School. Two old Bulldog friends—Jerry Savage and Mike Gallagher—soon formed a trio with me and rented a cheap apartment near the Las Cruces boxing arena. The crowded one-bedroom kitchenette cost fifty dollars a month split three ways—*cheap*, even for 1965!

While Jerry and Mike attended NMSU, I juggled two jobs day and night. During the day, the Western Auto store on Main Street hired me to uncrate and assemble bicycles and motorcycles. I'd also assist on the sales floor as needed. In the evenings, Jerry and I worked an eight-hour fry-cook shift at Neff's Topper Restaurant out on the truck bypass.

Jerry and I sometimes needed a car to haul his drum set, groceries, or large loads of empty Coke bottles around (which we sold for two cents apiece to buy gasoline). As luck would have it, we found a 1952 Ford station wagon sitting on Roark Chevrolet's car lot. It was advertised for sale at a hundred dollars, but we heard they were dying to get it off their property. We bought the bucket of bolts for fifty dollars—and what a great ol' rig it was, considering the investment.

As the first order of business, I installed a Citizen's Band radio in the old rig. I then painstakingly painted a flying stork on the driver's door: the stork was soaring majestically with a heavily loaded diaper in his bill. The graphic image was encircled by the hand-lettered: "*Savage Diaper Service – You Mess 'em, We Press 'em!*" (Thankfully, no one ever dropped off a bundle of diapers for us to clean!)

Mom was worried about me getting sent off to Vietnam, so she had a personal check hand-delivered to me to pay for my immediate enrollment at the university. Not wanting to disappoint her, I dutifully signed up for biology, math, and ROTC, a total of around 16 credits. Frankly, I felt lost back in academia—where I didn't want to be somehow, cooped up in crowded classrooms, plotting the curves of Xs and Ys and ancient, *useless stuff* that could probably wait awhile.

I kept getting letters in my mailbox from the Selective Service System, directing me to report for this thing or another—eventually for a physical examination. After a couple of long bus rides to the local Induction Center in El Paso, I found myself with a "1A" Draft Status, meaning I was a prime candidate to be involuntarily inducted into the military.

Cashing in two paychecks a week and living on the cheap, I scraped up enough *dinéro* to trade in my worn-out Honda for a new 250cc Yamaha Big Bear Scrambler. Mike Reynolds, an old high school pal, and I ran around on motorcycles in those days. He was extra-keen on his new 250cc Yamaha Catalina, so we teamed up for early morning rides down a vacant, brand-new Interstate 25 heading north out of town—side by side, taking it to the limit in the moonlight with our headlamps turned off.

One such morning we sipped hot coffee in a Las Cruces truck stop café after a cool ride. As the jukebox wailed, we admired our bikes parked under the lights. When the waitress came up with a hot refill, we noticed the tractor-trailer rig backing up—just missing Mike's Catalina, but running smack dab over my new Big Bear Scrambler!

I ran out the door screaming profanities to stop the driver, who hadn't seen the bikes in his mirror. The way I cussed that big fellow out, I was lucky he didn't punch me out, but he knew the score. With the tank smashed flat on one side and one wheel bent, the shine was rubbed off forever. I decided to strip it down and start dirt track racing the very next day!

The folks thought I was crazy and wouldn't sign my under-aged racing consent form, so I persuaded Harry Alejo's dad—a cool ol' guy in a wheelchair—to sign them for me!

Racing was in my blood, by then. I took an early interest in going fast and sideways around the big dirt ovals. It was right about then—January of 1966—that another official-looking letter came in the mail box; this one was from Lyndon B. Johnson, President of the United States of America: "Greetings," it began…

The Tape

*   Reel to Reel Hot Air

Looking back on the milestones of growing up, the Captain has sidestepped retelling at least one sordid tale of this particular era. Maybe it was the unmitigated embarrassment of *airing it all out*. There was a *tape recording* involved—not Richard Nixon's notorious missing eighteen minutes, but perhaps that's where this tape righteously should have gone—*missing!*

It was the sixties and the *transistor* had come of age. Practically overnight, audio equipment that used to be expensive and bulky become affordable and compact. I'm sure my mother's intentions were pure and educational in nature when she gave her teenage son a fine, new, battery-powered, reel-to-reel tape recorder for his sixteenth birthday. She probably figured I'd use it in my high school language studies or when playing the baritone horn—*Euphonium,* for all you classical music aficionados.

The tape recorder Mom gave me was made in Japan and was about the size of a metal lunch box. It came complete with two spinning reels, a robust speaker, and a high-fidelity plug-in microphone with an on-off switch. (Many "D" cell batteries not included.) Blanche recognized my fascination with *sound,* and that's how this all came to pass. Had she any idea what I would do with her gift, she would have had a cow right there on the spot.

When yours truly turned nineteen, I was living in Las Cruces in a cheap apartment near the boxing arena.

My roommates, recent Las Cruces High graduates Jerry Savage and Mike Gallagher, and I had collectively decided to move out of our respective parents' homes that summer. Mike was halfway toward his degree in political science at NMSU and worked after-hours balancing tires at an auto service shop. He had designs on the presidency.

Jerry was massaging a music scholarship with the NMSU Aggie Orchestra. Evenings and weekends, he and I worked at Neff's, flipping burgers, flirting with the carhops, and mopping the greasy floors. We earned enough cash to pay the rent, buy cigarettes, keep a hot motorcycle running, and an old '52 Ford Wagon gassed up. But only if we ate *on the cheap*.

Having lived in and around Las Cruces five years or so, I knew the local Mexican food was mighty tasty—and cheap, if you knew where to shop. My Yamaha Big Bear Scrambler and I frequently rumbled off toward Lucero Street where a great smelling roadside taco stand sold six bean and green chile burritos in a brown paper bag for a buck—the best deal in town! (These frijole time bombs had the usual pinto bean side effect, too!)

The tape originated from the following decadent scene: three tired, drowsy, bachelor burrito biters occupy three rumpled bunks in a dank, dark, one-roomed kitchenette. The paper wrappers from twelve volatile bean and green chile burritos have been littering the floor between the beds for over an hour.

Slumber is elusive! Crickets chirp, inside and out. Blankets stir. A tape recorder is clicked on. The tiny DC light from the recorder's "Vu" meter gives away the perpetrator. The perpetrator records a fart. He rewinds and plays it back. It is twice as funny over the speaker! Muffled laughter emerges from amid feather-stuffed pillows, prompting another playback.

We regarded the first one a *keeper*. Our illustrious baritone player proceeded to record another, straining for the upper registers. Silly giggles followed, giving away our three participants, who wished to remain anonymous. Belches were also recorded, the inevitable gastronomic backfire. Sleep was ignored. The microphone was passed. The baritone player motorcycled for more burritos as a new soloist grabbed the microphone.

Auditions were aired. Critics made their pitches. Matches were struck. Votes were taken, deletions and edits were common. When one's methane reservoir ran low, short rambling speeches were substituted, belching in idiotic tongues—inappropriately punctuated by gaseous outbursts in the background from Captain Methane and company.

(Note: If God was watching over us at this point in our lives, he more than likely had one Mighty Finger on the *Go Straight to Hell* button.)

Our frijole diets and impromptu duets didn't change much over the weeks ahead, and soon our illustrious trio had a truly inspirational collection, "Echoes of Burritos Long Gone." When we reached the end of our *thirty-minute* tape, we realized we truly had something!

By then, it was apparent even to my talented burrito brothers that I was indeed captain in the methane department, though the competition would gladly blow me off my pedestal should I falter or should fame ever go to my head. I bore the title with a degree of pride, figuring it was probably the first time on record that anyone had blown more hot air than an Aggie political science major!

Sadly, the story doesn't end here.

There was this milkman who lived in the adjoining apartment. He had a wife and a perennial screaming baby. Now, we had nothing against babies or milkmen, mind you. This couple's baby and the milkman's four o'clock in the morning tromping out the door seven-days-a-week routine had cost our tuckered trio plenty of shuteye. But, being the *gentlemen we were*, we never made an issue of it.

So you might understand how we felt one night when *somebody* in the milkman's kitchenette interrupted a good laugh we were having by banging rudely on the thin wall separating Unit 2 from Unit 3, allegedly to make us pipe down! The milkman no less!

The Burrito Brothers were not amused by such rudeness, especially when the wall got thumped a second time because we apparently didn't get *quiet* enough, *quick* enough. So we discussed the appropriate response quietly among us, and took corrective action.

You need to understand that there was a closet in the common wall involved here. We had a door access to the closet, they didn't. Being bachelors, there wasn't much in the closet, so it made an ideal echo chamber for devious teenagers with axes to grind.

After installing four fresh D-cells into the recorder, I loaded the celebrated fart tape on the left reel and threaded the lead through the playing head and back up to the take-up reel. I clicked the switch on, and as the tape started rolling slowly toward Classic Fart Number One of hundreds, I twisted the volume knob to *Max*...

As Mike held the closet door open, I set the tape recorder at pillow level on a shelf along the opposing wall and backed slowly away. Mike closed the door softly behind us as the unabated flaaaapping and fraaaapping began to *peeeeel the paaaaint offff the waaaalls*. The Burrito Brothers slipped out for twenty-five minutes and let the tape work its magic.

Sure enough, when we got back, there were no lights on next door and there was no more thumping on our walls, ever again!

And Lo! It wasn't much longer after that that my draft notice showed up from the Doña Ana County Draft Board, which beat goin' straight to *hell* by quite a margin, I reckon.

A Hole in the Wall

---

*   A **Blattella** by any other name is still a cockroach.

One thing becomes increasingly clear to me when I ponder my worldly adventures: Bugs will inherit the earth! Following a youth of concentrated religious upbringing, some misdirected years trying my hand at astral projection, and decades of hand-spraying powerful insecticides have done nothing to change my mind.

We humans are little more than a hiccup within the wisp of smoke that represents the total span of intelligent life on this earth. Before us came the bugs, and I am convinced that they shall frolic in our dust, long after our plastic milk cartons and TV sets have moldered into goo. Some think that killer bees will head the procession. Others side with the ant. My money is on the (suborder) dictyoptera (order) blattodea—the *cockroach!*

There are over 3,500 species of cockroaches on the planet; over fifty species in the United States alone. There's the *americana*, the *germanica*, and the *asahinai*, among others.

My first memorable encounter with *la cucaracha* occurred in the back streets of Old Juarez, Mexico. A resident of the-not-so-distant Las Cruces, I had arrived only a few hours before with my rowdy rabble of high school buddies and work mates, bristling with youthful hormones, attempting to consume all the mixed alcohol "Zombies" within reach.

We soon found our ranks scattered, disoriented, and stumbling aimlessly along dark and unfamiliar byways. No sidewalks, few friendlies, and no police protection.

I vaguely recall Frank and Nestor holding open a swinging saloon door for me underneath a horrid-looking neon sign; a curious *squiggle* instead of a word to mark *The Place Where We Might Finally Lose Our Male Virginity If We're Not Real Careful.*

The wretched little sign buzzed angrily, competing with several hard-shelled bomber beetles and suicidal moths that hammered away at its flaking sheet-metal cabinet. An old abandoned Plymouth with no windows, seats, or wheels seemed at home at the base of the sign's single pole. The light from one dim bulb on another concrete pole illuminated five slick-haired *pachucos*[11], glaring at us from the rusty fenders as we filed inside, *macho*-like.

We were thoroughly pickled by this time. My amigos' disjointed, sweaty faces told me that we were all on autopilot, so I followed along zombie-like, into the veritable Den of Iniquity.

Once inside, we were greeted in much the same way that Paul Newman's title character was welcomed to a raunchy bordello in the movie, *The Life and Times of Judge Roy Bean.* And if you're not familiar with the motion picture, gentle reader, follow along for a moment and you'll get the picture…

After another round of drinks for us and another round for the friendly young ladies who came to join us, we were separated from everything of value that we possessed and I found myself alone in a poorly lit, dank little room *waaay* in the back, one lacking any true comfort, or furniture.

I was leaning against the far wall, wondering how long it was going to take for the room to stop spinning, when a woman many years my senior came into the room, clutching a large roll of toilet paper. She looked like someone's sad, neglected mother.

The señora said something in Spanish about an *inspection*—then she suddenly gasped and jolted backward, her eyes wild with a look of terror

11   Popular Gringo name for their Latin American peers. "Chukes" for short.

as she let out a primal scream that stunned her *inspectee* and threatened to crack the dirty white plaster on the decrepit walls around us.

A split-second later, one of those previously mentioned Chukes suddenly materialized in front of mama-san, gesturing for the old woman to *get back* as he made a production of grinding out his smoldering *frajo*[12] on the cement floor.

A long lock of greasy black hair fell across his scarred face as his frowning eyes sized me up and his lips snarled. He juked kung-fu-like in my direction. Hesitating menacingly, he coiled for the attack.

The Chuke's cold brown eyes were focused on my left shoulder. (I figured he was severely wall-eyed or something!) My self-defense training was woefully inadequate at this stage of my development, but I managed to move my inebriated chin out of the way one microsecond before his left loafer came whistling by, deftly kicking away a monster cockroach perched on my left shoulder like a stereotypical pirate's parrot—unbeknownst to me—bobbing and flitting away!

I spun around in reflex, facing the wall as the monster roach clattered like a busted helicopter, landing on the dusty adobe just inches below an open window. As it scurried to escape, Chuko made like Fred Astaire, leaping for altitude.

Chuko's shoe became athletically super-imposed over the exact spot upon which the bug was clinging. A nauseating *crunch* shot around the dank room, followed by the thuds of attacker and bug hitting the floor, in that order.

The next thing I remember, I was back outside with Nestor, who wanted to leave *pronto* but was missing his shirt and looked even worse than when we went in.

"Where's Frank?" we wondered aloud, taking inventory.

A ruckus ensued, and who else but Frank was unceremoniously shoved out into the night through the now hostile swinging doors. Frank clutched a whiskey goblet in one hand, sneering like a man who has been pushed to the brink. He muttered hatefully, "*This* is what I think of *thieves!*"

---

12   Street name for a Mexican cigarette. They're flat and sweet; I smoked a ton of 'em back then.

As Nestor and I shouted *"Noooo, Frank!"* in disbelief, he defiantly kicked both swinging doors wide open and flung the half-full whiskey glass back from whence it came!

A chorus of screams and angry epithets followed. Suddenly it was time for our still virgin, would-be track-stars to head down the long dark street for the border—or we were doomed!

The Chukes had mysteriously doubled in number around the old Plymouth. As we spun to run, I observed them frowning fiercely, calling us *puta madres*[13] as they scrambled for some well-placed emergency caches of potato-sized rocks and Coke bottles.

Lacking a good exit line, we spun on our heels and broke into a wild three-man sprint as rocks and jagged bottles came crashing and splashing around us for an inordinately long time. Undaunted, we flew like the wind, and we had company.

We ran until our lungs ached, then slowed to a winded jog. The Chukes had stopped to puke and called it a night. In due time, we made it to the border and crossed under the ever-suspicious, disapproving eyes of *la Migra,* U.S. Customs, at the El Paso checkpoint.

"I'm an Okie!" I blurted out to the badge, who signaled me back over the line to my beloved America.

After sobering up, I realized what a dangerous sidetrack we had made in a notorious border town and just how close I had come to doing something I would have truly regretted later. *Instant dummy—just add alcohol!* From then on, when anyone mentioned a trip to Juarez, I had the uncontrollable urge to say *"Noooo!"* and flick wildly at my left shoulder!

(Four years later, in the Highlands of Vietnam.)

The Ghetto, as it was called, housed Alpha Company's warrant officer pilot corps. The Ghetto was comprised of two former infantry barracks converted into ten *hooches.* Halfway through my combat tour, I moved in with the *Left Bank* guys. Our humble four-room hooch came with a TV/card room, a hotplate, and our very own, dug-in, indestructible cockroach horde.

---

13   The ultimate insult in Spanish.

Our quarters, according to local folklore, had been built a couple of years previously by and for the South Vietnamese Army. Screened-in, twin rows of bunks; nothing in the way of a room or privacy. The South Vietnamese units moved elsewhere when LBJ ordered up more troops and the ground war expanded.

When Camp Enari was established, the 4th Aviation Battalion's "Blackjacks" and "Gambler Guns" moved in and, over time, scores of helicopter rocket boxes were hammered asunder to erect walls, doors, counters, tables, side-rooms—whatever! The hooch on the end of our row was famous for its continuous partying, psychedelic posters, black lights, and the occasional hungry jungle rat.

What was remarkable about our cockroach horde was, no matter how often we sprayed with the powerful all-purpose industrial-strength Pyrethrin GI aerosol bug spray, they always put on an impressive suicidal counterattack.

There were infinite legions of *Battella asahinai* living in our makeshift kitchen area, hidden away until lights out. Or until we saw one or two and reached for the ever-present olive drab spray can.

"Time to spray!" someone in the group would announce and we'd gather 'round. The trick was to aim the stream through a certain hole in the wall, mash the nozzle down for five seconds, hop up on top of the counter, and watch the show!

One of our guys we called "Mack" would truly get hysterical when the first fresh wave in a month or so came flooding out from under the counter, flailing their butts around and skittering the way they do when you've really fried 'em with nerve gas. Mack would shout, *"Their nervous systems are destroyed!"* over and over, until we finally had to *di-di*[14] outside before the fumes overpowered us or we'd be poisoned, too.

(Another four years later: it's 1974 and the scene, the Amazon Flood Basin...)

After becoming a commercial helicopter pilot, I ventured to South America. My cadre of pilots and mechanics worked and lived in the Amazon flood basin of northeastern Peru. It was there that I discovered the largest roach

14   Vietnamese slang for *run like hell!*

I've ever seen. I noticed it along the wooden boardwalk of our camp at Puerto Amelia following a tropical squall. It was *almost* dead (drowned? I debated) but in good condition otherwise, so I carefully rolled it up in sketching paper and took it with me to my observation tower, *La Torre de Paz...*

After making myself comfortable in my lofty perch, I began sketching the insect, full scale. I later sent the drawing away in a letter to my old pal Steve, back in Oregon, by writing all around the bug I just drew. I did this kind of stuff to share my observations with an old friend, and to educate/ entertain myself out in the middle of the jungle. *Know what I mean?*

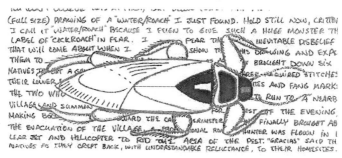

(The original sketch, returned by Steve Mankle.)

A little personal history refresher: as a kid growing up in Sundown, Texas, I always had my BB gun close by. Seemed to be the natural thing in our little town, and I seldom got into trouble with it. But I heartlessly thinned out the local grasshopper, horned toad, English sparrow, and lizard populations.

My single-shot, break-action air rifle shot faster and farther than the corner-store's repeater versions, earning me a sharpshooter's reputation at an early age. This skill I used as previously defined and to discourage any stray dogs that came 'round our place, lookin' for little kids to bite.

I'd pepper the mean dogs' flanks with a well-placed BB and they'd take off like a jet! The BB wouldn't break the skin, but it would send the message: *I've been bit once and it ain't gonna happen again!* My shooting skills would come in handy twenty years later when I encountered the *puta madre* of all cockroaches, right in our very own garage!

(One more cockroach to go: Rialto, California – 1980)

Whatever it was that I went into the garage for at that late hour, I fergit. As I opened the door, the light from behind me fell upon the darkened west wall of the garage where she was; above the washing machine—eight feet off the floor—clinging to the faded pink sheet rock, not moving a hair. Lordy! She's huge!

We'd only lived in the house about a year, but neither my wife Lourdes nor I had seen anything like the pregnant, three-inch *Periplaneta americana* on the wall, patiently waiting for me to turn the lights out so *she* could go about her *roach* business and eat Rialto, or something.

My latest version of the standard Daisy Red Ryder stray-dog-persuader stood in the corner by the patio door behind me, loaded; not cocked. Leaving the garage door ajar *per se*, I stealthily segued over to the BB rifle, cocked it slowly, and returned to the garage door, hoping beyond hope that she was still there.

Yes!

She appeared to be napping a mere ten feet from my air rifle's front sight. I drew a tight bead on her midsection, holding my breath as I began applying pressure to the trigger.

[Thhunnkk/ssssplatt!!]

She was apparently snoozing while she digested a large, gelatinous meal; something yellow and icky that would long stain the wall around the BB embedded in the sheet rock, where she *used* to be.

Section II:
From Jungle Warrior to Burger Flipper

Bad Boys

*   *Some Got Through – Some Didn't.*

I was pining to be a pilot by the time I reached second grade. Even then, a life without wings was unimaginable. Helicopters became my focus by the age of twelve, followed by a detour through three memorable motorcycles. I did okay in school, but as my high school peers flocked off to college, I found the whole academic scene way too stifling. I'm an outdoor, wind-in-my-hair kind of guy!

Soon after turning nineteen, I was on my own and working two jobs, day and night; but there was no money for flying lessons.

Lo and Behold, Lyndon Baines Johnson comes along with his Vietnam *conflict*, and my draft notice. Johnson needed lots of grunts (read trigger-pullers) and chopper pilots. I heard that a couple of the "1As" I had been taking pre-induction physicals with took off to Canada. My then-brother-in-law (the hippie art student) got drunk and—with the help of his wife—blew one of his big toes off in an alleged "shooting accident" to earn a draft deferment; others ignored the whole thing and/or took refuge in the local university.

The Explorer Scout in me concluded that our president must know what he's doing, and if he called, I was obliged to respond. I was not alone in recalling the somber pledge that we stood and repeated at school every morning for as long as I can remember: *"I pledge allegiance to the flag,* of the United States of America..." it began. So I signed up and filled one five-foot, ten-inch hole in the breach.

Standing at rigid attention, my fellow warrant officer candidates and I had just been summoned by our TAC officer,[15] a thin, menacing figure of a man we called SIR! Mr. Machina was a no-nonsense veteran combat helicopter pilot and a powerful chief warrant officer, so it was only behind his back that we called him Machine Gun. Why our flight of pilots-in-training was hurriedly called into formation was about to become clear.

Long before daybreak that morning, there had been a commotion at the PX store adjacent to our helicopter flight school barracks. A military policeman was making a routine security check of the locked facility. Spotting someone breaking into an entrance at the far end of the building, a challenge was shouted and a shot was fired.

The would-be burglar dropped dead on the hard concrete floor, wiped out by the MP's .45 pistol slug, which had first ricocheted off the metal doorframe near the burglar's head. Turns out, the burglar was also a veteran combat helicopter pilot—a chief warrant officer!

It was naturally a shock to those of us going through military hell in an attempt to achieve the coveted status of the fallen officer, who was revealed to have a large collection of *stolen guns!* Doing his best to explain how this could happen, Mr. Machina spoke with unusual *passion*...

"As a TAC officer, it is my job to see that only the most disciplined, the most deserving candidates pin on the wings. The man who was shot this morning is an embarrassment to the United States Army. Every now and then, one of *these guys* gets through the system. *Somebody* screwed up here at Fort Wolters over two years ago. He shouldn't have made it through flight school in the first place—he should have been *weeded out!*" growled *Machine Gun*, as he paced right and left in front of our forty-man formation.

When his speech was finished and we were dismissed, many expressed their disbelief about what had happened so close to home. At my first opportunity, I double-timed over to the building and took a look. There was a short line of us waiting to get a look at the infamous door. Sure enough, there was a deep telling gouge in the thick metal doorframe

15   TAC officers are drill sergeants on steroids.

where the heavy slug was deflected into its intended target, at about nose level. It made quite an impression.

I was beginning to wonder about all the background checks we had gone through to get this far, where even a minor scrape with the law or a less-than-favorable report from one of our schoolteachers would spell doom for an aspiring aviator. (Did they know about my wonderful fart recording, I worried?) How many *jokers* were getting through, I wondered?

Only two months before—during the non-flying phase of our training—a brand-new candidate took a stroll one Sunday afternoon, out to the Main Heliport flight line. He had no instructor with him and knew *nothing* about flying one of the scores of OH-23s quietly sitting there. Picking one that he liked, he opened a flight manual that was in plain view. Wherever security was that day, he was undeterred as he buckled himself in and started down the checklist.

As things worked out, he managed to get the helicopter started, revved it up, and began sliding and hopping around wildly, and in short order crashed hard at the edge of the ramp and burst into flames. An off-duty WOC by the name of Robert Davidson witnessed the bizarre incident and bravely ran to the rescue, earning himself a Soldier's Medal.

The would-be pilot made headlines days later when he pointed out to his commanding officer that he came to Fort Wolters *to learn to fly*, and *no one ever told him* he couldn't just walk out there and fire up a helicopter! As incredible as it sounds, he successfully avoided a military court martial with this ruse and was eventually allowed to continue training! (They corrected the *permission omission* in the orientation process, you can bet on that.)

Not very long afterward, someone noticed that there was a Hughes 269 sitting in several feet of water in a local Mineral Wells lake, not far from where the OH-23 had crashed and burned. A reliable source later divulged to me that the trainer's solo pilot became bored with boring holes in the sky and decided to unbuckle and switch seats in the 269 as he was flying. In the process, he fell out of the aircraft at low altitude, dropped into the lake, swam to shore, and disappeared. The helicopter was discovered later in the shallow lake, all alone and fairly bent.

As for my class, most went on to graduate, transferred to Fort Rucker, and eventually pinned on their silver wings. Among the exceptions was one of my roommates who couldn't hack flying instruments and had to accept the given alternative: "Welcome to the infantry!" Another decided that flying helicopters was too *stressful* and opted out—but I always wondered if the infantry was any *less stressful?*

And let us not forget the jubilant candidate who graduated with us that fine day and (many beers later) celebrated by sneaking into his ornery TAC officer's office, whereupon he rifled the locked filing cabinet open and relieved himself upon the deep drawer of neatly typed files therein. In midstream, the lights came on above him and *guess who* was standing in the doorway with his finger on the light switch? *Infantry,* make room for one more.

Many of those aviators fortunate enough to survive Vietnam eventually got out of the military and made the awkward transition to flying as civilians— although some were more *civil* than others. One acquaintance of mine had a day job flying Sikorsky S-55Ts in Arizona near the Mexican border. Turns out he also had a clandestine night job flying *weed* across the border, and was making a sizeable haul one night with his landing lights switched off. Upon landing, however, his fragile rotor blades took out a light pole, just as he was about to cash in. A few years in the cooler, and he was back among us, civil as ever.

The last bad boy in this tale pulled off a stunt that should have put him in chains for a decade: picture a heavily loaded, mile-long freight train working its way down a steep mountain grade somewhere in the great American West. A few hundred feet uphill from a railway tunnel, the train's engineer suddenly detects a bright light shining in his direction! He hits the emergency brakes, locking the engines' steel wheels in place as the train bears down on the tunnel, helpless to stop its momentum before impact.

Just as the engineer is about to jump, he observes that the light is attached to a French helicopter hovering over the tracks at the downhill entrance to the tunnel! Before the engineer can ID the culprit, the helicopter pulls up, disappears over the ridge, and is gone.

By then, though, the damage to the train's traction wheels was done, partially flattened by the effort to arrest the lumbering locomotives and all those heavy railcars. The engines were unable to continue downhill, and instead, had to *back up* several miles to a suitable siding, an effort that totally infuriated the train's crew and its bankers. All the wheels had to be changed out and/or re-trued!

Every effort was made to pin the crime on a certain chopper pilot working on a seismic contract near the remote location, but they had no "N" number and the pilot swore up and down that he was elsewhere. And besides, what would be his *motivation* for doing such a reckless thing?

A reliable source thought he knew the answer: The trains came and went by the bad boy's motel room all night long and disturbed his slumber—that was his way of getting even.

(Sheesh!)

Primary helicopter training was moved from Fort Wolters to Fort Rucker, Alabama in November of 1973. The grand old fort went from a once proud, rigidly policed, freshly painted, bustling flight school to a collection of neglected old buildings with tall weeds growing out of cracks in the pavement. Gone forever was the daily buzz of a thousand helicopters filling the sky.

Mineral Wells took over control of some of the old camp and renamed the facility Wolters Industrial Park. In the late 1980s, a Tennessee corporation by the name of Corrections Corporation of America leased a portion of the property to house 2,100 prison inmates at what is called Mineral Wells PPT, for *pre-parole transfer* facility.

Now—more than ever—the old fort is an unhappy home for hundreds of *bad boys* from all over the country—a thought which must sour the stomachs of the honorable graduates who marched between the gate posts of our old alma mater.

In time the Army took care of all that expensive flight training, and my helicopter adventure took off, with one *catch*: after training, I owed Uncle Sam three years of duty, starting with Vietnam. Fortunately, I made it through the 'Nam. Not all of us did. The twenty-two hundred helicopter pilots we left behind died hard, and young. The living returned to heartbreak and indifference for the most part. We learned to keep quiet about the war, what we did and what we saw. America turned her back on the Vietnam soldier.

My Purple Heart

Charlie woulda been pissed—knowing he had missed.

I kept having this stupid *combat dream*; the same one kept waking me up, time after time. Lying in my top bunk, I was bathed in sweat—my olive drab T-shirt clung to my flat chest, stinking of mildew. A *Playboy* pinup—an impossible, 1969 air-brushed blond sex goddess smiled back at me between my dusty black boots, reminding me of my obligatory abstinence as a married soldier[16] in Vietnam—and all the other things we did without for duty, honor, and country. The dream always ended in black:

I was down behind enemy lines, humpin' an M16, very much on the run. My crew didn't make it out of the shattered gunship. Grabbing the weapons bag, I raced for the tree line. Charlie[17] had me trapped in a deserted banana plantation; the lack of cover would be my undoing.

The gooks[18] were pumped up after shooting our C-model[19] down; they wanted revenge for what our mini-guns had been doing to their ranks. AK[20] rounds zinged by; one burned past my ear, turning me around. Two more bullets drilled their way into me—in slow motion—making small holes in my flat stomach, <u>from which my life</u> flowed outward—scaring me rudely awake.

16 My first wife left me while I served in Vietnam.
17 Charlie or Victor Charlie: VC—the enemy.
18 Popular grunts' term for the enemy
19 UH-1C Model Huey Gunship, preceded the Cobra in Vietnam.
20 AK47—The enemy's 7.62mm automatic weapon-of-choice.

Being a "Peter Pilot"[21] in Alpha Company entitled me to a bunk and the right seat of a Huey[22], but not much else. The guys with seniority had more refined hooches, meaning the usual rocket-box bar, a reel-to-reel stereo-tuner-amp with big speakers, and above all...

A **big-ass** electric **fan!** The steamy jungle air didn't move in the Central Highlands when the temperatures hit the high numbers in summer, so everyone either paid hard cash, begged, borrowed, or stole to get one. (Essential to a good night's sleep!)

But, like I said—I had a bunk, but no fan. Most of my combat pay was sent home automatically to a young woman who was already secretly boxing up all my belongings, getting everything ready for my funeral. Or a divorce, whichever came first.

With a little more cash I could have had a new fan from the PX, but I wasn't the best poker player in the Fourth Aviation Battalion. I liked the action, though—the players made for interesting company. But with monotonous regularity, they relieved me of my *expendable income*.

So I suffered through every sticky, tropical night like Charlie did until—one wonderful evening, some thoughtful Left Seater took a short R&R[23] to Saigon and suggested I use his spare bunk while he was gone. Lo and behold, there was a **big-ass fan** waiting there when I opened the creaky door!

It was one of those powerful, half-horsepower stateside models that sat near the floor in a short, homemade stand. The wire safety-cage was long gone. The ventilator's three dirty, curved aluminum fan blades had a grody buildup of ancient crud on the leading edges that I *dared not* disturb—for any reason. Left Seaters can get real superstitious 'bout stuff like that.

That evening started out wonderful. I showered up, down at the lean-to, and toweled down in the cool breeze. After a short read, it was a rare treat to hit the pillow and not stick to it. The mosquitoes couldn't compete with the nearby hurricane for my hide, and the noisy ventilator helped mask the eternal racket around the *Ghetto,* "A" Company's sector of hooches that housed warrant-officer-slick-pilots, mostly. *Finally,* I thought, *I am going to get a good night's sleep.*

---

21   New Guy in the Right Seat
22   (Bell) UH-1 Utility Helicopter (troop hauler)
23   Rest and Relaxation (One week in duration.)

Charlie had other ideas. Unknown to us, he had been busy humping bamboo racks full of 122mm Soviet surface-to-surface rockets down the Ho Chi Minh Trail over time. Someone among their ranks decided *tonight was the night* to terrorize the Fourth Infantry Division's base, Camp Enari.

The 122 had a range of about six miles, and anyone who has been on the receiving end of one of these killers can tell you, they pack a **wallop** when they hit! The shockwave that woke me up sent me diving for the floor. Shouts of **"INCOMING!"** were heard. In a strange, dark room at two in the morning, the Sundown Kid was lost! And he'd forgotten about the big-ass fan!

The big-ass fan was waiting for me—spinning wildly—as my diving, outstretched fingers crossed the event horizon of the dirty, swirling, finger-shredder. I yelled loudly in my sleepy recoil—my situational awareness mauled awake by reality—as the whirling mechanism ground to a buzzing halt. More rockets slammed into the southwest perimeter, sending more shockwaves, dirt, and shrapnel raining down onto our tin roofs.

In the shattered darkness, confusion was rampant. *Were they inside the wire?* I heard more shouts. *Who was running around out there, us or them?* I couldn't get my fingers moving again; they felt numb and throbbed with pain. *How many fingers have I lost?* I feared turning on the light, yet I couldn't find my boots—and I sure as *hell* wasn't heading for the bunker without my boots! I had my Colt .38 Special and holster, at least.

Trouble was, my fingers weren't gripping it very well; blood was running down my trigger finger, and I felt all that dirty crud stuck in my wounds. More shouts in the distance. The perimeter guards were returning fire across the rows of concertina; the quad-fifties were awake, too. Getting a little panicky, I threw the light switch on just long enough to ID my boots, and ducked back down as I fought my bloody bootlaces to get dressed for combat.

All lights were off as I sprinted for the nearest bunker. Ducking under the last clothesline, I was finally inside the dank sandbagged affair, the last pilot to report. I wasn't the only injured man; a tall lieutenant had forgot the clothesline, suffering a stretched neck, clothesline rash, and an angry Adam's apple.

I kept hearing *"Purple Heart! Purple Heart!"* meaning that the lieutenant and I had been injured due to hostile action, so that was that. Go to the dispensary and the medal will follow. I felt strangely ashamed, and told 'em, *"I'll wait for the bullet."*

And so it went. The incoming rockets fell silent, the outgoing artillery ceased, and finally, the *all clear* siren was sounded. I trudged back to the hooch in search of a first aid kit, and the lieutenant marched off to the dispensary and his Purple Heart.

The Elephant Brander

An Unbelievable Tale from Vietnam

"Mike finds the big rogues, Lieutenant. He has a sixth sense when it comes to the Highland Asian elephant." I nodded in Mike's direction (he was pouring a foamy head on his fourth or fifth beer) and returned to answering the stranger's loaded question.

"Just this morning we were headin' over toward Ban Me Twat[24] following a report by the Montagnards of a huge unbranded bull yonder ways. Mike here was on his scent as soon as we crossed the blue line," I continued.

"I kid you not, Lieutenant, Mr. Mullenix can root out the big ones like nobody. We were—what, Mike? Ten minutes out—when you sat up and rocked the Huey over hard left, shouting over the racket...?

"There he is! A damn' big bull at that!" Mike announced loudly over his helmet's microphone. ***"Get 'er hot!"*** he yelled to the Guys In Back[25] (GIBs).

Banking right, then hard left again, he headed our Huey into a hole in the jungle canopy that his right seater frankly didn't think was wide enough for

---

24   Ban Me Thuot—II Corps, a city in the Highlands about an hour's flight southwest of Pleiku
25   Guys in Back, could include navigators, gunners, technicians, etc.; abbreviated "GIBs."

fifty feet of rotor blade! I'll wager the GIBs were too scared to look as one of them closed the heavy copper switch, powering up the brander as we hovered straight for the elusive bull's big behind.

"Low limbs, twelve and three o'clock!" I blurted over the intercom, but Mullenix was on autopilot—in a groove, flying sans-error. Fully transformed into the decisive Texan we knew him to be—confident in his every move—he cinched up the collective pitch, reefing just-so on the cyclic control stick while milking in some left pedal to create a ground cushion as we came into a hover within reach of the behemoth's unbranded pink ass.

"Hit the horn!" Mullenix commanded. My left index finger jammed the black "horn" button into the detent position. The Huey honked loudly from the harmonic blast of twin air horns. Right on cue, the big Asian slowed, looking bug-eyed over his left shoulder to see what on this big green earth was about to marry him!

The end of the brand glowed neon orange, lighting up the short hairs and dirt on the bull's graphic posterior as Mike rammed it home with barely two feet of rotor blade clearance. There was a shudder in the airframe as helicopter-bumped-pachyderm, then we rocked forward again as the bull's burned-butt reflex kicked in and he shot ahead, trumpeting and venting copiously.

"Thar' she blows!" Mike bellowed as we observed the elephant's tail shift high into the air, his main exhaust forming a bulging, ominous "O."

"Ignitors!" The Captain piled on the work. Obediently, I snapped the task selector bar from "horn" to "ignitors" and took a deep breath as we headed into the shimmering methane cloud.

"Ignitors, aye!" I gasped, and into the vapors we blundered.

A thick arc of raw electrical current flashed between the brander's outside verticals, lighting off the fart before it could be sucked into our turbine engine—or worse: up our nostrils!

Fffwwwoooommmppp!

An eerie blue flame passed quickly over us and down both sides of our D-Model as the engine and ambient temps shot up twenty degrees and instantly back down again. It made quite a ripple! Through the dissipating smoke and pungent odor of *charred rump*, we proudly made out the "Ace-Jack" brand of the Blackjacks on the backside of the darting mammoth.

"Charlie'll never touch that bull," Mike drawled.

Mullenix spun 'er around toward the tight hole from which we came. With both feet on the gas pedal, he punched us back through it while firing up a short black stogie to help mask the stench—as the GIBs and I coughed, cheered, and laughed all the way back to Pleiku.

That's when I knew beyond a doubt that we were in the hands of the baddest of all the Elephant Brander pilots in Vietnam. And we were back and showered up in time for happy hour! It ain't every day **you bag a bull for LBJ**, sir!

Looking straight into the incredulous eyes of the formerly inquisitive lieutenant seated across the beer can-strewn table from us, I smiled overly sincerely and gently nudged Mullenix's elbow. He was seated right next to me, half lit up; I had just sloshed over his warm glass of beer.

"*True sh'tory*," Mike wheezed, never missing a beat.

"*An' how 'bout the time…*" he began again…

"I ain't believin' this shit!" the transient Army officer announced as he shifted his gaze from Mullenix to me—back and forth—frowning as he rejected our latest tall tale of an answer. He stood up disapprovingly and moved along to another table, away from us warrant officers!

Truth was, we were officially *Left Bank* pilots, crewing one of only three helicopters *in country* on a certain classified mission. Because of the distinctive look of the helicopter, we created interest here and there when we landed for fuel.

We opted to be creative sometimes, instead of being rude, by saying, "Gee, I'm sorry but I can't tell you what we're doing. You have no **need to know**. Sir."

So we told anyone who might ask, "What's that thing sticking out the nose of your helicopter and how come you got black curtains on your winders?"

Our standard reply was: "We're the Elephant Branders." That usually did the trick.

(Over Vietnam in 1969 – Photo by Warren Finch)

Burger Flipper Redux

The next few years after Vietnam were a struggle. It was a decade that came to be known irreverently as *"the Suckin' Seventies."* *Tricky Dick* Nixon was in the White House. Elvis was *back* and sold out in Vegas. And the *conflict* in the 'Nam—the Ten Thousand Day War—was drawing to a disgraceful closure.

As of early 1971, I had been back from *the 'Nam* for almost a year. Now assigned to the Army's Air Operations Directorate at Holloman Air Force Base, New Mexico, I had worn the Army's olive green uniform for over five years. There was a Chief Warrant Officer Grade Two bar on both shoulders of my Army flight jacket, and I had accumulated 1,200 helicopter flight hours—most of it in Combat Assault roles, piloting UH-1C gunships, and UH-1D and H slicks. That was about average for the returning one-tour helicopter aviator.

I was the proud owner of a brand-new Commercial Rotorcraft license, and a spankin' new private airplane (ASEL) license. Bob Holliday, a B-17 pilot and certified instructor with Black Hills Aviation in Alamogordo, saw to my Cessna 150 flight training.[26]

During all this merriment, I was heavily debating whether to stay in the Army or return to civilian life. If I completed my commercial flight training

---

26   Sadly, Bob was killed a few years later. A wing of his B-17 allegedly struck a tree while fighting fires.

in airplanes, I would at best be a bottom-rung civilian fixed-wing pilot anywhere I went. The word on the street was, nobody was hiring freshly discharged helicopter pilots.

On one hand, the Army brass were encouraging me to finish my commercial fixed-wing training so they could qualify me to pilot T-41s, Beavers, and Otters. On the other hand, Vietnam was winding down, and I sensed a *reduction in force*. The *Big R.I.F.* was coming, others said. Lots of nervous career-types were wondering what the future would bring.

And, like too many of my spat-upon soldier brothers, I was freshly divorced, broken-hearted, disillusioned, and desperately in need of something positive and meaningful in this elusive thing called *life*.

As my military tour grew short, the new movie sensation *M.A.S.H.* opened at the Base Theater to a packed crowd. After reading the reviews, I decided I had better check it out. Not surprisingly, I loved the helicopter scenes and the music.

And if I hadn't been an officer, I might have found *M.A.S.H.* to be highly innovative and knee-slapping funny in places. It provided hundreds of Airmen in the theater several opportunities to howl hysterically through one scene after another of dope smoking, officer bashing, and gross insubordination. But wearing the uniform, I couldn't enjoy witnessing Hollywood's dishonorable slap to the collective military face.

As a freedom-loving American, I'm distrustful of censorship. As an officer, I was shocked that the Base would show that movie in a military theater. I thought Donald Sutherland and cast did more harm to military discipline in two hours than all the West Pointers would be able to heal in a decade. Of course, he and Elliott Gould were merely *actors*, doing their jobs. Watergate's "Deep Throat" would teach us to "follow the money"…in this case, to the *producers?*

Only in America could such a film's producers get rich off the success of their farce, while irresponsibly shaking up an already demoralized American military force. And everyone knows the *M.A.S.H.* TV series (with Alan Alda) was also a huge success, setting new records for a television series.

This is definitely a good time to get out, I decided that day. Things are going to continue to decline for anyone in uniform. *The hippies have won.* I was more determined than ever to say good-bye to military life and get my civilian helicopter career kick-started.

While mailing out a plethora of resumes, an Army captain from Yuma Proving Grounds befriended me and suggested I contact his former Jaycee[27] acquaintance in Oregon, something about a restaurant chain that was looking for a helicopter pilot. I telephoned Keith Andler, the VP of Operations, and he encouraged me to come up for an interview.

A month or so before my release from the Army (April Fool's Day, '71), I bought a round-trip ticket from El Paso, Texas, to Eugene, Oregon for the interview, my first real trip to the region. It was also my first flight in what was then a *new* airliner, the Boeing Model 737. (I had to wear my familiar Army dress green uniform to get the military discount.)

Keith was waiting at the fence when I arrived at the terminal. He was a tall, handsome ex-Marine captain (quartermaster) who resembled the actor George Hamilton. I found him to be quite charismatic. Keith had all the traits of a middle-aged aristocrat, exuding class and confidence with every step. He was a senior partner with the firm, and destined to be rich.

We sped off toward the company's newly completed restaurant nearby, when a fluttering airport parking ticket pinched under his left wiper blade began to go crazy. I figured Keith hadn't noticed his parking violation and would pull over to retrieve it, but he simply turned on the wipers for his thundering Pontiac Grand Prix. The offending ticket disappeared right over the roof and settled onto Route 99 well behind us (Type "A" personality, anyone?).

Turns out, there were several whom one might label *Type "A's"* in this outfit. The top two were flamboyant entrepreneurs who had built several modern *fast-food* family restaurants in the northwest, and more were popping up like toadstools after a spring rain. Nice, new 100-seat facilities for the most part, competing with such establishments as Denny's and Sambo's. All operated under a motivated staff that was determined to provide quality food, clean washrooms, and "personality service." They even had a big, jolly corporate chef!

---

27   Junior Chamber of Commerce—Popular young businesspersons' organization of the time.

The CEO was a flashy guy and he loved his big-boy toys. He drove his Citroen-Maserati through the busy streets of Salem like a man possessed. I soon learned that his brother had been killed a few years before in an unfortunate single-engine airplane accident. "Bob" consequently set his sights on acquiring a *twin-turbine* helicopter—allegedly within a few months—and he would have me fly the overhead and his guests around the Northwest.

After I underwent restaurant manager training, of course. The plan was—according to Keith—I'd be their corporate pilot, yet I'd be available to relieve the other restaurant managers when they took their annual vacations. Manager training started at the very bottom: the dishwasher.

Pearl diving again. My teenager-burger-flippin' days at Neff's Topper Drive-In back in Las Cruces were payin' off, I mused to myself. A strange return path to a corporate flying job, I mulled. At least, I'd be out of uniform, and that appealed to me.

This was during *the good ol' days* before the government dictated workplace anti-discrimination hiring practices. It was clear that this outfit hired the most attractive young women from among the many applicants. There were no "grannies" or "Hash-house Harriets," as they called 'em. From a lonely soldier's perspective, this meant there were available, nice-looking young ladies all over the place!

Naturally, we were discouraged—per company policy—from fraternizing with our female employees, a draconian rule that worked just fine for your average eunuch. But if you happened to be a gregarious twenty-five-year-old Scorpio, the virile son of a Scorpio woman...*mission impossible!*

After an overnight stay in Portland, I got a tour of their prized Doubletree,[28] a fine dinner house. The swanky establishment featured a popular lounge that flowed with the latest libations and a rockin' dance floor.

I was pretty dazzled by Keith's red-carpet introduction. Eventually, he motioned me to a discreet leather-clad booth to talk terms. Mr. Andler was, to no one's surprise, a master negotiator. I soon heard myself agreeing to the lowest starting salary I felt I could afford. We shook hands on the deal, and in little time, I was on my way back down Interstate 5 toward Eugene's airport.

28   Another firm had already registered the "Doubletree" name, and a successful lawsuit followed.

On the return flight to El Paso, I felt anxious to put my last few days in the Army behind me, and begin my new life as a Manager-in-Training-slash-Corporate Pilot. My initial training was to take place in one of their busiest "stores" in Portland, the twenty-four-hour "Truckadero."

As the big bird clipped along, I gazed out the airliner's window from 29,000 feet. Oregon's lush, green, forested mountains looked cool and inviting compared to the parched New Mexican desert I had grown accustomed to.

Back at the Base, I soon bolted an after-market trailer hitch to my gorgeous 1970 "Bridgehampton Blue" Corvette Stingray Sport Coupe's stylish rear end. Her 350CID/HP mill would easily pull my earthly possessions in U-Haul's smallest trailer, a one-way rental from nearby Alamogordo.

The mysterious young lady named Aletha (also from Alamogordo) whom I had been dating a few months beforehand didn't seem to understand why I was leaving for Oregon and not taking her with me. The thought had actually entered my mind, briefly.

We had—after all—made fabulous love in the New Mexico moonlight, right there on the ice-cold cement picnic tables of the Lincoln National Forest—more than once. (The Corvette did *not* accommodate going horizontal.) But Aletha had a steady job with a defense contractor and, heck—I was still getting over my divorce and we'd never even *discussed* matrimony. With me having no appreciable savings, and just starting out, I sensed that taking Aletha with me was asking for trouble.

Aletha appeared to take the news graciously. She acted like she was over it, even invited me over for a homemade dinner at her folks' place before I headed south for Fort Bliss. After dinner, she patiently clipped my already short fingernails and trimmed my hair and eyebrows—catching every hair and nail. During this touching little ceremony, she sweetly explained that she was making a *going-away present,* which she would ship to me in Oregon.

On April 1st, I said my good-byes to a small gathering of friends at the Holloman AFB Officer's Club and headed south down lonely Highway 54 to Old Fort Bliss. Standing in one more line to collect my last Regular Army pay, half a handful of *President Grants*, and an Honorable Discharge to send me on my way.

I was suddenly a free man, after a five-year-and-one-month military hitch. I regarded those years as an almost forgettable experience, highlighted by learning to fly and serving in my beloved America's only military defeat. There wasn't a lot to celebrate in 1971.

Remembering it was April Fool's Day, I delayed my departure long enough to locate a pay phone, where I telephoned my old Army buddies Jimmy Williams, Dennis Freeman, and "Nonie" Orósco—informing them in turn that I had changed my mind about getting out, that I had instead *signed my life away* and went *"Voluntary Indefinite!"* To a man, they detected the mirth behind my mischief, and called my bluff. *"Get outta town, Wingo!"* they cried.

One last stop near Old Mesilla to say *adiós* to my folks. Blanche and J.B. still resided along the Rio Gránde in the middle of their one-acre fruit orchard; their fifty-plus trees were looking good. These were the golden years for my parents.

Afterward, heading down that terribly corrugated, dusty Mesilla Valley farming road one last time—the smooth asphalt of Highway 28 looked mighty attractive. I couldn't wait to get off the dirt roads and put some miles behind me; to shed my unrewarding past and begin anew.

Rainy Beaverton, Oregon became my new home for the next several months, and although I worked my butt off at the Truckadero and Lake Oswego restaurants, I was barely earning enough to rent a decent apartment and make car payments. The expense of owning and maintaining a Corvette was eating me alive!

One rainy afternoon, Aletha's *going-away present* arrived, parcel post. I was quite surprised to find in the gift box a fierce-looking, handmade figure. The ghoulish balsa wood form had some familiar-looking hair glued to its spiny head, along with bits of my finger and toenails. There was no note. It was not something I would send to *her,* if you know what I mean.

My good Bangkok Army pal—Jimmy Williams—paid me a visit a few days later, and he was shocked when he saw "the doll." After discussing what it might be, he took his worries with him back to Los Angeles, and called me after he had done some research.

"It's a *curse*, Wingo! You gotta kill a chicken and bury them together under the full moon to undo the spell of the witch." He was most sincere. Now, I knew that some people practice the black arts, and have for centuries— but I also had no fear of such mean-spirited humans, so long as they aren't shooting at me (had I actually hurt her so?!).

When the next full moon came and went, I called Jimmy and told him I had complied with his suggestion. (Then I tossed the haunting figure in the trash, head first.)

On to the next problem: refiguring my modest civilian budget, it was obvious that the 'Vette had to go. On a rare day off, I left her sitting in a Portland "Corvettes Only" sales lot, the keys clutched by a conniving, grinning, greasy-looking car buyer who simply took over the payments. And I literally walked on down the road.

Hoofing it slowly back toward the apartment, I pondered the fact that my Army pilot friend Dennis Freeman had had a great affection for his VW *Bug*. My Air Force pilot/brother Jon had also been a contented Bug owner. And up ahead was none other than a Volkswagen dealership. I decided, *What the heck!*

In the VW sales door I waltzed, and an hour or so later, with no money down (and a radical step-down in horsepower, flash, and dash) I putt-putted away from Sunset Motors in a brand-new (orange) 1971 VW Super Beetle. With the pricey after-market FM stereo-multiplex, of course!

I felt strangely relieved to have the expensive status symbol off my back. Driving slowly through Portland's *friendly* Washington Park, I kicked back among the hippie freaks and admired the sunset. A familiar sweet fragrance filled the air around me.

As the sun languished in the late afternoon, I passed along a doobie and cranked up a Moody Blues *"To Our Children's Children's Children"* cassette. Wingo was beginning to feel like a displaced hippie. And those gossipy, hard-to-please, rain-fed Oregon girls I had been so attracted to were beginning to make me wonder if I could ever love another *American woman.*

Three months came and went, and no one even *mentioned* the word helicopter. A year went by, and another. *And another.* I was moved here and there to solve managerial problems or take over new restaurants, and although everything else about my employment was satisfactory, I was really beginning to wonder about this *flying position*.

What about that *twin-engine* helicopter, my old Army buddies wanted to know? As it turned out, my hiring was, well—*premature*. That became obvious one day when Jack Brown, the company's area manager, dropped by for an unexpected visit.

Jack thoughtfully timed his arrival for the lull between breakfast and lunch so we could have some time to talk. He usually dropped in during the lunch-business rush hour so he could watch the employees under the pressure of maximum capacity. I joined him in the empty dining room and slid my weary butt into the chair opposite him. Loosening my choking necktie, we commenced to shoot the breeze.

Jack and I had developed a good relationship over time. In fact, we golfed together now and then and occasionally played chess at his home in Portland. He had recently married a widow of the Vietnam war, a beautiful blonde about half his age with three kids.

Mr. Brown was around sixty years old, and had a rare gift of personal power. He was a highly confident speaker, and reminded me of the actor Jack Nicholson. He could be very gruff and heartless, if he judged that you were doing less than your best. But after three years, he knew me about as well as anyone, and we got along, *after* he stopped pouring salt in my coffee when I wasn't looking. (That was his favorite stunt to test the resolve of rookie restaurant managers and/or make them look stupid.)

Eventually, the subject of the *company helicopter* came up, and Jack let slip that the CEO, when informed of the $110,000 purchase price of a (single-engine) Bell JetRanger,[29] reportedly exclaimed, *"Hey, I can build another restaurant with that kinda money!"* Jack measured my reaction and fell silent while I glared at my cold cup of coffee. At least he had the grace to tell me; he realized what flying meant to me.

So there it was. The helicopter was nothing more than an elusive carrot! Though the restaurant work was entertaining, my departure was inevitable: after three years of exhausting, six-days-a-week, twelve- to sixteen-hour work shifts—busing tables, serving coffee *ad infinitum*, flippin' burgers,

29   Approximately $110,000 in 1972 for the basic model, plus tax.

chasing waitresses, and depositing lots of hard-earned cash for our flashy *entrepreneurs,* I sadly concluded that Wingo was wasting his time. My dream was going *nowhere.*

Meanwhile, my ol' buddy Freeman had finally left the Army. After a messy divorce, a frustrating period of insecurity (which included no work, no money, and *mondo* spiritual meandering) he magically landed a truly *cool* chopper job in remote northern Alaska. He was soon tormenting me to no end with his lengthy, meticulously penned letters.

Patiently hand-wrought in ink on long yellow sheets of legal paper, Dennis wrote of his enviable exploits in unabashed, glowing script: flying rugged utility choppers into the vast reaches of the Brooks Mountain Range, he was happily strapped in next to two intriguing travel companions who knew no fear and uttered nary a discouraging word. *And the skies were not cloudy all day.*[30]

Seasoned explorers all, the trio flourished in the bush. Camping alongside virgin trout streams, they roasted small, tasty grayling skewered on alder sticks over a fragrant campfire for breakfast. A large, blackened pot of *cowboy coffee* got their collective hearts a-thumpin' for the aerial adventures a-waiting.

Climbing into their trusty Hiller 12E—in the endless Arctic summer daylight—they navigated throughout the remote Brooks Range, landing frequently to survey major peaks, saddles, and ridges. There were countless breathtaking vistas along the way, and with a keen eye, Dennis recorded scene after glorious scene through the lens of his Canon 35mm SLR camera.

Of course, he was also sleeping on the cold, hard ground at night and feeding infinite swarms of blood-sucking insects, but he was being paid handsomely for such minor discomforts! His tortured soul was on the mend, and he may have rubbed it in a little, knowing my frustrated, big-city-restaurant-manager state of mind.[31]

Putting those eloquently penned letters aside, I resolved anew to get the

---

30   Sentiments borrowed from the old cowboy song, "Home on the Range."
31   Mr. Freeman and I still correspond after thirty-odd years. Dennis enjoys tenure as a famous professional storyteller from Arizona. His third wife, Marilyn, is a lively Italian who was once a belly dancer.

heck out of the restaurant business and escape the designs of scheming entrepreneurs and the gossipy castration-minded women of the metropolis. I vowed to toss the suit and tie *forever,* and exchange them all for one of those faraway helicopter *adventures* I'd been reading so much about!

Cranking out the resumes again, I started looking for any hint of chopper work in *Rotor & Wing* magazine: lots of applicants, few flying jobs. I spent my limited spare time licking envelopes, working the phone, crossing off one operator after another. Rejection was routine. But my scanners were on *maximum,* and my eyes were on the horizon.

Looking back, the three-years-plus spent in the American Northwest were educational. I had moved what little I owned a total of six times, living in three different states. (I even got back into those olive-green fatigues once again, for a brief tenure in the Washington Army National Guard, all so I could stay close to the controls of my beloved Hueys. A job transfer to Sacramento ended that; a new over/under restaurant awaited me.)

Wingo—with the help of some highly motivated sales girls—won three company-sponsored sales contests in succession at two different restaurants, in as many states. After six months in Sacramento, I was promoted to Employee Relations Manager at the home office in Salem, Oregon—down the hall from Keith and the CEO. I was becoming a freaking bureaucrat!

Not long after, I gave it all up. With no job waiting in the wings, I handed Keith my thirty-day notice. When the big day came, my stuffed-to-the-roof '72 Volkswagen Delivery Van *upgrade* waiting patiently outside in the rain, I suffered through a small, poorly attended farewell party, with not one flashy *entrepreneur* in sight.

Eyeing the seemingly frozen time clock, I washed down my cut of the ubiquitous farewell cake, and whispered to the eyes-black-as-coal and highly ambitious training manager, Teri Cunningham: "I've got to get out of here!"

With all of $700 to my name and dragging my farewell gift behind me—a colorful (laminated cardboard) steamer trunk—I headed blissfully out the door and into a steady downpour. (That ol' trunk served me well in the years ahead!)

Section III:
La Torre de Paz

Adventures Recalled

On the table in front of me sits an old photograph, a diminutive three-by-five print of a simple hardwood pole structure with a thatched roof. This image, long ago burned into a now tattered piece of Kodak paper, is my time machine back to a rewarding, far-flung odyssey: parrot-infested jungles, hardworking helicopters, and new vistas beyond description. Add that to a cast of outrageous characters, and you have an *adventure!*

I rediscovered the photo recently, somehow forgotten in and among my "bachelor days" photos, and now I can't seem to put it away. It has rekindled the romantic fool in me, and I know I will get little rest until I finally document what was for me a very interesting and challenging time, in a jungle far away.

The tower in the photograph was a breezy, lofty, off-duty retreat, built as *far away* as possible from our little jungle camp's howling chainsaw shop and two massive yellow "Cat" diesel generators. In the dense surrounding jungle, "far away" meant to the edge of the bulldozed clearing...which was where I built it: high up on the riverbank, facing west and directly into the quarter-mile wide, on-rushing *Rio Huallága!*

A fifty-foot-deep, muddy, meandering river—the Huallaga slams into the bend at Puerto Amélia in front of the tower at an impressive five knots, then makes a broad turn northerly toward the nearby *Marañon*. Their combined power flows relentlessly onward into the mighty *Amazon*. Giant tasty catfish, anyone? *Plátanos*[32] with that?!

So, if you were to twist my arm real hard up behind my back, I'd confess that this little jungle-based "wildcat" drilling operation was one of the most *primo* assignments I've ever been paid to fly, and it happened way the heck out in the Brazilian flood plain. There lies the *Oriénte, la sélva*, the land east of the Andes.

"Have I forgotten the Amazon, Earth's greatest river? Never, never, never. It has been burning in me half a century, and will burn forever."

John Muir (1838-1914)

---

32   Fried plantains were frequent substitutes for potatoes.

Back in the Saddle

Dennis Freeman and I had discovered early on that we were merely two guys among thousands of shell-shocked, Agent-Oranged, low-flight-time ex-warriors trying to *maintain* in the early '70s. We were doing our utmost to land a decent flying position, to finally get a finger hold on America's young commercial helicopter industry.

Awaiting me down the road was more of what Dennis overcame to find work. Foremost on the list of rejection phrases facing the jobless flying veteran was this standard: "Chopper pilots are a *dime a dozen!*"

How *true*. The Army pinned a thousand sets of wings on a thousand young men's chests every month for....how many years?! In all, more than 23,000 young men flew choppers in the Republic of Vietnam. I was not alone in my frustration.[33] There were many who made it back to *the World* in one piece, and they were searching high and low for any outfit that was hiring pilots.

On yet another rainy day in January—the restaurant gig many weeks behind me—a fresh haircut and a shiny new passport in hand, I headed for an interview in McMinnville.

---

33   There were 23,438 helicopter pilots who flew in Southeast Asia during the Vietnam Era and were known to the Vietnam Helicopter Pilots Association as of 2007. Source: VHPA Membership Directory.

Driving through the heavy Oregonian *sunshine*, I pulled into Evergreen's attractive new facility, east of town. Out back stood several new-looking civilian Hueys lined up smartly on the south tarmac...a sight that made my heart leap. I appeared at the west entrance well ahead of time and slithered in, dripping wet.

After three disappointing years as a grounded civilian, I was being interviewed by Evergreen's vice president of marketing for a *sales position*, to sell helicopter services. In a moment of joyous inspiration, I managed to turn the interview around, convincing the man that I'd be much happier and more productive flying their choppers!

And, lucky me, Don New picked up the executive-style telephone on his huge desk and mumbled a few magic words into the receiver. I was suddenly and miraculously back in the helicopter-piloting business!

What followed was a virtual whirlwind of employment forms, training manuals, etc. It was the usual nine yards of tedium that would easily bore the most enthusiastic bureaucrat thirty feet into solid bedrock. Or so it seemed at the time.

Then I got to fly! I also learned to tolerate the surly chief pilot and his subplots to convert us all into *ag-pilots*. (He soon became *"Agyard,"* one of my favorite cartoon characters, months later, in a strip about *"Neverspin Helicopters,"* and the world of the twirling rotors).

In the spring, I was dispatched along with five other pilots to hover over a 1,200-acre almond ranch in central California. This was mostly night flying in periodic frost conditions, guaranteeing a bountiful crop of almonds for a well-known candy conglomerate.

When May came around, it was off to Fairbanks, Alaska, for a short BLM fire contract, which was great until the seasonal rains took over. Heading south, I landed another Huey fire standby assignment based in Boise, Idaho, and then it was back to the McMinnville base.

(The flying had been kinda boring so far—for an ex-warrior—but I can assure you that this kind of work beats the *crap* out of flippin' burgers!)

By then, I knew that McMinnville was *not* the place to hang out! The more experienced line pilots actually hid from *Agyard*—the frowning King of Pesticide—until a "real" flying job appeared, and I was fearful of becoming one of his victims. (Good-bye *Huey*, hello *Bug Smasher!*)[34]

A week spent milling around home base exposed us to several rumors, none of which produced a warm and fuzzy feeling. I soon found myself among a sizeable group of Vietnam veterans seated outside the infamous Operations office. Picture a nervous, insecure beehive…

Word was that Evergreen had just inked a lucrative heli-drilling contract with a big-time international oil company. Out on the ramp, two gorgeous green and white Hueys were being readied for a C-130 ride to South America. Civilian Hueys? In the Peruvian jungle? *South Honkin' America??* Where do I sign up?! (Whom do I have to mug?)

The smoky waiting room was packed with bored-looking strangers. I took a seat, wondering if I knew any of these characters. There was a former First Cav scout pilot standing by the water cooler, twitching and chain-smoking Pall Malls. He was skin and bones. Did DFCs[35] mean anything to this outfit, I wondered?

A scowling figure with a humongous gold watch faced the entrance. Had to be an *Air America* type: the heavy gold bracelet on his Rolex Oyster Perpetual timepiece gave him away. Several more daring aviators were

---

34   To a dyed-in-the-wool Huey pilot, any helicopter smaller than a Huey is a *bug smasher.*

35   Distinguished Flying Crosses – Most scout pilots had a drawer full at home.

carrying on in the corner, oblivious to any *new guys*. We were all different; we were all the same.

Some of us were rumored to be destined to fill vacancies in the dreaded aerial-spraying division, flying piston-powered H-12 Hillers. This encompassed spraying all kinds of stuff that you definitely don't want to get on you! Organo-phosphates, chlorinated hydrocarbons, you name it.

Some debated openly if it wouldn't be *safer* to be piloting a "Death Stranger"[36] on some bucolic Fire Standby contract way out in Po-dunk, Idaho.[37] Those of us who were left seated at the end of the day would likely get the ol' pink slip.

"Dime a dozen." *"Bye-bye now!"* (*Back to the burger joints.*)

Then came a nerve-wracking lull in the decision-making process. The company kept us pilots-in-limbo busy during the attrition phase with unskilled entry-level labor, the worst of which was shoveling ten cubic yards of gravel underneath their rain-flooded administrative building foundations. Record rainfall had saturated the water table under the new building. The architect called for tons of river-run gravel to help displace the surplus water.

Picture several heavy, gravel-heaped wheelbarrows creaking along under low-hanging flooring beams, their overloaded tires hissing over waterlogged wooden planks...kept upright by filthy, exhausted, grunting ex-combat pilots on either side—their hairy arms weeping dirty sweat onto heavy gold bracelets.

The more fortunate ones were put to work building and brush-painting heavy plywood "support boxes" for the lucky few about to ship out. Still, I noticed our ranks were shrinking somehow. No one had taken a head-count lately. The next day, "backaches" popped up; a few called in "sick!" A lot of military survival expertise was resurfacing in my cluster of pilots!

---

36 Pilot's put-down nickname for the JetRanger, which was also known as the "Jet-Danger" in the earlier years of its introduction. (Keep in mind that almost all of this group were die-hard Huey drivers at heart!)

37 If there *is* any town in Idaho by that name, they most likely know what Po-dunk means.

Agyard appeared suddenly (still scowling, ever more the aerial spraying menace) to inquire: "Anyone seen that *Air America* driver?" (Dead quiet.) "Well, where'd that First Cav guy go?" (Maybe that JetRanger gig wasn't so bad after all!) "And Rick-what's-his-face?" "Oh, he's getting his wisdom teeth yanked today!" And so it went.

In the small group left standing, we were eyeballing one another between heavy shovelfuls of gravel… wondering who would buckle next, who had the right stuff, who would get the gold mine…and who gets the *shaft?!*

Time passed like it does when you're in the "Start Here" line of the local California Department of Motor Vehicles. (Take my word on that one.)

I just happened to be sitting outside the closed Operations office door the next foggy morning when I heard voices from inside. Some poor fellow was pleading for his job. Ward Eason, the head of Operations, was hearing no part of it.

"You did a stupid thing!"[38]

Ward's response was audible even in the parking lot, I reckon. A few seconds later, a freshly unemployed chopper pilot huffed out the door and back into the bread line.

Sensing a fresh vacuum in the pilot roster, I surreptitiously placed a hand-wrought cartoon/note on the director of operation's desktop early the next morning: a goofy version of yours truly, depicted boasting, "*Hablo Español!*" (I speak Spanish!)

To be fair, I spoke *poquíto* Spanish back then, but when pressed, I usually managed to skate around the issue with some clever phrases that I learned from the *bracéros* on Bobby Mayfield's cotton ranch, back there on the Rio Grande. Bobby spoke the lingo *muy bueno*, but like the misguided youth that I was, I studied German and Russian in high school…after all, who in *heck* needed to speak *Spanish?!*

(¡Hay, que gríngo!)

I can't say for sure if the cartoon made any difference, but *sports fans,*

---

38   Poor fellow (and his mechanic?) forgot to remove the air intake cover-tarp from a Bell 205A-1 and brought it to a hover, over-stressing an expensive engine! (*D'oh!*)

before the sun set that wonderful day, I had turned in my shovel! Judiciously submitting to *one more* haircut, I carefully packed my spacious parachute bag, stuffed all my other earthly possessions into my steamer trunk, and locked 'er up inside the VW. There it would molder in the designated dirt parking lot for the many months ahead. And I was on the 727 to El Perú before you could say *Sundown Shoeshine Boy!*

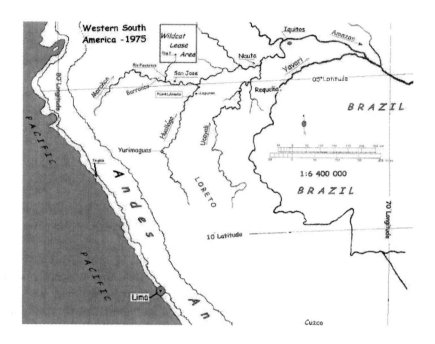

New Horizons

On the flight over, Evergreen's South American sales rep, Robert Fox, thoroughly briefed us as to the prevailing Peruvian political scene, ergo, the military-run government. *Adiós* democracy, *hello* dictatorship. The military ran the country, period. This would take some getting used to.

The big airliner touched down in Lima on a cold, overcast morning and spewed several of us adventurers forth into a cavernous gray terminal building. The customs goons were the first to greet us, acting as though their hemorrhoids were on fire, and it was *our fault.*

Walking stiff-legged from the long flight, our little entourage hobbled into the International Flights inspection area of Lima's terminal. I immediately felt *unarmed* and vulnerable in the face of the heavily armed Peruvian military types. These guys gave me a very *un*-welcome feeling, but remembering my political orientation speech, I put on the big smile.

Next in line, I unzipped the heavy bag. A mean-looking military customs agent, *La Aduána,* stared down at the tall stack of stiff, brand spankin' new Levi's, right on top. All that was missing were the original factory labels.

The finely machined 9mm Luger at the agent's side looked sinister in its shiny patent-leather holster, practically daring me to click my heels together and shout at the very top of my lungs *"**HEIL** freakin' **HITLER!!**"*

I took a deep breath and smiled obsequiously instead. I had to keep my cool—this flying opportunity meant *everything* to me. *Discipline!*

The agent coyly inquired why I was bringing in so many *new* garments. "I'll be working in the jungle for several months, *Jefe,* and I've heard that our inferior cotton garments rot quickly in the jungle."

"*Páse, gríngo,*" the bored inspector whined.

He didn't have to say it twice. I re-zipped the bag.

Kaa-*ching!* The Levi's had just doubled in value. The factory labels for the jeans were hidden elsewhere, ready to be reattached for the right moment. "*Blue jeans are one of the great bargaining tools abroad,*" a wise old traveler once told me. The sage would have also approved of the *bonus* behind compartment number two: extra pairs of new Ray Bans and a couple of those newfangled HP pocket calculators!

(I've found that some foreign governments have an inflexible importation or "luxury" tax. All too often what they call a *luxury,* you and I call a *necessity.* The road ahead promised to be a little smoother already.)

Following a speedy taxi ride into Lima's modern hotel district, we were reunited with a distinguished Evergreen bush pilot, Charles Johnson. "Horseshit Charlie" was his handle, and that's what *everybody* called him—even the Evergreen secretaries!

On my rookie firefighting assignment, I had worked briefly with Charlie in Fairbanks, Alaska. While there, he taught me how to hover-dip water out of the fast-moving Tanana River with a Bell 205. We used a 300-gallon Griffiths water bucket, slung under the cargo hook. He was a good instructor, and his reputation as an Alaska bush pilot (and prankster) was legendary.

Charlie had cleared customs the day before. Rising from the sofa with a big grin to greet us, he laughed kinda like Tommy Lee Jones and shook our hands with exaggerated care, as if he might break our sissy little fingers if he wasn't careful.

And his *hair!* I couldn't believe the long hair springing straight out under that old-style red BELL helicopter hat! Between his full beard and his hat, there was enough hair on Charlie to stuff a mattress. And Evergreen required *me* to cut *my* short hair *twice* before I could get on the plane? Whose idea was *that*, I wondered?!

To the experienced eye, Charlie looked like he had just walked out of a porta-camp on the Arctic slope, because he actually *had*. Given his choice, he probably would have wintered in Alaska again—but regardless, we were happy to have him with us.

Here was this gaudy foreigner with the ever-twinkling eyes, that bushy brown beard, and a big, round Santa Claus belly. Add a ten-gallon-sized Texas drawl, and one could assume that the average Peruvian's first impression would be: *"Gringo feo,"* one of those *ugly Americans!*

Nothing was further from the truth. Turns out, everybody just *loved* this guy, and his unique brand of Texas charisma would be sorely appreciated out in the brush. Evergreen sent us a smart, good-natured fellow to keep the show going straight.

Having spent my early adolescence in Texas, Charlie's familiar Texas accent put me in a sociable mood. However, after a polite round of *new-guys-in-country* banter, it became clear that both Charlie and I were *hungry*. I knew from experience how he loved to eat, so I didn't waste any time to get Horseshit properly acclimated to the local cuisine. Well, you know, I could order the food because I speak the language, right?

"Vamonos a caminar, compadre!...or 'Let's mosey, Tex!'...as they say back in Sundown!" I said to Charlie. As wiser pilots unpacked, Charlie and I excused <u>ourselves and strolled</u> purposefully down *La Calle de Los Payásos,*[39] where we

39   The Street of Clowns, reflecting our fate (but don't expect to find such a street in Lima!).

would soon come to know *Atahualpa*, a fifteenth-century Inca ruler who fell victim to the conquering Spaniards' treachery. According to legend, he returns every now and then to wreak havoc on naïve *estraños*…like me and Charles.

We ended up seated in a quaint fly-blown open-air café, casually ordering the house special, *cevíche*, which I had heard was as popular in Lima as *kímche* was in Korea. I don't think it registered that we were eating putrid *raw fish in lemon juice* until later, but after a few hours, Charlie vowed he'd never forget it, *or* the little café. (And thank *you* for the two extra *haircuts*, pal!)

Yes, sports fans, we were both introduced to a galloping version of food poisoning that evening, Inca style! Not "Montezuma's" revenge…*Atahualpa's* revenge! Cancel all appointments. Take the phone off the hook and lock the door. Stay close to the head! Drink tiny sips of beef broth only. *No milk!*

Charlie lost the *Big Mo*[40] during this ordeal. He didn't seem to be in much of a hurry to get on the airliner for the infamous bouncy flight over the towering Andes toward Iquítos to join up with our helicopters. We were already taking the usual diarrhea remedies, but Atahualpa was not impressed by our feeble medications, and we suffered into the night, and on into the next.

After three days, I finally shook the porcelain monkey, but poor Charlie was looking *thin,* and thin didn't look good on Charles. Nor did the slack, *clammy* expression…in lieu of the *twinkle.*

"More beef bouillon, Charlie?" I asked, clanging a large soup spoon against the borrowed saucepan. (Only moans from behind the heavy wooden bathroom door.) "The hot plate is my *domain!*" I volunteered, cheerfully.

Finally, a weak voice…sounding more like a pitiful Marlon Brando's *Godfather* than our beloved Charles …mumbled from atop the crapper. "Please…don't feed me *no more,* Wingo."

But—amazingly enough—when the time came, Charlie cowboy'd up and both of us got on the plane, a Brazilian job with two stuck wings, two real jet motors, and a cramped little toilet way in the back. And that's where Charlie rode out his first-ever crossing of the majestic Andes, sweating bullets while I had a cold *Bohémia* in his honor, way up front! Man, it was one bouncy flight! Poor Charlie musta had a death-grip on the appliance! Oh, the in-flight meal? …Cevíche!

---

40   His motivation to proceed.

The Andes were mostly obscured in clouds, but the flight over the clear, boundless jungle was inspirational! Hundreds of fresh spiraling *ghosts* were streaming up from the lush greenery below—evidence of a recent thunderstorm, high ambient temperatures, and 100% humidity. The unstoppable Ucayáli and Marañon rivers crashed together yonder, forming the headwaters of the Amazón, as we banked steeply toward Iquítos.

Charlie had an unflattering *sheen* when we helped him down the ramp at hot and steamy Iquítos International. Across the ramp we could see the large parts of our two Bell helicopters being eased down the ramp of a C-130 Hercules. The big bird had flown in overnight from stateside, saving us a heck of a long ferry flight in the process.

Our weary-looking young A&P mechanics had been out on the blazing tarmac all day and would allegedly have the ships ready to fly by morning. Their sunburns were just beginning to blister when we arrived to give them a slap on the back and wish them *happy wrenching!*

Charlie normally would have stuck around to shoot the skinny with the mechanics, but he was instead out in front of the terminal bartering curbside with the taxi drivers for a trip to the hotel, *pronto!*

Our party soon taxied off to "the finest hotel in town," La Turísta. Poor Horseshit was having cramps when the elevator finally reached the top floor. However, during the night, he streaked to the *baño* only once. He moaned even less toward morning and began showing signs of rejoining the living.

Up at sunrise, we hit the elevator together, bags in hand. Charlie seemed almost cheerful and was beginning to show some color in his cheeks. Looked like to me that Sir Charles was *back!*

But when the elevator halted abruptly at the restaurant level, he rocked back and gasped, grabbing the handrail. He had that terrified look on his face again, and started stabbing the "up" button with abandon!

I quickly stepped out as the metal doors began to close. The sweat popped out on poor Charlie's forehead as if on cue, and his eyes rolled back. "*My regards to Atahualpa,*" I offered, as the doors rumbled sssshut.

I moseyed on into the virtually vacant restaurant to begin what can only be described as a Hotel La Turísta ritual: being totally *ignored* by the numerous surly white-coated *meséros (waiters)*, who acted as if *turístas* were *freaking invisible!*

(Patience, gringo…patience! You could be spraying turnips or something!)

It was just under an hour before Horseshit reappeared behind door number two. He walked slowly in my direction like he was stepping on *eggs*. Taking a seat at my white linen-covered table, Charlie watched nervously as I drained my second cup of crusty old *Nescafé*, the closest either of us would come to a *real* cup of coffee for the next six months.

I moved the cups and condiments aside as Charlie spread out his aeronautical *sectional* and began briefing me on our 160-mile flight upstream to *Puerto Amélia*, our new jungle base camp. Since there were no aeronautical navigational aids at our destination, we'd be using the time-honored method of dead-reckoning navigation: time, distance, and heading. We'd stay close to the Rio Marañón en route, as this was the only "highway" between Iquítos and…well, anywhere west or upstream. If we had any problems along the way, we'd need the river's distinctive topography to help isolate our position and work out a rescue plan.

The Bells we were flying were like *new* and capable of ferry flights of over two hours. This would be one of the rare occasions where we actually topped off the fuel cells with *turbosína*.

"Those birds are *aerial tractors*," the silver-tongued marketing guys liked to say of Evergreen's rotorcraft during their sales pitches. That usually meant we pilots had to take on only enough Jet-A1 to get us to the first external load; re-compute the useful load at that point based on wind, density altitude, the distance to be covered, and the time it would take to fly the load there and get to a refueling point; plus a "reserve."

Then all we had to do was fly the aircraft on the ragged edges of its performance—regardless of the wind or the heat—to attain the projected sales numbers, and repeat for many months. There was actually very little room for error, and in the jungle, there was no place to park it if things got goofy!

Since these machines had a twenty-minute low-fuel warning light, the jungle rule was to fly for ten minutes into the light and not one minute longer. And that usually worked, *gracias a Dios*. I'll wager that each and every pilot who ever *worked* the Amazon Flood Basin with a helicopter has a "low fuel" story to tell, and I've got one! (Another time, perhaps.)

By midday, the mechanics had the big bolts torqued, the rotors tracked, the logbooks signed off, and both birds had "a full bag of gas," as they say in the genre. We marched our flight plans over to the Peruvian version of the FAA authorities at Iquítos International—who, like the tower operators, spoke just enough English to take our money, stamp our permits, and send us on our way—with few questions asked!

(And no firing squads! Things were looking up.)

Walking on the hot tarmac through the shimmering heat waves to where our nice, shiny helicopters and sweltering mechanics were waiting, Charlie and I paused briefly in the shade of the only other helicopter parked at the airport, an old Sikorsky S-62!

This flying antique had once been the backbone of the US Coast Guard Search and Rescue fleet longer than either of us could recall. She had a single engine, three main rotor blades, a cavernous interior; was *slow as hell*, and—with the hull of boat—she could float! A *great* ship for low-altitude work, and everywhere around us for hundreds of miles was about a hundred feet above sea level or less!

This particular old Sikorsky belonged to a stateside operator who'd done a major part of the early seismic work in preparation for us *wildcatters*, but this ship had obviously been parked for *months*, which caused us to make inquiry. Turns out the helicopter kept getting shot at, in flight. And hit! In the last incident, the tail rotor had been peppered by double-ought buckshot. It was no secret that twelve-gauge shotguns were the weapons-of-choice in *la sélva*.

Yep, somewhere along the way, someone had offended the locals with their whirly-copters or their politics or their superiority complexes or their *pínchy dinero*—their wealth. Or all of the above. And the rancor ended up shutting down their operation.

The once-grand old Sikorsky remained a dusty airport monument to futility for over a year, as we wildcatters would document in our comings and goings through this piquant airstrip at the headwaters of the Amazon:

"Is she still there, Paul?"

"Still there, Bruce."

"Damn shame!"

Rejoining our mechanics, we got N1496W and N59438 loaded up, fired up, rotors *in the green* and *gone* before you could say *"Puerto Amélia!"* Headed west in a loose trail formation, I admired the way Charlie had the Peruvian air traffic control guy eating out of his hand with that wonderful Texas *twang* of his. *Cariñoso! So charming.* Charlie was back!

I was impressed by the track and feel of "438," a Huey at heart. Dennis Hingston rode left seat, a skinny young mechanic with long blond hair and one hell of a sunburn. He looked at me kind of funny, and shouted over the bedlam, "Hey Wingo, did you get a *haircut?*"

Dennis could be a smart-alec, too. But that's okay. He and his sun-burnt buddies would soon be outside every evening, working on these maintenance-hog *flying tractors*, all the while involuntarily feeding the mosquito herd for miles around. Lots and lots of *pínchy sancúdos*…blood suckers. And the pilots would be all nice and snug inside their screened bunkrooms, snoozing!

438 was quickly up to 110 knots, straight and level. The mechanics had trimmed the vibration levels to "under point two ips," which is rotor-track-and-balance parlance for "smoother than a baby's behind." Keeping 'er right on Charlie's tail was no strain. Still, our combined rotor-racket projected a wide noise footprint around us, especially at 500 feet.

We could see by all the heads turning along the riverbanks and rafts below us that Bell 205s were a new sight and sound in these parts! Flying in trail formation over the jungle gave me flashbacks to Vietnam.

I could almost hear my old Cobra-drivin' buddy Dudley G. Hale,[41] who would shout over the din: "We're burning ninety gallons an hour, pal. We'd *better be* makin' some freakin' *noise!*"

41   As a bad-ass Cobra pilot with the 1/9 Cavalry, Dudley was known in 'Nam as "*Deadly Hail!*"

And sports fans, that's the way I *love* to go to work: the big rotors rocking my world, making the familiar thundering noises a Huey driver learns to love; skill-testing challenges with every takeoff, and new horizons through yonder windscreen. And they *pay* you to do this!

(Momma, if I'm dreamin'—don't wake me up!)

Puerto Amelia

*"Let observation with extensive view
Survey Mankind, from China to Peru."*

Samuel Jackson (1709-1784)

Just over an hour into our amazing low-level jungle flight, our little formation passed over the village of Lagunas, a kilometer or so east of our destination. The Marañon is wide here. Lagunas's population? I'm guessing less than a thousand. (Looks fairly primitive!)

Westward we whirled, another kilometer before getting our first aerial view of Puerto Amelia: a wide meadow carved out of the jungle, adjacent to a left-hand bend in the mighty Huallaga. A harbor—large enough to park a couple of river barges—had been dredged out recently. A dozen buildings with jungle-style corrugated tin roofs, a couple of warehouses, and—lo and behold—two virginal, yet-to-be-touched-by-a-helicopter concrete pads awaited us, in addition to a helicopter hangar. (Make that a one-holer.)

Circling to verify wind direction and feast our eyes, Charlie keyed up the VHF radio and called attention to the floating dock along the riverbank. A Pilatus Porter on floats bobbed along next to the pier. "There's our taxi back to civilization, boys," he drawled.

Out in the middle of the meadow was a massive, vine-draped, hundred-foot-tall-plus *Lupuna* tree, the lone survivor that was spared the chainsaw and bulldozer. Standing there majestically, it was instantly a *Wingo magnet.*

Pulling my head back inside to face the dials, I copied Charlie's directions. "Ease 'em in nice and pretty now, Wingo—we done drew a crowd!"

And sure enough, the oil company's overhead had flown in by float planes to meet us. Add to that group the regular camp staff, and they had the elevated walkways near the helipads jammed as we made what Charlie would call a "707" approach. More like two noisy, oversized iron butterflies, fluttering right up to the helispots. *Nice and smooth.*

That's one of the things I liked about Horseshit—he didn't showboat. When you had Charlie as a pilot, you were in good hands. Magic carpet rides—professional and stress free. (Well, he did have some shady stories or two about flying "Mattel Messerschmitts"[42] as a civilian maintenance pilot back at Fort Wolters…a story that gathers momentum with the line, "Git your foot up, Horseshit! Here they come!")

Following the standard two-minute turbine engine cool-down, I was anticipating a lengthy bureaucratic indoctrination once the introductions and handshaking were over. We first met Jim Duncan, the customer's head engineer. Jim wobbled forward and wasted no time informing us we were just in time for a tour of the drilling operation, fifty miles or so northwest of Puerto Amelia.

All hands pitched in to help unload the luggage and supplies, as Charlie assisted an overweight, flushed-face Duncan into the left front seat. Charlie had shut down 96W and took over the right front seat of 438 as I helped unload our gear. I had the distinct impression that Jim was intoxicated; and he was sweating profusely. But he was giving Charlie clear directions to the lease location. I'm sure Charlie noticed his condition, too—but Charlie was a *company man,* and pretended to not notice.

Going along for the orientation, several passengers strapped into the rear bench seats, from the ten or so available. Charlie's conservative departure over the broad, churning Marañon signaled the first *air-taxi* flight for our little wildcat operation.

42   Army-aviator speak for the once popular Hughes 269A, a primary helicopter trainer.

After a two-hour orientation, 438 returned with half our *pax* and no cargo; the rest had been dropped off at Rig Nine, the *plataforma*—as the locals called the portable H&P drill rig. After Horseshit shut the engine down, our small group of pilots reconvened in the mess hall to go over the maps and points along the route to use for VFR navigation.

The mess hall was well appointed, with large freezers and refrigerators. Several ceiling fans kept a gentle breeze going over the paperwork while we sized up the jungle lease boundaries and noted magnetic headings[43] to important locations, as well as the prevalent radio frequencies. As we looked ahead to the next day's production, Charlie made flying assignments and we retired to wash up for dinner.

I was immediately impressed with the friendly nature of the Peruvian staff. Some were *obreros*, vaguely defined as day laborers. The mess hall staff wore white uniforms and were all smiles, always ready to scoop us up some *sopa* or a slice of cake. The coffee urn was full of hot water, all one needed to make unlimited cups of the aforementioned instant coffee. It was also a surprise to learn that cold beer was available (for those off duty) in the mess hall, not something found in every oil camp, I learned.

There were others from Iquitos or Lima, depending on their pecking order and job description. There were never more than twenty or thirty people in Puerto Amelia at one time; most of the company's manpower stayed at the *plataforma*, either in porta-camps[44] or crude temporary shelters, again depending on the nature of their responsibilities.

Being the designated rookie pilot of our flock of five, my flying challenges would begin soon. The first drill site, "Rig Nine," was in danger of being abandoned after numerous cave-ins at a depth of around 10,000 feet. Last year's seismic research told them they would have to drill deeper—perhaps 18,000 feet—to reach crude oil.

But the first exploratory hole was a big loser, so they were considering pulling out of the hole, disassembling the rig, and moving the equipment by barge to a staging area several miles northeast and upstream—known as "Line 22"—alongside the Pavayaca River. From there, we would have to

---

43   This was before the time that the Global Positioning System was available to commercial aircraft.

44   Picture an insulated box with four bunks, one door, and one window. The toilets were elsewhere.

chopper everything by air, eleven miles over the flat, triple canopy jungle to the next prospect, "Drill Site 305."

When the inevitable drill move came, Charlie began supervising the short-sling operation from dockside at Line 22, while Alaska-based pilot Dick Izold and I flew the first loads to the new drill location. The Bells performed well at one hundred feet above sea level, so Charlie worked with the staging manager to keep our external load weights up for maximum efficiency.

(Horseshit rarely flew as part of the daily rotation. He had plenty else to do: schmoozing with the customer; managing parts and supplies for two Hueys; scheduling his four pilots; and motivating our three A&P mechanics. For the most part, his capable pilots required little supervision.)

Charlie had apparently forgiven me for the tainted ceviche episode back in Lima, but when I blew his coveted red Bell baseball cap off his hairy head and into the piranha-infested Rio Pavayaca, he was one pissed-off unit. There was no diving in to save the cap—carried away by a five knot current. He could only watch as a whirlpool sucked it up. Charlie's prized headgear was on its way to the Marañon as I clattered off with my lumbering load of pilings and he bowed his shaggy mane in the waning of my gale.

In the dazzling Peruvian sunshine, Charlie was reduced to squinting a lot without his cap, the well-weathered unit he had picked up years earlier going through the Bell Helicopter factory's 205A-1 transition program. The faded red ball cap was unique—they had large bills on them in those days. The rotor-wash from my heavy load had caught him off guard as he straddled a deck portal on the jet fuel barge—away it sailed! The way he pouted afterward, I knew he wasn't going to get over it any time soon.

If You Can't Stand the Heat...

*   *Stay the Heck Out of the Kitchen!*

From ten thousand feet, the Amazon Basin looks like a wet pool table on a good day, and a wall of black-and-coral thunderstorms on a bad day. In between (and down at five hundred feet) we were free to sling the oil company's equipment by helicopter over the flat, featureless jungle. There was plenty of sweltering work for the next two weeks, in fact.

This was to be my second complete drill move—flying a Bell 205A-1—but this move was for a different customer. We were filling in for one of their Sikorsky 58Ts that perished with an engine fire. Union Oil was heli-drilling near Soledad Bartra, along the Rio Tigre and the Ecuadorian border. They were just starting to move the big pieces when I arrived with N59438.

We were under the gun, however—because another fill-in pilot before me had pickled a valuable load of steel pipe valves the previous day. Thunderstorms had obscured the destination and I suppose he freaked out, punching off the load (to fly faster) when he ran low on fuel. (He was searching for a job after that.)

The remaining 58T and I got things going again. "Tito" took the heavier loads by virtue of more lift capacity and a detailed game plan he had worked out, giving me all I could handle in terms of bulky block-shaped items, such as the *porta-camp* living quarters, the mess hall, and the kitchen.

While the obreros nailed the shipping panels back in place around the mess hall, Tito headed south with a load. I took on just enough jet fuel to short-sling the first big box forty-eight nautical miles at forty knots—and land with a low fuel light.

Signaling me into the chute, the heli-director knelt at my one o'clock and gave me hand signals while I verified the hookup man's work via the convex belly mirror. I felt the familiar *clunk* as the shackle slammed past the keeper onto the belly hook's load beam, and the hookup man headed for cover. The director held on to his hard hat with one hand and gave me the ol' *let-'er-rip* signal with the other.

A slight application of power took the slackness out of the rigging. Pulling collective pitch to *max-gas-producer*, there arose a mighty commotion! My EGT was in the mid-yellow, and while trying hard not to move the cyclic, I was sandblasting the poor director. A lot of *wop-wop-wopping* was going on, but not much was else was happening. (The Staging Area *sucked* today, for want of a steady breeze.) Give it time, I kept telling myself—*poco-a-poco*...

Slowly, the bulky box lifted off the ground, teetering against the four-way rigging and jostling the bird. Daring not to move the cyclic more than a *hair* forward, the beautiful Bell somehow understood, inching ahead. More shaking, as her fuel load began to disappear on the gauge; her abundance of moving parts were getting a noisy workout.

Our *walking pace* gradually increased to a *canter*, then came the welcomed clatter of the main rotor-blades, the long-awaited *dip* toward earth as the subtle ground-cushion shifted aft and we punched through to translational lift...and the Captain began breathing again.

The mess hall swung and thumped, though—and started to rotate. Regardless, I kept the nose down and held takeoff power for the brief climb. We would need forty knots to make *Drill Site Bravo* with this fuel load, and the overhead didn't want these loads comin' back. Like all the other loads, it was gonna spin "one way or the other." So said Tito, an experienced pilot.

The mess hall was almost a perfect square, I noted—as its four corners rotated clockwise under my skids; finally maxing out at ten rotations per minute—at forty knots. The thunderstorms were on the waning side of the first daily drenching, so at least I would have good visibility—although the atmosphere was very steamy.

Twenty minutes into the flight, I helplessly noted that an entire wall panel had departed the mess hall! As I eyeballed the convex mirror, an explosion of white particles followed—which I later confirmed was the camp's impressive collection of Louis L'Amour paperback novels, now lying tattered and scattered throughout the jungle behind me. The monkeys should appreciate this, I mused as I augered along...

And—since there was no place to land and no time to waste—I plowed ahead as *one, two, three, four* Samsonite folding tables shot out the open hole in plain view of my mirror. After the tables split, I started wondering about the chairs—and here *they* came, shooting out like cards out of a dealer's shoe, every last one. We were a bit lighter now...

Eventually I spotted the familiar broken snag above a year-old, dilapidated JetRanger seismic helispot, one of only two course markers along the otherwise obscure magnetic track that led us to *Bravo*. *No room to land there*, Tito had cautioned—*keep everything moving*. A few minutes later, the freshly graded clearing for *Drill Site Bravo* came into view abeam the refueling point, where our loads were beginning to stack up.

As I took on fuel, the ground handlers appraised the missing panel and equipment. I suggested *screws* versus *nails* and *more of them*. The man in charge nodded in complete agreement. He then changed the subject.

"If we're gonna eat anything tonight," he drawled, appraising the ever-changing sky, "you better git back with the kitchen before the next wave of storms." Which meant to me, we can always eat standing up. *Tables and chairs can be added to the list!* Off I clattered.

Right as rain, the storms began fluffing up for the second daily drenching as I headed back northbound at cruise speed, determined to get the kitchen back in time for the evening meal. Inside the cabin, I was back-hauling some rigging for the Staging Area hands; otherwise I was empty and made close to 120 knots.

The director at the other end was *mondo* unhappy to hear about the lost tables and chairs, but he assured me I'd have no such trouble with the kitchen. "Long screws," he said, holding several up for me to see. After a touch more fuel, I hovered toward the slot; the kitchen was waiting as the Bell floated into position.

The kitchen was a tad smaller than the mess hall, but it was a heavy load. Max power (and a little headwind this time) made the launch go well, but I'd be flying against those same southwesterlies on the way back. As I leveled off at five hundred feet, the kitchen stabilized in an eight-revs-per-minute rotation, and appeared to be holding together.

Dark thunderclouds on the horizon made the imaginary course line difficult to perceive, but twenty minutes into the flight came the familiar old snag and rotten LZ—right on course. Ten minutes later, the only exception to the monotonous flat terrain glided by, a small hill off to the right. *Home free,* I said to myself, as the graded strip finally popped out of the clouds at my twelve o'clock, five hundred yards away.

On short final, I had the power pulled in and was still decelerating as I noticed a previously undetected dirt berm crossing under my nose, perpendicular to my approach path. Applying aft cyclic, I tried to avoid having the load strike the berm on the way by.

No such luck! *Shudder, clunk* went the kitchen, as the load bottomed out on the dirt hump at around five knots and stopped rudely, bringing the ship to a halt as well. Easing off the power, I pickled the rigging to one side and landed for fuel.

While refueling was underway, I jogged back to the kitchen to make sure I hadn't damaged anything. The other hands were busy rounding up the loose rigging as I twisted the door knob and stepped in to take a look: Standing between the big gas grill and the prep sink—where nobody should have been—stood Jaime, the Peruvian cook—manning a broom!

Jaime was mumbling about *the mess* but didn't look my way as I stood there in slack-jawed disbelief. Some flour had spilled out of one of the cupboards, yet the cook had swept most of it up by the time I opened the door! "*No problema,*" he kept saying, as I reconsidered the appropriate words.

I felt like screaming as I shut the door behind me, knowing our macho cook had flown every rotation inside the spinning kitchen—no doubt getting the ride of his life! As I prepared to strap back in the helicopter, the director waltzed over nonchalantly and handed me a list titled "Staging Area Passengers." Several pax were waiting for me up north, my last load of the day.

As he looked on, I slowly drew a line through "Jaime" and handed it back to the director. He gazed at me with a confused expression as I angled my head in the direction of the kitchen. He turned toward the kitchen, a disbelieving look on his ashen face. As he stood there, his dusty mouth beginning to open wide, I climbed in and revved her up for the last flight while Jaime hurried to prepare our dinner.

Cargo We'd Rather Not Haul

---

* *Two of the worst sling loads one might fly...*

The swift Pavayaca was instrumental in a tragedy that occurred a few weeks later. There was a celebration of some kind one Saturday afternoon at the obreros' camp alongside Line 22. Two of the senior native labor supervisors got to partying with their men, and the beer and whiskey flowed late into the evening.

At around 2 a.m.—and against the objections of some—the two bid *adios* and made their way to the small outboard that was to return them to their comfortable cabin on a barge, just downstream a ways. In the inky darkness, the inebriated supers stumbled boarding the boat. The boat immediately capsized and the men disappeared from view. They went missing for over two days.

Three days later, I was asked to fly an unscheduled mission to our distant riverside staging area. The bodies of our two local labor managers had bobbed to the surface in a piranha-infested[45] river. The dead men's supervisor—a young Peruvian oil engineer—explained that I was to retrieve the bodies and fly them to the village where they both were born and raised. A wooden box suitable for a temporary

---

45 *Serrasalmus nattereri*—the red variety swims in large schools, grows up to twelve inches long, and prefers calm water to swift.

dual-coffin was being loaded into my shiny Bell 205 A-1 as I was briefed.

No stranger to hauling the deceased,[46] I gently asked the young man if he knew what he was asking me to do, as there were no body bags available for the occasion; and once loaded, the flight to their village would take at least forty minutes. Due to his inexperience and emotional attachment, he didn't fully catch my drift.

About then, Horseshit Charlie walked up to lend me a hand. After a short private conversation, the two of us nonchalantly loaded up a long line and some choker straps—*just in case*. Charlie hadn't shared my combat experiences—but he *was* from Texas, where common sense is handed out in bushel baskets.

We maintained a solemn silence on the ferry flight to the staging area, as the mourning engineer sat strapped into one of the rear seats. Charlie thoughtfully fingered his tangled beard while scanning for dazzling formations of colorful parrots, and let me do the flying.

An outboard motorboat had towed the bloated victims two kilometers upstream by a short piece of rope. Negotiating a five-knot current, the boat pulled up to the crude cargo dock just as we shut down. Charlie and I waited as the engineer ran to identify his old friends. Within seconds, he came running back with his handkerchief clutched over his mouth, tears streaming down his face.

"Hor-**rí**-ble!" he cried. "We cannot carry them inside!" Charlie consoled the distraught man while I helped unload the wooden box and rigging.

We ended up long-lining the victims with a one-hundred-foot braided wire rope and swivel for the return flight to the village. The box rocked and spun slowly; forty knots was as fast as our non-aerodynamic load would fly. An hour later, the village came into view.

Hundreds of villagers were silently awaiting the noisy chopper as we approached the ancient, bald, dirt soccer field—our designated LZ. There was no security in place for the crowd that had gathered. This became a safety factor as the slowly spinning box inched down toward the ground; the crush of humanity rushed to retrieve their loved ones.

46   Our least favorite mission in the Vietnam war: hauling out our dead.

Looking out the left cockpit window, my concern switched to the living as I gently lowered the box to within their outstretched fingers, at which time the Bell's rotor wash swept over the box and upon the crowd. Immediately an opening formed—as the closest villagers caught wind of our cargo and reeled—shoving back at the crowd as they fought for fresh air. Word spread like wildfire; there was suddenly a clearing below the box, and we lowered away.

(I shiver, just *thinking* about our options without that long line…)

A few days later—the fertilizer hit the ventilator again. While idling at the staging area for my next sling load to the new oil platform, I saw several obreros wrestling a large, heavy roll of *something* from under a tarp. They made faces as they wheeled it awkwardly around, and began rolling it slowly down the boardwalk in my direction. As the cargo rolled closer, it hit me: this thing is *ripe!*

A month previously I had heard one of Evergreen's pilots—Paul Lloyd—describe in glowing, Shakespearean terms what one must endure while transporting a one-ton roll of crudely dried (Corvina) fish to the plataforma, where scores of laborers worked hard and dined ravenously on the local fare—and suddenly, it was my turn.

The exposed roll was *food* after all, therefore not something that they wanted slung under the Bell. As my Okie nostrils winced, the rotting roll barely cleared the sliding door's upper frame; the obreros manhandled it onto the cargo deck and cinched 'er down.

Drawing a deep breath from the open right side window as the cargo doors slid shut, I eyeballed the important gauges and did a max-performance takeoff. I was soon sailing over the triple-canopy jungle on a magnetic bearing for the eleven-mile flight to the oil platform. Just shy of two minutes later, I finally had to exhale and gasp for air, but it was *rotten perch* that hit my lungs, not oxygen. *Five more minutes to go……*

I could go on, but you get the picture. This is the domain of the Utility Pilot!

Perhaps a good moral for this story would be for utility pilots to carry one of those little tubes of aromatic *white stuff* those FBI guys smeared under their noses in *Silence of the Lambs*.

So heads-up, pilgrim! When it's your turn to haul some *thing* or some *body,* be *prepared.*

El Papazzo and La Torre de Paz

---

*   *The Boss, the Bug, and the Bully*

A month into my Peruvian adventure, our celebrated top guy on the job—Mr. Duncan—had a heart attack while on break at his home in Lima. His recovery was forecasted to take *months*, so daily control of the Puerto Amelia operation was turned over to his old drinking buddy from southern Louisiana. Broussard was a big *Cajun*. He was a tough, experienced dredge operator—and he had (in my opinion) one-third of his predecessor's managerial skill and tact—unfortunately for the rest of us.

When the reins were passed to Broussard, he made himself at home in Duncan's hooch and office, spending a lot of time on the short-wave radio, where he got over-the-shoulder instructions from the other side of the Andes on how things worked at the next level.

Had Broussard just kept to his job, things around Puerto Amelia would probably have sailed smoothly. But dredge operator Broussard brought some baggage with him that soon began to grate upon those of us who expected a little courtesy among our group of combat veterans. That baggage included—again, in my opinion—being a bully—and becoming a **tyrant** once he broke in the big shoes that Jim Duncan left behind.

I think it all started with Broussard's new rule: **No hats in the mess**

hall. I mean, here we were, about as far from a hat rack as a civilized man could get, and he lays this silly rule on us. He was asking for it, as far as Huey pilot Dick Izold was concerned! Dick was a big man, inches taller than Broussard, stouter, and ten years younger. And Dick had a cold stare that would stop a charging grizzly bear in his tracks.

(In preparing to write this story, I located Dick Izold's address in the Vietnam Helicopter Pilots Association Directory and wrote to him in Alaska. Dick's email response came soon, as did photographs of the rig and big Captain Izold himself standing next to a Pilatus-Porter floatplane. His memory of Puerto Amelia and all the characters there was still sharp, and over the days that followed, he recounted some thoughts that serve to complement the Puerto Amelia story, starting with....)

"Do you remember when Broussard unilaterally declared we couldn't wear hats in the mess hall anymore? One day we were in the mess hall playing 'Hearts' or something and Broussard sneaked up on Horseshit and knocked his hat off. The instant he did that I put mine on, stood up, and stared him down. He didn't say a word."

The card game sorta froze at that point, I remember distinctly. All eyes were on the big fellas. But it suffices to say that Broussard *blinked*, and left the building! We didn't hear any more about Broussard's silly hat rule, and the three of us were proud of Dick that evening for reminding Broussard he wasn't in high school anymore.

Broussard had no inkling of, nor any respect for the skill level and courage it takes to sling-load heavy equipment from a single engine rotorcraft all day long, so it was inevitable that we would come to odds. It wasn't just me—the jungle camp's pet monkey learned real quick to *disappear* when Broussard's hand-wrought slingshot materialized in the bully's hands and painful stones began to fly.

The native employees recoiled in shame when he started shooting at the camp's pitiful stray dogs; the bony-ribbed mongrels only sought a scrap from the bountiful trash drum just inside the kitchen's screen door.

Weary of the generators' noise and Broussard in general, I got inspired one day and started building an observation tower at the edge of the jungle, solely to have a quiet place to go to on my time off. This afforded a treetop view of the massive eastbound Rio Huallaga as it turned north to join the Marañon, and on to the Amazon. Broussard stayed away from my *Torre de Paz*, and things started to improve. Then my boss showed up—from far, far away.

My antagonist slash dredge operator had called the home office the week prior. He wanted me fired for challenging him over the right of the mostly native employees to play soccer in the small compound near the mess hall. That was the only stump-cleared, flat place for many, many miles. An errant forward pass had popped the screen-wire loose on an adjacent building, and Broussard decided that was **that.**

Puffing himself up like some kind of demigod, Broussard summarily cancelled that match and all future games—the only real recreation that the pilots, mechanics, and natives had at our disposal!

Outraged by his brand of bullying, I blew my top! After all, the bully himself had shot more than one rock through other screens while target practicing at the mess hall monkey. I stood my ground, screaming Hispanic insults at him and shaking my fists.

Broussard glared at me like I was nuts, but didn't come after me—fortunately. He could have broken my neck like a twig with one punch. Unfortunately, he went instead into the radio room and picked up the shortwave's handset, letting his distant boss know the score. Hence *my* boss's arrival, a few days later.

Life in the jungle got a little more interesting the morning the boss was due to arrive on the oh-eleven-hundred Pilatus Porter: I discovered a *Callipogon armillatum (Linnaeus)*[47] clinging to the screen wire outside my humble jungle hut. Commonly known as " the longhorned beetle," this is considered *the* largest of all beetles on the planet. I'd never seen one before and didn't even know they existed. (The native's name for the huge bug is *"el Papazzo."*)

Dashing back into the hut for my Pentax, I snapped one photo with my hand nearby for scale, while the aggressive beetle hissed and thrashed his long antennae around. I convinced one of the braver Obreros looking on to grab hold of it for a close-up of its underside. Being a night flyer,

---

47   Courtesy of Al Samuelson, Natural Sciences, Bishop Museum in Honolulu and
       Steve Lingafelter, Ph.D., Systematic Entomology Laboratory, the National Museum
       of Natural History, Washington, D.C.

el Papazzo was temporarily grounded by the nightly DDT fogger that kept the mosquito herd at bay while our nocturnal A&P mechanics wrenched on the beautiful Bells.

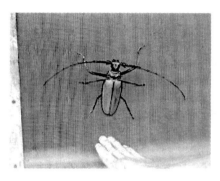

Curious about the power of his imposing mandibles, I offered the behemoth a plastic card, which he perforated like a train conductor on steroids! After three snapshots, I left *el Papazzo* hanging angrily to the screen wire and hiked reflectively toward yonder tower. If this was going to be my last day on the job, I wanted to spend it in my tower.

Ward Eason arrived by float plane right on time and, glancing in my direction with a stern look, marched with his out-of-place-looking briefcase up the long floating ramp toward the Camp Boss's hut. An hour or so later, he strolled (head bowed) past the dock, in the shade of the hangar's eave, and through the tall grassy path in my direction.

I was about to learn that Ward was an unusually thoughtful person for having such a lofty position in Operations. With few words, he negotiated the rough-hewn pole ladder's ascent to the crude, two-man recliner. We were soon gazing westward—silently observing the incredible, ever-changing *Huallaga*.

A lonely river raft loaded with platanos floated peacefully toward us and drifted quietly around the bend; blind white fresh-water porpoises played in small schools; carpenter birds dive-bombed for chubs. *Sancudos* nibbled our exposed skin while we perspired in the light breeze.

I sensed that Ward had already *seen* the problem he came six thousand miles to exorcise. After a very pleasant silence, he spoke. No harsh words came forth—just some suggestions that a friend might offer another to help resolve differences of opinions.

Gently changing the subject, I asked Mr. Eason if he had noticed *el Papazzo* clinging to the hut. His crafty right eyebrow lifted up a millimeter. *"Papazzo?"* he inquired. *A fellow amateur entomologist,* my

Okie sensors deduced. He headed gingerly down the trembling ladder after I invited him to check "el" out before his final meeting with Broussard.

Imagine the consternation the bully must have felt when he heard the commotion outside his office moments later. He glared out the office's window as a handful of natives and three greasy mechanics laughed and hooted: Ward Eason was walking merrily along the boardwalk behind the giant, flying beetle. He had tied a long thread around its thorax! Ward was in heaven, a kid drawn back in time by a bug and a piece of string.

Minutes later, the float plane pilot waved *adios* to those at dockside as Ward situated his briefcase for flight and snugged up his seat belt. He had good reason to be pleased with himself, having quelled a potentially nasty *wrinkle* in the field so easily. I wondered if ol' Broussard would have agreed, as I admired a paralyzing sunset from the tower and he sulked up a storm in his steamy office.

The tower was the best idea I'd had in a long time, one that probably saved my job and cemented my excellent relationship with the Peruvians. They took a shine to it, especially after I added the thatched roof and Peruvian flag. They were the ones who named it "Torre de Paz," *tower of peace*—the appropriate mechanism for distancing myself from you-know-who.

As fast as the Obreros named it, Broussard was heard swearing an oath during a drunken rage. He was "*by-gawd-gonna cut it down,*" before he left Puerto Amelia. (So long as he didn't do it while I was around, my hands were tied—and I let the bully's threat molder.)

Wildlife in the Jungle

Ever since I was a kid in Sundown, Texas, I have been an admirer of Lepidoptera (butterflies), owing to a lethargic Monarch migration that fluttered through our tiny town in the mid-fifties. Puerto Amelia was home to so many species of butterflies, I got moderately excited at the prospect of collecting some specimens. They were in abundance, I noted—tearing my eyes away from the alluring red and blue formations of free-ranging feathered scarlet *Macaws* and *Birds of Paradise*. Butterflies were *much* easier to catch!

Most of the butterflies around camp gathered by the riverbank or along the edge of the jungle. A few parked overnight on the illuminated screen-wire entrance to our jungle quarters, alongside gorgeous moths that were over twice their size.

Having a net-fabric tropical shirt in my travel bag, I decided to sacrifice it for *the cause*. With a needle and thread from my sewing kit, I fashioned a butterfly net (with short sleeves) out of the shirt by sewing it to a stiff loop of coat hanger wire, and mounted it on a stick.

The crude net worked great, much to the amusement of all who saw *el Gringo Wingo* dashing helter-skelter across the compound in full pursuit of an elusive *thecline lycaenid* (or *hairstreak*) butterfly.[48] The hairstreak

---

48   Identification (via a photograph many years later) courtesy of Al Samuelson, Bishop Museum, Hawaii.

was the smallest and speediest trophy in my collection. I observed only two during my six-month tour. Both flew out of the dense jungle during thunderstorms.

There was a Peruvian medic based at Puerto Amelia who assisted my efforts by donating a spare hypodermic needle and a small bottle of alcohol for subduing my catches in a ghoulish but humane manner. I soon had a few prized specimens stuck on straight pins on my barracks wall, but I was clearly in need of a trophy case to protect them.

Consulting with the local camp carpenter, I offered up a few *Soles* to commission a wooden display case. Motioning at the few supplies at hand, the carpenter said he'd have to order a half-sheet of glass and some cabinet hinges from Iquitos for the folding lid. There were none in camp. The rest would come from materials available in his little shed.

It took over a week for the glass to arrive, and although it rippled in clarity, I was happy to have a 20-inch by 20-inch cotton-blanketed case hanging on the wall when it was finished. Turns out, some of the most beautiful specimens in my collection were moths. I had visions of returning with the case to the USA someday.

When work took us north to the Rio Tigre, my butterfly net followed. One sunny afternoon, one of the natives working for Union Oil saw me running myself ragged, chasing some speedy swallow-tailed butterflies around camp. He suggested urinating near the river bank to bait the insects, an idea which worked so well that my display case was filled in short order! (*Sheesh!*)

There were thousands and thousands of other interesting critters just waiting to be discovered in the Oriénte. Some of the more intriguing were members of the "lantern fly" group (order Homoptera), classified as *fulgeroids*. These were large, sucking insects that fed on toxic jungle foliage.

Fulgeroids process toxic chemicals in what amounts to little "factories" in their heads, which resemble leafs, peanuts or alligator heads. Some of the natives in camp truly feared being bitten by the *cacahuate* or *peanut* bug—a bite they claimed was poisonous. Dick Izold was quick to remind me....

"Don't forget the big bugs that looked like miniature bowling pins![49] The natives were deathly afraid of them. I remember two natives refusing to go into our little hangar at Puerto Amelia because there were two of them hanging on the screen wire there.

And the big spiders! Those bunches of bananas [platanos] we hauled were usually good for a spider or two. And grubs! Think back, Dorcey, when we first spent a night at the rig, the native help was sitting around the campfire cooking and eating four-inch long grubs and telling us how good they were. But I didn't eat any. I think Charlie did; you'll have to ask him if it tasted like chicken.

And how 'bout the way every bird in the jungle would take off thirty seconds before an earthquake? How the hell did they know? The day we had a good shaker at noon, everyone ran out to watch the rig topple over— which it never did."

---

49   Fulgeroids again: bowling pins or peanuts, your choice.

Losing One's Load

Early in the drill move from Rig Nine to "305," something happened that would shake us all up. One of our experienced pilots hooked up to one of the heavier H&P rig's steel base pieces and took off for the eleven-mile flight to the new rig location. About one minute after takeoff, the pilot heard and felt a violent **clank** of metal-on-metal, and clutched the cyclic control grip hard, by reflex.

Unfortunately, his right ring finger tripped the electric cargo hook release button, triggering the release of the 3,300-lb. chunk of steel. Falling from around five hundred feet, the rig piece impacted a hardwood tree and disappeared into the ever-present watery muck at its base.

What happened was not *new*, especially—as we all had instances where one of the four weight-bearing screw shackles suspending the load would cock in the "up" position. This can sometimes be observed in the convex mirror, but we were dependent upon the Staging Area Manager to signal us if one got *cocked*. Not that we'd set it back down—which is an option—but doing so doesn't always un-cock it.

We'd usually continue with the mission—keeping our right hand cupped over the top of the cyclic grip—fully expecting the rude **thump** that would follow seconds, or minutes later. (Some shackles would ride the entire distance that way, keeping the pilot in white-knuckled suspense the whole time.) It was our pal's bad luck that he made contact with the cargo release button when the shackle flipped down and jolted the whole aircraft.

The following morning I was scoring a cup of caffeine in the mess hall when I had the misfortune of overhearing Broussard voice his opinion of the incident to one of the engineers. "Seems to me the *mother f---er* shoulda *known better*......" at which point I had to leave before I let him know who I thought the *real mother f---er* was! It galled me to no end to hear such criticism coming from such a crude individual—who had no tact and no flying expertise of any kind.[50]

There were no back-up parts for the main rig, unfortunately. After sending an engineer out to inspect the piece that fell,[51] it was determined that an identical piece would have to be flown to Iquitos by C-130 and we would have to go after it in one of the 205s.

This was no simple feat. When the part was said to be on its way to Iquitos, I drew the short straw. Another ship pre-positioned six barrels of Jet-A ahead of time for me. Three fuel barrels were prepositioned at Santa Elena and three more at Requeña, making for a 6.2-hour round trip.

When I landed for fuel at Santa Elena, scores of young school kids came out to witness the spectacle, getting far closer to my hovering helicopter and dangling steel cargo than I would have preferred. It was the same thing on takeoff, even after cautioning the crowd to stay back! I was relieved to get the missing rig piece to its destination safely. For my efforts, I was given another 2.3 hours of rig support-flying to do before dark.

When things were going well, a pilot on the Puerto Amelia rotation could count on working twenty days and getting a week or so off. If a pilot got sick, it could really throw things into a dither, so *that* meant sometimes flying with a cold, a hangover, or as in my case, under the influence of a strong antibiotic—for an infection I came down with. (Had I bothered translating the whole label, I would have noticed that the prescription cautioned me to *avoid strong sunlight* while on the medication.)

My first day back in action was spent hauling those dreaded rig-platform pilings in the broiling sun. The staging manager would hook me up to

---

50   To his credit, no personnel action was undertaken for the frazzled pilot, who stayed on until the end.
51   The rig base piece was too bent to be salvaged, and was left to rust in place.

over three thousand pounds of wooden pilings in a rectangular bundle and give me the *go* sign. The pilings were thick, wooden eight-inch-by-twelve-inch-by-twenty-foot-long beams, on top of which the rig would be assembled.

Paul was flying the other bird that day, and we compared notes over the tendency of the loads to start *bucking* in the relative wind at cruise speed, repeatedly pulling the nose of the helicopter down—making even an unmedicated pilot nauseous in short order...[52]

And then it happened... along about noontime, I was in the final seconds of my long, galloping approach to the new rig when I realized I wasn't going to make it. Concentrating as hard as I could to keep the roiling contents of my stomach down, I finally got the load on the deck, pickled the slack rigging, and hovered aft and sideways to land on the designated spot.

Unfortunately, I tossed my cookies before the skids hit the planks—a disturbing sight for the poor *obrero* who was standing nearby, giving me hand signals. He ran to open my right front door for me as I weakly heaved another load over my knees, onto the floor, and into the chin bubble. (Sorry—even *pilots* puke periodically. But I'm not done yet.)

I motioned for the signalman to stand back until I caught my breath, at which point I shut the ship down and took off for the *obreros'* latrine, a short trot down the elevated walkway...but not in the shade. I was finished throwing up, but now my bowels were in an uproar—so I was fortunate to reach the privy's wide-open bench seat with multiple *portholes*. (Oh good, I noticed—they have *paper!*)

After only a minute or two, I made it back to the ship to find the thoughtful signalman had already swabbed out the chin bubble and other affected areas with a rag and a tin can full of water! I was plenty embarrassed, but very much appreciative of the man's willingness to pitch in. And back to work we went.

On occasion we could hear other *Americanos* talking over the VHF radio from jungle bases distant, but one pilot in particular became an object of ridicule. On the common 122.9 MHz air-to-air frequency, this one S-58T

---

52   Later on, drogue parachutes were attached to the rigging to help keep the loads from oscillating.

pilot was frequently heard screaming at his would-be dispatcher—a native fellow who tended to stray away from his radio. This was allegedly near a place that sounded like *"Arequipa."*

The 58 pilot always seemed to be in need of *something* that only the dispatcher could give him, and the dispatcher was apparently tired of hearing the pilot's foul mouth day in and day out (as were we)...so the dispatcher made it a point to be *gone* a lot.

"Ar-e-keep-a, Ar-e-keep-a, Ar-e-keep-a! Answer the f---ing radio, you stupid slope bastard!" came the acidic radio calls. *"I'm gonna fly down there and drop a f----ing brick through your f---ing roof if you don't get on the f----ing radio!!"* he screamed.

(Our crew was—for the most part—enjoying our adventure in Peru, so we made it a point to be civil, especially with the locals. We found it shocking the way a few others steamrolled over them in the guise of commerce.)

Finally one day, I had heard enough and radioed Dick Izold, who was slinging drill pipe in the other Huey. *"Richard, can you hear that trash-mouth pilot?"* To which Dick replied, *"Yeah, disgusting, isn't it? I wish he'd shut up."*

And the 58 pilot must have heard us, for he *did* shut up right then and there, and we never heard another uncivil word out of him. Had we known how easy it was going to be, we would have said something sooner! (I wonder—many years later—if the pilot was suffering from Post-Traumatic Stress.)

There comes a time on every contract where a chopper pilot gets the feeling he should be moving on, and the feeling came to me when we cleaned out our jungle barracks and moved into the porta-camps way out at the drill rig. I sadly watched my empty tower disappear from view as we flew off into the sunset.

Accommodations at the rig were basic, at best. There were now up to four men to a box, double bunked. The restrooms and showers were some distance away. The boxy mess hall was open most of the time, and the food was *okay.* Hanging my butterfly collection on the wall, I unpacked my bag and made the best of it, but I already missed La Torre de Paz and the option to retreat to it when boredom or frustration struck.

I spent a lot of my free time at Rig 305 watching the roughnecks run the drilling platform. When they saw me studying them, someone handed me a hard hat and pointed to a safe place to observe the action, close up. Unless you've had the opportunity, you might not appreciate the many ways a man can get mangled by spinning oil-drilling machinery. Our guys were sharp, though—I don't recall any injuries to a roughneck that required a flight to the medic.

It was strangely satisfying to see the mountain of ninety-pound quickset concrete bags going down the ever-deepening hole, after flying so many bags so many miles. I remember the respect I felt for the sweat-soaked chain of muscular obreros as they piss-anted the bags one by one into a gigantic pile inside the warehouse that was built close to the rig. (As I recall, they earned less than three dollars a day for their backbreaking labor.)[53]

As the hole was drilled, concrete was pumped down it to form a solid casing above the drill. This accommodated the exchange of rock cuttings and mud that was forced up and out of the hole, splashing at long last into a gooey lake on one side of the rig.

The multihued lake was pretty disgusting to look at, so it didn't take my cartoon-based brain very long to come up with a name for it. On my first "off" day, I fashioned a neatly lettered sign on a slab of wood, nailed that to a long stake, removed my rotting sneakers, and put on my shorts...

When I got the head driller's attention, I held up the sign and pointed toward the mire. He grinned and waved me on. It was quite a struggle to wade through the sucking muck, but when I sank the stake, I heard a cheer or two from the platform crew as I oriented the name *Lake Broussard* in full view of the camp.

---

53   The Peruvian government determined the laborers' wages, allegedly designed to minimize inflation.

Giving Notice

It wasn't long afterward, I received word that my mother back in New Mexico had been diagnosed with double phlebitis, a serious inflammation of the arteries in both legs. I could tell from her letter that she was worried sick and wanted her faraway son to come home again. After serving two and one-half years overseas in the Army, I could read between the lines. I saw the end coming six months into my adventure, like it or not.

The monsoons arrived about that time, and my treasured butterfly collection—whose display case was not airtight—molded practically overnight into a sad-looking green mess. I was crushed. It was only five months into the project when I voiced my intentions to return home.

It had been a truly excellent six-month adventure, overlooking one dredge operator. As a young captain, I was pleased to log 333 flight hours over seventy-three workdays, rising and falling with heavy equipment or putrid fish rolls. There were more "down" days than anyone planned for, but such is the nature of the work. That's a good time to have one's spirit of adventure and curiosity kick in.

During all that flying, the following problems occurred:

- Nov.17—Tail rotor struck a wooden stake that a none-too-sharp surveyor sank in the ground, right in the LZ we were using— miraculously, there was no damage.

- Jan. 10—Lost hydraulic pressure, hover-landed on slippery jungle helipad during a rainstorm.
- Jan. 31—DC generator failure.
- Mar.18—Lost hydraulic pressure.
- Apr. 10—Flamed out while refueling at Line 22. The Jet-A barge had sprung a leak and took on several hundred gallons of water. Much work followed to clean out both vessels.

I also had an engine hot-start after shutting down briefly at Line 22 one afternoon, catching me flat-footed. Evergreen's future Chairman of the Board—Tim Wahlberg—was Director of Maintenance in those days. Unfortunately for him, he was also a mechanic and was visiting our field operation that afternoon. He and another mechanic spent all night doing a hot end inspection on my ship, which determined the engine's hot section to be *okay*.

The best part of my adventure may have been the free time I spent perched in La Torre while Peru floated by, taking short, sweaty power naps, writing long, illustrated letters to friends, and sipping cold Bohemia beer from an iced-up bucket the mess hall crew gladly prepared for me. This was made sweeter if some thoughtful traveler flew in with a week-old newspaper or news magazine to read from *The World* (as we still lovingly referred to the United States). Or perhaps it was exploring the outer fringes of the jungle with the obreros, observing a new side of nature while giving my anemic Español a good workout. Or simply flying along hour after hour with my head half out the window, marveling at the dependability of my anti-gravity machine and how lucky I was to be alive.

I am frequently reminded of an item that appeared in a long list of *"Tips for Student Pilots"* a wise old Air Force pilot sent to me. The one that really hit home read: *"You start with a bag full of luck and an empty bag of experience. The trick is to fill the bag of experience before you empty the bag of luck."*

I would be remiss in failing to mention the humongous *catfish* that inhabited the Huallaga near Puerto Amelia, although I never did manage to photograph one. Some might not believe it, but these river bottom dwellers frequently weighed over four hundred pounds!

When I was first told about them, I must have had a look of disbelief on my face. That was before our Peruvian chef invited me to follow him into the kitchen and inspect the contents of the camp's walk-in freezer.

Lordy, there were *three* frozen *motas*[54] hanging from meat hooks in plain sight as he opened the door! Each was big around the middle and four feet to five feet in length. Their whiskers were longer than their bodies! The chef explained that it took at least two men to catch, clean, and hang them on the meat hook. Even with a thin layer of freezer-frost, the cats were a lovely speckled blue and white in color.

Here's the prescribed manner for catching a big mota:

1. First, take an eighteen-inch-long piece of "number nine" rebar (concrete reinforcement bar) and bend one end into a barbed hook and the other end into an eyelet, using a welding torch, vise, and hammer.
2. Finesse a sharp point on the hook using a grinding wheel. For the sinker, fill a coffee can with quick-setting concrete and trap another rebar eyelet in the mix. Then tie one end of a sturdy sixty-foot-long polyurethane rope securely to the eye.
3. Five feet above the sinker, tie the rebar hook securely to the rope.
4. Next, take an ordinary rod and reel and catch a small mota—a three-pounder or so—for bait.
5. Slap the unfortunate baitfish on the hook.
6. Lower the bait and sinker into the river, after tying the free end onto a stout tree trunk.
7. Go find something else to do for a day or two.
8. When you come back, test-lift the line. If you can't budge it, you have probably hooked a full-sized mota!
9. If so, **summon help**, and enjoy the feast. (The meat: delicious, with the taste and texture of pork loin chops.)

My departure from Puerto Amelia was uneventful, although I was sad to leave in many ways. One of the natives working for the Tool Pusher bought my last pair of Ray Bans off me as I headed for the floatplane. The Levi's and other items had long been sold or traded at a nice profit, adding a small bonus to the six grand I had managed to save. The hard-earned cash came in handy later that summer, when I had to put down some earnest money on ten acres of riverfront property near O'Brien, Oregon.[55]

---

54   *Surubim mandi*
55   As described later in *"Pedo Heights."*

Going Against the Flow

By his fifth month in the jungle, Dick Izold let Horseshit Charlie know that he could make better money working in construction back in Alaska and be home every night. (He made his decision after Ward came to visit us at Puerto Amelia…)

Dick wrote from Alaska in March of 2001…

I remember Ward coming to camp for a short 'You guys are doing a great job' pep talk, and to tell us the contract had been extended. As I recall, he thought an 'atta-boy' was better for us than a raise. He was wrong. One of the photos that got away from me was of him flying one of our giant bugs around on a string. I always thought that picture summed up the corporate policy perfectly: 'We don't pay much…but we have fun!'

Dick eventually got his wish, returning to Alaska six days after I left for New Mexico. Before Dick caught his floatplane home at Puerto Amelia, he described what transpired his last night in the jungle, as told in another e-mail:

*Duncan and Broussard were thick. Could be because I think they were from the same town. Weren't they from Mississippi, a town named Broussard? Maybe it was Louisiana, I'm not sure. I do remember them calling each other **Coon Ass** and **Redneck** or some other unpleasant name. They didn't come off as very educated and I'd be surprised if…they had ever* read more than one book between them. For sure they were asshole buddies. I don't mean they were tail-gunning each other—I mean they'd pal around and laugh at each other's sorry-ass jokes.

'Sid' was one of the H&P Tool Pushers who worked two weeks on and two weeks off. It turns out that the evening I'm back at Puerto Amelia (I was leaving for Alaska the next day), Sid had just come in to switch with the other Tool Pusher. So there was me, Broussard, Sid, and Jim Duncan in camp. I no longer had a room at PA because we'd been living at the rig so I had to share a room with Broussard.

When I got tired I went to bed; the other three stayed in the mess hall drinking beer. At oh-dark-thirty here they came and woke me up with their arguing. I saw Broussard punch Sid in the mouth and knock him down. A short while later, after Broussard had gone to bed, here comes Sid with a huge knife he got from the mess hall. He announced very loudly (and woke me up again), 'Broussard, now you die!'

I didn't want to stick around filling out papers forever if Sid killed him, so I intervened. After a half-hour or so I got Sid to put down his knife and walked him back to the mess hall where he washed off his bloody mouth. We sat around and I drank another beer with him—then finally got him to bed.

The next day Broussard and Duncan asked me not to say anything about what went on and I agreed and left. I didn't hear anything else about Broussard until I ran into Charlie a year or two later when he told me the story about someone almost killing him. I think he said he crapped or peed his drawers on that one.

Broussard was a very sorry excuse for a human being; he should never have been placed in a position of authority over another person. As a Squad Leader in Vietnam, he'd have taken ten full magazines in the back the first time there was lead in the air. If you'll think about that for a minute, you know it's true!

Paul Lloyd was one of the pilots on the Puerto Amelia job who was there at the beginning and—like Horseshit Charlie—saw it through to the end. A former Army officer and chopper pilot, he eventually hung up his helmet, got his master's in chemistry, and went to work for NASA.

Before he left Peru for good, he had the unique experience of flying one of the Bell 205s all the way back to Oregon as oil exploration played out in Peru.

(I tracked Paul down the same way I did Mr. Izold, and he was kind enough to respond to my request for some input. Mr. Lloyd wrote a detailed letter from Houston about the same time that Dick Izold began collaborating with me (*story follows*).

What I remember most about our Peruvian pilot, Tony - aside from his great looking wife (God she was good-looking) - was his efforts to get a couple of shotguns to Lima. Remember, this was Peru. Also, this was when we were winding down, sending helicopters back to the States, etc. Tony had been talking about trying to get these guns back to Lima. Originally, Charlie Johnson ("Horseshit") and I planned to take one of the S-61s back to Lima en route to the States. As it turns out, we ended up leaving Iquitos and heading straight to Cali, Colombia.

So we're in Iquitos (my girlfriend Rosie in tow) in late December 1975 packing up all of the company's stuff to ship back to the U.S. Charlie and I are debating the route. I'd made the trip before, in August, flying a 205 and I wanted to take the same route I'd followed then, through the "Marañon Pass" to Tumbes in Northern Peru.

From there, generally up the coast, across Mexico, and eventually up to Tucson. Remembering that Charlie is the 'Chief Pilot,' he has decided we should go direct from Iquitos to Cali, Colombia. I can still hear him now: 'We'll save a day and 900 miles.' I had pointed out that the map was loaded with large white areas ('unsurveyed') and that there was no indication of any passes through the Andes with this projected route.

But then, he's the Chief Pilot, and it's just my job to do or die so, dutifully— on about 3 or 4 January '76, we set off on this 'Save a day and 900 miles' plan. Mostly it was boring with the terrain being the usually flat-as-a-pancake Amazon basin stuff. We lost ADF[56] direction fairly soon, and lost count of the number of rivers we'd crossed, etc. I remember turning the map every which way to try and figure out where we were, and also Charlie saying 'Where do you think we are?' I responded, 'How the hell should I know?!'

---

56   Automatic Direction Finder: A none-too-accurate WWII-era radio-based navigation
      system used prior to the advent of GPS navigation.

We were going along through the Colombian Amazon area when the mechanic comes running up with the news he had found a shotgun wrapped up in tape and hidden back in the cargo area. We immediately slowed down to about 40 knots, had him open a window, and throw the damn thing out into the jungle below (probably supporting the narco-trafficos today). To this day I'm convinced Tony was trying to smuggle a shotgun to Lima.

So we truck on and eventually hit the Andes where the weather is down. We flew back and forth trying to find some decent weather and a pass. Eventually we don't have enough fuel to make it to Cali, so we land at a place called Nieva, Colombia, which—from the air—seems like a nice little town.

Well, the local 'officialdom' noted we didn't have a Colombian visa. This being in the days when you just showed up at a local international point of entry with the good old 'green passport.' Unfortunately, Nieva wasn't one of these points of entries. So, we went 'downtown' to the local jail.

The jail was a porticoed building with a guy sitting at a desk out front who literally had flies buzzing around him. They took our shoelaces, belts, etc. but, for some reason, left us with our money (about $5,000 US). We had to carry all that cash because we stopped in out-of-the-way places and they weren't interested in credit cards, and forget about the local currency.

Anyway, they threw us in a cell facing a courtyard. About 10' by 10', concrete floor, no furnishings, and an alcove which contained the toilet. The toilet had been stuffed up for months, but since there was no other place to go...

There was also a Colombian in there for beating up his girlfriend. His family brought him some food, a mattress, and a pillow as the sun was going down. We had to bribe a guard to get us some rotten chicken.

As we bedded down for the night, the Colombian let us use the part of the mattress he wasn't using, for a pillow. During the night we were awakened from time to time to find whole families outside the bars looking in at the 'gringos.' I mean Mom, Pop, and three kids. We were the biggest attraction in town that night.

Next day, I think they actually fed us some breakfast. We then made about three trips out to the aircraft so the Gestapo could 'inspect it.' The last trip was in late afternoon when, while returning, one of the guards asked me if we had $300. I said, 'NO WE DON'T HAVE THREE HUNDRED DOLLARS.' Of course they knew we all had money.

After we got back to the cell, we talked it over and decided to give them the money and get out of there. We were just getting ready to rap on the bars with a cup (our traditional way of getting one of them down there) when one of them showed up and asked, 'If we let you out can you get to Cali tonight?' We of course responded, 'Absolutely!' If they'd waited another fifteen seconds, they'd have had their money!

They took us to the airfield and, remembering we needed fuel (real aviators here) we asked about jet fuel. None available, so we filled up the center tank with AvGas.[57] The S-61 has three fuel tanks which can be cross-fed. We'd decided we'd had enough of their hospitality, so if we couldn't make Cali, we'd set down on a road somewhere.

After takeoff, we switched to the center tank. Everything seemed to run okay. We ended up at around 15,000 feet in a helicopter that was tail rotor limited to 11,500 and we were burning AvGas. Both Charlie and I smoked in those days, and I remember the mechanic running up and saying he could smell AvGas and if either of us lit a cigarette he would kill us.[58]

15,000 foot peaks as far as you could see in any direction, and dodging peaks and clouds, what a trip. All the temperatures seemed to be running normally. Eventually we could see the valley and dived down to find Cali.

After landing we went through customs and immigration, etc. eventually ending up at the Inter-continental Hotel. What a change from the previous night. The clerk at the front desk said to me, 'Sir, the police have been calling about you.' I replied, 'Yeah, we've been having our problems with them, thank you.' Great night, room service, shower, bellhops wanting to know if we wanted a girl, etc. First class hotel.

Next morning we took off after filling up with jet fuel and everything seemed to be running normally. Eventually we ended up spending the night on the <u>beach in Mexico</u>, in the middle of a storm (another story, which was also

57   Aviation gasoline for internal combustion engines.
58   Lead Mechanic John Harwood, a great guy whom we all miss. RIP, John.

Charlie's fault—at least that's what I tell him every time I see him).

As it turns out, we were the second helicopter returning from Peru which had failed to report in to corporate headquarters in Oregon the night we were in jail. Bob Nash, the American we hired from a Peruvian helicopter company, had also headed back to the States in a 205 the same day. He'd left a location on the Rio Ucayáli, headed for Lima.

Bob got into turbulence and crashed at about the 10,000-foot level in the Andes. He and the mechanic waited about three days, and then walked for about three days to find a village. The Peruvians, of course, never started a search effort. You'll remember they always insisted you file a flight plan, but never cared if you closed one.

Bob was okay; he was the guy who had crashed several times. Had major nose surgery from a previous crash, and was sort of tall. He was eventually killed offshore in the Florida area. They found the wreckage but never found him.

I guess this ended up being a long story about Tony. All said and done he was your basic Latino with impressive family connections. Eventually he was killed in an airplane crash in Mexico City. This must have been in the early eighties. Never cared much for him (but damn he had a great looking wife!).

My buddy Mike Pond was in on the fun as well, arriving at Puerto Amelia in March of '75. We later shared an interesting spraying assignment in Mexico where I met my second wife, Lourdes. Mike flies choppers over Colorado's Royal Gorge for money and races jet-cars for excitement. He passed along three Amazon tales, ergo the following...

Oh, by the way—Were you there when myself and another 205 moved the drill cable? The Peruvian Mil 8 couldn't move it because it was too heavy (7100 lbs) and they didn't want to cut the cable and wanted it in one length. I said I think I could do it with two 205's. Of course the other pilots said I was crazy. Tito asked if it was possible and I explained how we could do it. (Each ship picks up one end of the cable and shares the load.) Having gone over my idea with him, off we went to the staging area to get the cable. Back we came with the cable in tow much to the delight of the head driller. It was sort of like formation flying with a common sling load. Wish I had a picture of that! Wonder where Tito is nowadays?

(And…regarding whether the wildcatters struck oil on our customer's lease…)

I think all the holes were dry including the ones where I was on the S-61. I think that was for Hispanoil. The Company wanted me to come back to the States early, so I was only there for two holes with them. I remember that all but one of the S-61 pilots had quit, so we had to learn to fly the S-61 on our own. (When [the pilots] got their first pay check…they walked.) [The Boss] said to keep it in the air no matter what!! The S-61 driver that stayed with the Company showed us how to start it and we taught him how to longline since he had never done any sling work. We flew the thing for two months before Bob Brown came down to give us our type rating and make us legal. The SAS system never worked on the aircraft for the two months we were flying it and we amazed Brown at how we could work the machine without the SAS[59] working. Us dumb shit Bell drivers didn't know any different, although it was nice to fly when they got it working.

Plus… I didn't see Broussard's departure [from Puerto Amelia]. I was flying the S-61 when he left, although I had heard it was a quite a deal, as some of the Indians wanted to kill him.

Dick Izold sent me the following joke around the same time, knowing—for those of us who have plied the sometimes hostile skies of the Amazon Basin—it would hit home:

*An explorer in the deepest Amazon suddenly finds himself surrounded by a group of bloodthirsty natives. Upon surveying the situation, he says quietly to himself, 'Oh God, I'm screwed.' The sky darkens and a deep voice booms out, **'No, you are NOT screwed. Pick up that stone at your feet and bash in the head of the chief standing in front of you.'** So with the stone he bashed the life out of the chief. Standing above the body, breathing heavily, facing over one hundred angry Indians, he hears the voice boom out again. **'Okay…NOW you're screwed.'***

Broussard must have come to the same realization when the time came for him to leave Puerto Amelia. The night before, he drank his fill of

---

59   Stabilization Augmentation System, which reduces pilot control input to keep from over-controlling large helicopters.

Bohemias, then grabbed a chainsaw and fulfilled his pointless oath by sawing through the four legs and ladder of La Torre de Paz, shoving it over the bank and into the river.

Now it was morning. His bags were packed, the weather was clear, and the floatplane was right on time. Everyone in Lagunas and Puerto Amelia knew that the bully's time to say *adios* had come.

Broussard had to be concerned as to why so many natives were waiting outside near the floating dock. One might wonder where his despised pistol was at a time like this, the one he had recently substituted for his malicious slingshot to kill the starving stray dogs that begged for scraps. Who was there that morning to back him up, I wonder—to lend some support in his time of need?

I know not. After digging around for all these years, I believe that Horseshit Charlie may have been present, but the man didn't respond to the two letters I wrote him, asking for his input. Can't say I fault him for keeping it to himself, after hearing from a pilot here and a mechanic there that things had gone rather poorly for Broussard, as time ran out and he made way for the dock. Charlie was a *company man*, after all.

One thing I do know: folks from Lagunas and around camp were up to *here* with the bully for his drunkenness, his foul mouth, his stupid rules, and shooting the mess hall monkey with rocks. And killing the stray dogs, instead of just scaring them off. Couldn't he see where his cruelty was leading? Was he so blind?

I don't think I ever saw a gathering of obreros where at least half of them didn't carry their machetes. Yet I never feared for my life, and I was alone with them many times, attempting to learn their lingo or something about their incredible land. Broussard was another matter.

I actually worked pretty hard to get Broussard's version of his departure from Puerto Amelia, to be fair. This story lay largely unfinished for almost thirty years. I had come to an unsettling end, not having an eyewitness statement about his *going-away party*.

It was by coincidence that in June of 2003, I signed on for a heli-logging job in the swampland a few miles from Broussard, Louisiana. The helicopter

I was supposed to go grapple-logging with was said to be *in the shop*, but by the time I drove the two thousand plus miles to Broussard, it was allegedly going to be *ready to rock*.

I wondered how much time I would have to dig around for the old bully once I got there, and how to go about it. He would have been well into his seventies by then. Turns out the poor logging helicopter's problems wouldn't be solved any time soon, and the well-intended fellow who sent me all that way eventually had to admit that they were short of funds to buy parts. So while they tried to raise money, I settled into a cheap motel room in Broussard and began surfing the phone book.

Knowing there had to be a bunch of Broussards in Broussard, I was nonetheless shocked by all the Broussards with his first name, and/or his first initial. It took me a couple of days to get up the mustard to start making phone calls. In between calls, I became a regular at the Broussard Public Library, checking my email and learning something about the town and its illustrious history.

Broussard was originally named *Coté Gelee* (frozen hills), dating from a hard winter in 1784. Vasil Broussard formed the first Vigilante Committee to protect the local residents from outlaws, and eventually founded the town of Broussard in 1884.[60] His famous old house is now a historical monument on West Main. There is a handsome plaque honoring Vasil in the Town Square, which I photographed one stormy afternoon in the rain.

I thought it interesting that—besides Vasil, an Indian, and a pioneer woman—the plaque pictures a train, a cannon, and a pistol; so heavy equipment and handguns appear to have run in the family.

In the ten days I waited for my alleged logging job to start up, I went back and forth from the helicopter hangar to the Broussard Public Library to the motel—periodically chatting with the mechanic while I wiped grease off of the helicopter, read relevant texts, and made more telephone calls.

Now and then I'd get an answer, but when I mentioned *working in the oil fields*, it usually narrowed the answer down to a *no*. Not many of them seemed to want to talk to a guy who asked a lot of questions, either.

A visit to the Sacred Heart Catholic Church was most pleasant, meeting with folks who knew many of the Broussards on the adjacent cemetery's

60   Courtesy Lafayette Convention and Visitors Commission

markers. After explaining the purpose of my visit, I was disappointed to learn that no one at the church could say if they even knew the Broussard I sought or if he was among the living.

Well, there was that one old fellow at a local dredging outfit who seemed eager to help. He thought for a minute, looked at the sky and back down again, and said, "I think he died not too long ago." Not having a middle initial or anything else I could take to the local police station, I was about ready to give up.

There were three calls left to make on the long list I was slowly eliminating in the phone book, and the first one I called—around eight in the evening—might have been the bully. When I said his first name, he answered gruffly, "Yeah?"

I introduced myself.

"Whadaya want?" he responded, none too friendly. (Did the man on the other end of the phone sound old enough to be him? I wondered. After all these years…could it be?!)

I explained that I was trying to locate "an old dredge operator who once worked in the jungles of Peru."

(CLICK!)

Getting back to the moment of his departure then, *hearsay* will have to suffice in following Broussard, laden with his bags and no one ahead of him to part the sea of waving machetes and angry faces between him and the floatplane to freedom.

As the uniformed Peruvian Air Force pilot watched from alongside his Pilatus Porter on floats, Broussard attempted to reach the floating dock. He was likely nervous by then and may have attempted to try some *command presence* or disarming mirth, but *the natives were restless* and in no mood to listen.

He was soon surrounded by well over two dozen Peruvians of varying backgrounds, all of whom had a bone to pick with Señor *Coon Ass*. One man in particular was anxious to get in Broussard's face. When the crowd of mostly shirtless, muscular natives pressed into a circle around him—blocking his advance—a pistol appeared in the Indian's hand.

Shouting *"Mata lo! Mata lo!"*[61] the rabble converged as the pistol was brandished in Broussard's face, closer—the nickel barrel threatening, the snub-nosed revolver's .38 slugs ready to take their turn in the firing chamber. Strong, dark brown hands yanked away his luggage, as the shouts condemning Broussard grew louder and more profane.

"You go nowhere, Broussard! You die here! You die today!" the instigator shouted, aiming the gun with both hands as Broussard tried to back away. Encouraged by the furious obreros, the gun barrel was pushed harder into Broussard's scowling face.

Within seconds, Broussard fell backward and was on the ground, his travel outfit no longer fit for travel. Little light fell on his hated head as the vigilantes stood defiantly over him, cheering—their long blades held high above him.

The instigator took the pistol's barrel and ground the gun sight into the bully's nostrils, making clear to the dredge operator from Louisiana that he was about to *disappear* into the Huallaga, and no one would ever find his body—*ever.*

Pleading for mercy, Broussard shivered in fear. He had come full circle with his own sick karma. Now *he* was the helpless dog. *He* had become the shivering monkey.

But Broussard did not die that day. Nor did his plane take off at the appointed time.

God willing, I'd like nothing more than to team up with one of my old Puerto Amelia buddies and take a boat cruise up the Amazon to Lagunas someday. I'm confident that some of my younger native pals—should they still be around—can say if I got it right or not. It must be quite a yarn after all these years. Another adventure awaits!

Regardless, I feel it safe to say that no one—before or after Broussard— was more relieved to fly away from the harbor he dredged than he was. Soiled pants or no!

---

61   Kill him!

Section IV:
South of the Border

El Gringo Wingo de Chilpancingo

* *The Norte Americano packed some angry laundry!*

President Nixon's administration financed a first-of-its-kind joint anti-drug task force in México during the mid-1970s called "Operation Cooperation." I personally thought the name was rather unimaginative, but I was nonetheless pleased to accept a captain's seat in one of six new Bell 212 helicopters donated to México as part of the program.

Five other captains, a Spanish-speaking maintenance foreman, and yours truly were flown to Mexico City in January of 1976 to kick off the mission. As experienced 212 pilots, our job was to serve as pilots-in-command to train an equal number of indigenous co-pilots in the manly art of spraying illegal crops with micro-foil[62] equipped, twin-engined Hueys. This was one of those *low-profile* assignments; we were officially *tourists*.

As the appointed hour came for our first official briefing, Alfonzo Gertz—the political head of Mexico's *Procuraduria*[63]—made a celebrated appearance on the tarmac at the Mexico City Airport. Gathering around México's top cop, we were informed in perfect English that our mission was to fumigate illegal crops in México, specifically opium poppies and any marijuana that we came across. In doing so, we would train México's

---

62   Micro-foils emit *drops* of water (versus tiny *droplets* as with sprayers) allowing for application at a higher altitude.
63   México's equivalent to the Federal Bureau of Investigation.

pilots in the task of eradicating tons of raw heroin and *evil weed* destined for the United States.

As lead pilot Mike Pond suited up to give the Mexican brass a quick demonstration of the micro-foil spray system, we were informed the herbicide chosen for defoliating the targeted crops was *Gramexone,* México's version of the herbicide 2,4D.

For the demo flight, Mike's 212 was loaded with 300 gallons of water (without the chemical). As the sun sank into late afternoon, Mike got the tower's okay to spray an idle east-west taxiway down with water, flying along at fifty knots and altitudes up to three hundred feet above the concrete.

At the end of his first westbound swath, Mike hauled the nose back sharply, climbing and slowing the ship to about twenty knots, which allowed the engines' torque to turn the big helicopter 180 degrees to the right and spray the eastbound swath. Mike's smooth flying style was impressive, demonstrating the skill he had honed over the years applying 2,45-T[64] to brushy clear-cuts in the Northwest.

As Captain Pond swooped past, our group followed Gertz out onto the tarmac, observing firsthand the precise flow of millions of identical droplets raining down like a curtain upon the dry concrete in straight, parallel rows. The new-tech micro-foils replaced conventional spray-heads for this mission—allowing the helicopter to fly up to three hundred feet over the terrain—yet assuring a lethal shower on any crop below it.

Noting that there were literally no gaps in the pattern on the ramp, Mr. Gertz allowed himself to be relatively impressed by Mike's demonstration. Turning to his subordinates with a knowing smile, he voiced his approval: "*Bueno.*"

Shortly thereafter, we were given our regional assignments and sent packing for the field. My Mexican co-pilot and I were dispatched to a Mexican army infantry outpost on the west edge of Chilpancingo, where we were under the command of the unit's commanding general. In hindsight, I guess it was poetic justice for me to draw the assignment in the mountainous state of Guerrero, about two hundred miles southwest.

---

64 A brush-killing herbicide similar to the notorious *Agent Orange* applied in Southeast Asia.

I was anxious to begin work, but there always seemed to be a built-in delay of some sort everywhere we went. Our ship's spray system had yet to be fully installed, so while the mechanics labored on our 212 (XC-BEI), my left-seater and I were invited to try the mess hall coffee at the Army outpost. I was doing my best to get to know "Juan," although my Spanish was not all that good in the days before meeting my Mexican wife. Juan was in his mid-twenties, a novice helicopter pilot, and he spoke even less English.

Two meals per day were served in the division's mess hall, amid the usual military fanfare: while we were served coffee at the linen-clad junior officer's table, the general made his entrance and someone shouted *"Atención!"*

He strode right in, gesturing flamboyantly with his right palm out and up like Saddam used to—acknowledging his subjects with aplomb—while returning diners to their heaping plates of rice, beans, and chilés with a cheery *"Provecho,"* a courteous directive equal to our military's *"carry on."* He then took his seat at the head of the *comandante's* table, and we quietly returned to the subject matter at hand.

After an hour or so, Juan and I were informed that the helicopter would be ready for a recon flight the following morning. Juan made arrangements to be housed—free of charge—in the nearby Bachelor Officers' Quarters. I'd seen enough BOQs in my time, and besides, we *capitánes* were allocated per diem, so I bid Juan *adieu* and commandeered a ride to the local hotel. That's where a *turista* would be staying, after all.

My logbook notes do not include the name of the elegant, historic old hotel, but it might as well have been *El Grande*. The main lobby was a beautiful vaulted affair with tall, adorned columns and a spiral staircase leading to the upper floor. The courteous male clerk who registered me smiled, handed me the standard Schlage room key hard-wired to a cumbersome wooden gizmo of some sort, and gestured politely toward an ancient-looking elevator. Dismissing the baggage handler with a small tip, I hoisted my own bags and made for the stairs.

Nothing fancy room-wise, but it was clean and quiet. I wasted no time unpacking, lathered down in the basic unheated tile shower, slipped on some *turista*-looking threads, and returned to street level to do some exploring while it was still daylight. A narrow side-street headed north into an enormous shady park, so I followed my instincts and in short order stumbled upon a sidewalk vendor who was selling some shiny green *footballs*. Upon closer examination, they turned out to be *giant, tasty avocados* from nearby Uraupan, ripened to perfection. I sampled one and thought, *This is worth the long voyage to Chilpancingo!*

I must have looked quite the tourist: walking along with a fresh green avocado under one arm, a Pentax dangling from my neck, while consuming another giant avocado with a plastic spoon. I hadn't seen any other gringos since we left the Mexico City Airport, and then it hit me: *Lordy, I'm the only gringo in town.* The locals will know me as *el Gringo Wingo de Chilpancingo!* I decided not to verify my assumption, remembering my *low-profile* situation.

There seemed to be no hurry to start our recon the next morning, as Juan and I loitered in the mess hall over a strong cup of coffee, waiting for a certain *guide* to show up and tell us where to fly. Finally he appeared—coming straight from the *comandante's* table, of all places—and within minutes, off we clattered—westbound and climbing toward the legendary Sierra Madre del Sur.[65]

Verdant valleys dotted the steep mountainous terrain, reminding me that agriculture was *tops* in the economy of Guerrero. Unfortunately, too many growers were reportedly focusing on illegal crops—which paid handsomely—compared to corn, which produced *maiz* for corn tortillas and animal feed. The latter was legal, though—and the former carried with them the risk of arrest, confiscation of assets, imprisonment, or *worse*.

Our recon flight lasted just under two hours, and during that time surprisingly few *plantios* (cultivated crops) were pointed out to us. I expected to see some of the legendary *acres of red* that opium poppies allegedly produced, but flying over one as the guide directed me, I saw scores of poppy plants with short stalks, not quite ready to blossom.

Flying up-slope to nearly nine thousand feet, there were suspicious-looking plots here and there, but our guide steered us away from those and over to less interesting stuff. Another small field or two of weed appeared (the notorious *Acapulco Gold*, I wondered?) planted in the direct sunlight in neat hillocks. I fought to remember its location without the assistance of <u>modern navigational</u> aids.

65   *The Mother Mountains of the South*, recalling Hemingway's *Treasure of the Sierra Madre*.

Returning to the Army garrison, we were told not to begin spraying until the next morning—another waste of daylight and resources, I lamented. Between the short recon flight and the glacier-like pace of "Operation Cooperation," El Gringo Wingo was rapidly forming the opinion that something was rotten in Denmark.

As the sun climbed into the sky for our third morning on the job, XC-BEI's three-hundred-gallon water tank was being topped off via a portable engine, pumping from a nearby fresh water well through a series of leaky canvas fire hoses.

Simultaneously, 2,4D concentrate was being sucked from five-gallon plastic jugs, introduced into the flow via a "Y" in the plumbing *ala* the *venturi* effect. As the noxious, sloshing liquid reached the upper mark on the translucent plastic tank, I noted a darker band along the bottom: dirt!

We didn't expect clean tap water everywhere we went on this mission; indeed, natural streams were destined to be the primary source of water for much of our spraying needs. I decided that the onboard pump (powered by a remote-controlled, eight-horse Briggs and Stratton engine) could probably deal with a little sand, so we capped off the reservoir and headed west toward the evil weeds.

We found the closer crops with no problem; most were small plots of poppies that someone had tried to conceal along a dry creek bed. Pointing them out to Juan, I powered up the pump. Doing my best imitation of the illustrious Captain Pond, I made one straight pass at about two hundred feet, hit the flow switch, and observed the familiar curtain of herbicide trailing away, scoring a bull's-eye at about fifty knots.

Midway through the second *plantio*, I thought I heard the onboard pump laboring slightly. Checking my three o'clock, I noticed the volume spewing forth from the micro-foil had dwindled to a mere trickle. Something was amiss, as our chemical tank was at least three-quarters full. Making our way down into the valley floor, Juan suggested we land near some thatched dwellings and check the system over.

It dawned on me that we could get shot this way, but we were too far from the garrison to consider going back to the mechanics, and I was frustrated by our lack of production—so I reluctantly agreed with Juan and put the big white machine down in a farmer's field. Juan stayed at the controls while I unbuckled and climbed aft into the cabin. I soon discovered that the inline chemical screen was clogged with sand!

The three-inch metal screen was just downstream from the pump; its job was to keep small particles from plugging up the tiny downward-pointing micro-foil tubes along the spray boom on either side of the helicopter. I flicked the screen against the skid tube several times and rendered it clean, reinstalled it, and went back to the task at hand. We were relieved to see the system performing perfectly over the next target.

With a minute or two, however, the flow subsided and we were forced to make another landing. And another. After the third episode, we were beginning to fume over our inability to stay over the targets. I closed the red switch on the aux-control panel, shutting the pump off, and we headed back to the base with more than one-half tank of chemical that we couldn't dispense.

Back inside the walled compound, our mechanics listened intently as we relayed our successes and failures. They suggested we *call it a day* while they cleaned out the tank and compared notes with the lead mechanic, who was working in another state.

Back at the hotel, I showered up and relaxed a few minutes before resuming work on a ribald cartoon I had been sketching. The protagonist in my parallel-cartoon tale was a rather handsome but thick-headed, greedy spray pilot who—on his first day in a strange Latin American country—managed to come down with amoebic dysentery after gorging himself in a local fly-strewn café.

I progressed to the frame where the emaciated pilot was perched atop the *boca-grande*[66] and stopped to sharpen my pencil. Then came a knock on my door. It was room service, inquiring if I had any laundry needing washed. I had, in fact, made a sizeable dent in my bag of clean clothes by then and gleefully handed it over to the señorita with the promise that it would be returned to me "*mañana.*"

After consuming a strange-looking plate of *something* at a local fly-strewn café, I returned to my room and resumed work on the sketch of the stricken spray pilot, who was anticipating being able to walk in a day or two. Then came *another* knock on the door.

---

66   Popular Hispanic slang for the standard porcelain toilet..."the big mouth."

I was taken aback by two menacing figures I spied through the heavy door's peephole and almost didn't respond, wondering if the local Mexican Mafia had found me! Turns out they were U.S. DEA[67] agents who decided to call on me and check my progress.

"Rocko" and "Nestor" introduced themselves, allowing me a quick glance at their credentials and the .38 snub-nosed revolvers in their hidden holsters. I invited them inside and fielded several of their questions about the mission as I sat on the corner of the bed, shielding my artwork. They didn't do any double back-flips when I suggested that things could be going better, listening as if they'd heard the story before. Exchanging glances now and then, perhaps they were just verifying their own suspicions.

Before long they got up to leave, after suggesting that I drop in at hotel *such-and-such* on the beach in Acapulco the next time I was down that way. They promised to introduce me to some airline stewardesses who *loved to party*, slipping me an official-looking DEA business card with a room number scribbled on it.

Opening the door slowly, out they slid—walking softly down the hall, descending the staircase. Through the curtained window, I watched them climb into a familiar-looking beige two-door Dodge sedan. The universal *Procuraduria* rig, I chuckled to myself. Some disguise!

Returning to the cartoon, my next frame soon featured two new characters— *Nestor* and *Rocko*, knocking on the spray-pilot's hotel door as he hurriedly fashioned a diaper for himself out of a nearby bedsheet…

Back at the compound, the mechanics explained that they had cleaned the spray system from stem to stern and reloaded the tank. The lead mechanic was out of reach for the time being, so Juan and I decided to launch and see how far we could get.

Precisely 1.6 flight hours later, we were back, hot and as frustrated as ever. Today had been a repeat of yesterday, except we landed *four* times to dump sand out of the screen. Both Juan and I were more than surprised that we hadn't been picked off, considering the exposure we created for ourselves spraying over hostile territory and landing here and there.

As the mechanics scratched their heads and considered ways to filter some of

67   Drug Enforcement Agency

the sand from our water source, another 212 approached to land inside the compound, creating quite a scene with a hot-dog approach and tornado-like landing. There were no spray booms on this ship, but its interior was crammed with people, cargo, and livestock.

As the Mexican pilot slammed the skids down, several uniformed soldiers jumped out, escorting two battered, blindfolded *campesino* prisoners toward the compound's lockup at gunpoint. Two other soldiers unloaded crates of sodas and melons, tarps tied around scores of wilting marijuana plants and confiscated water pumps: contraband from an illegal farming operation the soldiers had just raided. Another soldier guided a squealing pig toward the mess hall's kitchen, a crude rope tethering one of its rear hooves. There would apparently be some fresh *carnitas* for the comandante's table this evening.

After they passed, Juan and I both shook our heads, wondering what might become of the campesinos. He sided with me in the grim assessment of our mission's impact on those who dared test the resolve of the Procuraduria. I replayed the local AM radio's daily announcements in my head, warning violators that the consequences were *muy graves.*[68]

As we watched the mechanics toying with their fire hoses, Juan and I noticed a commotion to our nine o'clock. None other than the commanding general himself was striding our way, flanked by his junior officers. All were grinning broadly and apparently in a festive mood.

I stood up with Juan in greeting the general, somewhat fearful as to what would bring him out to our problem-plagued aircraft. "Congratulations!" I understood him to say. "You have successfully fumigated all the illegal crops in Guerrero!" Juan translated the rest for me, after the general shook our hands and informed us that we were to pack up our gear and head back to Mexico City, where we would be reassigned to do combat in yet another hot spot.

"That's absurd!" I protested to Juan as soon as the comandante was out of earshot. Juan looked at me knowingly, but quashed my animosity gently with the tilt of his head and an upheld hand. His smile was weak; we were resigned to follow orders, regardless.

I felt a new character about to pop up in my cartoon strip, but I wasn't happy with my part in what was going down around Chilpancingo. We had only sprayed a total of three hours! Despite our resources and capabilities, I

68   Very grave.

realized that we were mere pawns in the grand scheme of things.

The mechanics seemed clearly relieved to be sending us away, although they had just learned from the lead mechanic that someone had sent us here with the wrong filter screen for our pump! The replacement screen had just arrived; it had a coarser mesh that would allow much more of the pesky sand to pass through it. We could only shake our heads as they installed it and tossed the old screen into the trashcan.

Back at the hotel, I explained my unanticipated departure to the clerk and hurried upstairs to pack up for our afternoon flight back to Mexico City. Looking around the empty room, my bags were quickly packed but only half full when I remembered the señorita and her promise to return with my clean laundry! Then came the familiar knock on my door.

The little lady was good for her word, but she mumbled something about my shirts as she handed the bundle to me, accepting no gratuity, and vanished as if she'd done something wrong. Unwrapping the bundle I soon discovered that—in her haste to meet my new travel demands—there wasn't time to dry my shirts! This would be quite a problem in the humidity we lived with—the prospect of packing them away along with the clean, dry stuff didn't sit well with me.

Standing by the checkout counter, the courteous clerk slid my bill across the glass top as I juggled the plastic cards in my wallet and three wet shirts on hangers. He was obviously mystified by the sudden unhappy look on my face and asked in Español if everything was all right.

"No!" I replied impatiently. *"Mis camísas están enojadas!"* I had mistakenly replied in fractured Spanish, *"My shirts are angry,"* confusing the word *enojado* (angry) for *mojado* (wet).

The poor clerk's brow became furrowed about then, struggling to understand how my shirts could have become so angry in time to spoil my departure. He exchanged looks with the cashier, who hastily took my payment and handed back a receipt before any of my other garments became outraged.

It was sometime down the road that the relevance of my faux pax hit me, and in explaining my error, poor Juan almost lost control of the helicopter laughing along with me!

The Forbidden Fruit of Tierra Blanca

*   *Living Dangerously in Lulu Land.*

Crusty Pilot Logbook Number 2 (of 4) documents two traumatic events that occurred in the not-so-friendly skies of northwestern Sinaloa, México, in March of 1976. I recall both events more clearly than I'd prefer, and they were separated by a mere forty-eight hours. Between event number one and number two, the Gringo Wingo from Chilpancingo fell in love!

On March 27th, my competent Mexican left-seater and I were ferrying a micro-foil-equipped Bell 212 (XC-BET) from our overnight spray assignment in Tópia to the airport in Culiacán. We had recently sprayed one hundred seventy-one illegal crops and were headed west for a well-deserved day off.

"Daniél" was an affable, full-sized spray-pilot-in-training. His command of English was above average for the rotating group of trainees assigned to our dangerous mission, and I felt safe flying with him.

Daniél had customized the back of his flight helmet with a perfect marijuana leaf, preserving it *forever green* under a layer of epoxy sealant. Since he carried the credentials of a pilot working for the Procuraduria (the Mexican Attorney General's *top cops*) nobody gave him any grief over the leaf, certainly not me. Our eradication mission was fraught with peril, and such bravado helped keep things in perspective.

So there we were, descending to the hot valley floor from lofty Tópia, a small, remote mining community in the rugged mountains east of Culiacán. There was a grand, desert-like mesa to our twelve o'clock low, but a splendid drainage cut through it precisely in the direction we were going.

In our line of work, drainages meant water, and water sometimes meant illegal crops. With half a tank of herbicide riding along behind us, we weren't about to let any targets of opportunity go unchallenged.

Daniél was looking out his left window and tapping his fingers to the ADF radio's Latino station-of-choice when I lowered the collective pitch. Hitting the herbicide pump switch and nosing the big white spray ship over, I aimed for the east edge of the mesa. We would soon be able to peer down into the narrow ravine. Feeling the sudden changes in our course, Daniel bolted upright in his seat, spotted the ravine, and gave me a flashy grin.

"Ándale!" He chuckled into his microphone, letting me know he was up for zapping plantio number one-seventy-two. **"Git 'er hot!"** I chimed in, remembering my Elephant Brander Days.

The sun was almost straight overhead when we reached the drainage. Visibility was fifty miles if it was an inch, which is probably why I'm here to tell you about the *wire* that suddenly appeared at eye level, close enough to see the crappy insulation along its weathered span. I think we both saw it at the same time, tearing our beady eyes off the small plot of opium poppies growing down in the shadows not far below.

How we missed a direct hit on our Bell's vital control tubes with that wire is still a mystery to Captain Wingo, who thought it was *all over* for him and his happy-go-lucky left-seater.

We hit something, though, because what followed was a loud **thunk,** and the wire was suddenly behind us!

Looking out my right window, so was the spray boom! At least that was my first impression—as Daniél shouted shrill Hispanic expletives above the din, I reduced power, looked all around, and felt for any anomalies in the ship's controls—expecting the worst. Turns out the right side of our micro-foil spray boom had impacted the span of wire, snapping the spray boom sharply aft, where it virtually rode along against the right skid tube.

With nerves quite shattered, the two of us plowed straight ahead for the airport, deciding not to make a precautionary landing or turn around and search for the bad guys who had laid a trap for us; that would have to wait for another day. For the moment, we were glad to be alive and more than ready for the day off!

Sunday morning found Captains Wingo and Pond in cutoffs, fully engaged in the time-honored Yankee ritual of Frisbee-tossing in the shade of our spacious hotel courtyard. Mike and I were stretching our muscles and passing time after a big breakfast. When Dora drove up in her two-door Ford LTD—hot off the Camino Real—we should have realized that something was up.

Mike had met Dora Trejo Soto a week or so prior at one of Culiacán's better nightclubs, and hit it off. They were becoming regular dancing partners, so Dora wasn't bashful about coming to El Camino Real de Los Tres Rios Hotel to visit her new friend. She may have known that Mike and I whiled away a couple of hours per day playing Frisbee and lounging around the Olympic-sized pool.

Dora had a surprise for us on that sunny March 28th: she brought along her best pal, a beautiful young Mexican lass by the name of *Lourdes Maria Medina Alarcón*. Lulú—as her friends knew her—was a tall, twenty-one-year-old raven-haired executive secretary from Culiacán.

Turns out the girls were on their way to the beach about forty miles west of town. Tambór was an undeveloped retreat on the Gulf of California favored by the locals. It was off the beaten path and virtually unknown to tourists. And Dora was thoughtful to invite a couple of *Norte Americanos* to come along for some fun in the sun.

I was kinda lukewarm on the idea until Mike and I walked over to her big brown sled of a car to be introduced to Lourdes, who smiled her dazzling smile, said "Hola," and giggled "No hablo Inglés," in the same breath. (*Charming!*) Well, I thought—maybe a trip to the beach wouldn't be such a bad idea. Mike fetched the Frisbee while I grabbed our beach towels, and off we went.

Minutes later we were thundering along westbound with the windows rolled down. Dora did the driving with Mike riding shotgun and sweet little Lulú and me in the backseat. We combed through her tiny English-Spanish dictionary, trying to make sentences and laughing at our awkwardness. Lourdes had taken an English class at the local university, but I dare say my Spanish was a little ahead of her English. Regardless, I found her so lovely and charming that it didn't matter.

Unmarried virtuous ladies of Lourdes' category were traditionally accompanied by members of their family when seeing someone new, so she and Dora were risking the wrath of Mama Celia and no less than *nine* brothers and *three* sisters by driving around with us. Yes, Lourdes came from a large family, one of the many things we discussed on the way to the beach.

Her family needed not to worry about me, however. My heart had been thoroughly smashed by my "ex" while I was away fighting the war in Vietnam, and I was in no hurry to start up a relationship any time soon, especially with a virgin. Still, it had been six long years since my divorce, and something told me that the luscious-looking lips of Lourdes could do me no harm.

There was another thing about her appearance that I found intriguing: Lourdes has a small, dark brown speck of pigment in the white of her right eye (called a *lunita*, a little moon) close to her dark brown iris. I thought it made her adorable *Spanish Eyes* extra intriguing. Before long, I realized I had a crush on the pretty young lady!

I soon learned that her father, Francisco, had passed away suddenly a little over two years before, leaving his devastated family unprepared to deal with the hardships that followed. Their cherished two-story home near the river had to be liquidated, and Mama Celia had no choice but to move her family of fourteen to a small, split-level concrete dwelling in an unincorporated area of Culiacán known as Tierra Blanca.

Just across an old bridge northeast of town, Tierra Blanca was known to be a refuge for fugitives from justice, a home for *gomeros*[69] and the Mexican Mafia...the very people that the Procuraduria intended us pilots to help put out of business!

---

69   Those who illegally harvested the raw opium gum from poppies.

Arriving at Tambór, Mike and I were somewhat under-whelmed by the absence of the usual tourist amenities found in Mazatlán and Acapulco, but the señoritas said they knew where to find a nice stretch of beach. It was a zigzag, brushy hike across some low, rolling sand dunes to get there, but worth the effort. We practically had the clean, wave-swept beach to ourselves.

Fortunately, there was a beachside café-shack set up for business that day. I recall having a cold beer with my *camarones al natural* (butter-basted shrimp), which Lourdes and I devoured with gusto. (She didn't drink alcoholic beverages, opting for a Fanta.)

After lunch, the girls joined us in a game of Frisbee in the strong, westerly breeze. Mike and I then tried our hand at paddleball, the more popular pastime among young Latinas at the beach. Dora had an infectious giggle, and her aggressive play kept all of us laughing. We spent the rest of the afternoon beach-combing, tanning our hides, and chatting with the ladies.

On the way back into town, Mike asked the ladies if they'd like to see the Procuraduria's helicopters, parked in a secure area at Culiacán International Airport. They said "Si!" We gave them the royal tour of the facility, including sitting in the pilots' seats, where they pretended to be spraying—trying to make light of our risky business. Little did we know, the ship that the girls sat in that afternoon would be a crumpled wreck within twenty-four hours.

Early the next windy morning, March 29th, I took the controls behind Captain Mike's helicopter and hovered XC-BET up and over a 3,600-pound black rubber bladder filled with jet-fuel. Both spray ships had to sling out a heavy *rollagon* that morning, as we were on our way east to the Arroyo Sinaloa, a long way from fuel.

The plan for that day called for us to preposition our fuel bladders alongside the streambed as we began spraying in a new, remote sector known for an abundance of secluded plantios. An additional Bell 212 supported our two spray ships by carrying along the herbicide concentrate in plastic tubs and several armed Mexican soldiers, in case they were needed.

The wind intensified as we augered eastward, gaining altitude over the rugged terrain. Finally, Mike slowed his helicopter and began a right-hand orbit about a thousand feet above the Arroyo, sizing up how to land his heavy load on the sandy riverbed safely.

"Raúl"—my Mexican co-pilot for the day—and yours truly orbited out of the way as Mike negotiated the swirling wind, wondering all the while if Mike might abort the mission for the day in the face of such strong winds.

Mike took the path I predicted he would, turning dead into the wind for the final two hundred feet of his approach. Once he set the rollagon down, Mike keyed his radio: "Heads up, Dorce – it's blowin' pretty good down here."

"Roger that, Mike," I replied, glancing at Raúl. Raúl was a relatively inexperienced helicopter pilot, and from the looks of it, not all that happy to be bouncing around in the cockpit and carrying a heavy sling load. I took the controls and asked him to *follow through*.

I began my approach in the same manner that Mike had, staying high over a razor-sharp ridge west of the intended set-down spot. As I started the downwind leg, I noticed that the grass in the flats off to my right was standing straight up, out of the wind. I had enough space to turn in that direction and decided it would be a good alternative approach.

The rough air smoothed out as I passed below the level of the sharp ridge, and I was about to congratulate myself for finding a "better" way onto the riverbed when we inadvertently flew into a pronounced downdraft and the ship fell like a stone from about one hundred feet.

Realizing I had to punch off the rollagon to save the ship, I clenched the cyclic grip with my right hand to reach the pickle button. Instead of hitting the red cargo hook release button, my hand closed over the bulky spray switch, which was jerry-rigged in place near the button, and I missed. By then it was too late to hit the manual release pedal between the rudder pedals, and the earth rose up to smite me!

The rollagon hit the riverbed first, bouncing back toward the helicopter as the ship continued forward and rose slightly. The rollagon fell back to earth and the short cable between the ship and the load quickly became taut again, giving us a violent jerk and nosing the ship over onto its left front as her twin main rotors smashed into the sandy river bottom. As the blades shattered, we rolled over on our left side.

Now it was my turn for some choice expletives, realizing I had just wrecked a new helicopter, harmed my co-pilot, and screwed our important mission in one stupid maneuver. Raúl was calling for God's intervention but otherwise okay, just shook up. I shut the engines down, undid my belt, and lowered myself to his seat area.

Squatting low, I beat out the overhead plastic skylight to make a hole for us to egress. We got thoroughly soaked sliding out through the hole into two feet of water, and I managed to cut both hands on the sharp plastic, despite the Nomex gloves we both wore.

By the time Raúl and I made it to shore, Mike had landed on the opposite riverbank, and I waded back across to meet him—helmet in hand. As I came sloshing up angrily to my big friend, I muttered the F-word. He asked rather politely if we had hit a downdraft. Tossing my helmet down in disgust, I replied **"Yes!"** Captain Wingo was having a bad day, to put it mildly.

Armed military guards were assigned to protect the helicopter overnight as we loaded both ships for the depressing ride back to Culiacán International. I had no excuse for losing control of the ship, admitting *pilot error*, and—following a physical exam at the hospital, that's the way I wrote up my report—handing it in to Mike when I returned to the hotel. (The remarks section of my logbook for March 29th reads: "Crash-smash-bash-thrash.")

The next day's mission went on without me while the powers that be conferred as to my future with the Operation. There came a knock on my door early that afternoon, when three representatives from the Federal Aeronautical branch from Mexico City flew in to meet with me. I told the gentlemen that—had I flown the same route the lead pilot selected—there wouldn't have been an accident. After a lengthy Q & A session, I was asked if I would like to return to my flying duties, to which I replied to the affirmative. And that was that!

Yours truly was greatly relieved to be given an opportunity to return to work, owing in large part to the support of my friend Captain Pond and the fact that no one was hurt. Yes, it was a high-risk mission, but I learned from the incident. I'll always feel bad about wrecking their ship and casting any doubt as to our group's expertise.

The only good news to come out of the accident was that XC-BET was eventually stripped down to two or three sling loads and flown back to the airport. It was rebuilt in due time, and—I'm sure—at considerable expense, as all six 212's were uninsured.

Trying to explain to Lourdes and Dora what had happened was more than my Spanish was up for, but the accident was mentioned briefly in the *Noroeste* newspaper. Both girls knew Mike and I were living on the edge, so little was said about it and I was able to go on with life....*except* for a new *nickname*, courtesy of the lead Mexican pilot, Lomalee. He started calling me *"Rollerball,"* as in *roll-it-into-a-ball!*

Part of the healing process was—in fact—being with Lourdes, once I made the trip with Dora to Tierra Blanca to meet her extended family. Mama Celia and her children welcomed me, but wasted no time cautioning me to stay in the house and not to go walking around by myself in Tierra Blanca. (I personally thought—being dark-haired and tanned—that I blended in pretty well with the locals; but when I suggested that to the Medinas, they just laughed and told me that *"everyone* would know you are a *gringo!"* *Sheesh!*)

Mexican pilot Juan Rangel soon joined the Culiacán division, after working afar with another regional spray operation. He and I had been spraying partners early on in Chilpancingo, and when he came north, he drove his plush late model Ford Thunderbird up from Mexico City.

By then, Mike and Dora's relationship had cooled off, so it came to be that Juan and Dora were a team and the four of us went dancing at the clubs on a regular basis. I recall many an evening Juan would speed through the narrow side streets of Culiacán with Dora shrieking and giggling, Barry White blaring on the eight-track player while Lourdes and I cuddled in the big backseat, falling in love.

I was invited to a fiesta at the Medinas' house one sunny afternoon, a birthday party for one of her brothers, as I recall. I was cautioned to be on guard as there might be some *mafiósos* there, so the word for the day was *look out for the guys in straw hats*.

Sure enough, I spotted two likely suspects having *cervezas*[70] in the rear of the enclosed patio when I arrived, and avoided eye contact thereafter. The Medinas allowed certain "old friends" from Tierra Blanca in their house, but I think everyone was more than a little nervous about how this gathering might shake out.

"They won't try anything in the house, so just stay close and you'll be safe," Lourdes whispered to me.

Strangely enough, several beers later I was cooling off outside when one of the straw hats appeared alongside me and suggested that we *get together* soon. I politely answered, "Sure, amigo—when do you suggest?"

"Tuesday, in the afternoon," he said, but there was no frivolity in his tone.

Sunday morning I was sitting in the shade of an orange tree, struggling to finish the final book in Tolkein's *Ring* trilogy when Dora's LTD came flying into the hotel compound, skidding to a stop nearby. Dora didn't notice me in the shade and ran to knock on my door. Seeing that she was in a panic, I dashed over to her and asked what was wrong.

"Did you talk to one of *them*?" she asked.

"Yes, they said to meet them in Tierra Blanca Tuesday," I said.

"The word is *out*, Dorcito. *Don't go!*" she gasped, out of breath from her anxiety.

I assured Dora that I had no intention of meeting with the Mexican Mafia—today, tomorrow, or even *Tuesday*. And I thanked her for caring about me.

Despite the Medinas' sound advice, I found my way back over the old bridge once or twice more, taking a local taxi and doing my best imitation of a chameleon. Lourdes was too precious to ignore for long, and I always felt safe among the Medinas. Perhaps this feeling came from her work connection to three federal judges, who prosecuted the cases brought

70   Cold *Pacifico* beer, brewed in Mazatlán.

forth by the Procuraduría. Or perhaps it was an illusion, and I was just damned lucky.

By mid-April I had sprayed my last plantío in México, having fulfilled the terms of my six-month oral agreement with Operations. By then, I had stared down the barrels of two chrome-plated .45 pistols and one Mexican soldier's assault rifle, and had come to the conclusion that *El Gringo Wingo de Chilpancingo* had used up all his luck in México.

It wasn't easy to say good-bye to lovely Lourdes, but we had come to a comfortable feeling between us by then. I trusted her and I think she knew I would continue to be in touch, even though I was leaving the Operation.

During one last trip to Tambór, the possibility of matrimony was briefly discussed. Lourdes was a major contributor to the financial well-being of her siblings. I was hesitant to suggest that she could come live with me in one motel room after another and ignore the needs of her family. They were close, after all—closer than I had ever been with my own clan, so I honestly felt that marriage to Lourdes just wasn't meant to be.

The bottom line was, I was content with my career as a roving helicopter pilot, going anywhere the work sent me—and there would be no one to miss me if I got killed. When the topic came up, I gave her my most sincere answer: *"I don't think you would want to be married to a helicopter pilot, Lourdes."* A long silence followed, and I think it dawned on her that I might be right.

But you know what they say about *absence* and the *corazón*. After my departure, Lourdes and I began a lengthy correspondence with each other that continued for over a year. During that time I fought fires in Oregon and worked on my rustic cabin there, whenever possible. I also bought a late model Dodge Power Wagon pickup, choosing an automatic, with her in mind.

I was able to translate most of her wonderful letters, but had to have some help now and then. I wrote back in English, knowing she had a *confidant* there to translate for her.

When a work break came in May of 1977, I bought a diamond ring and a round-trip ticket to Culiacán and headed south once again, aiming to return with my darling Lourdes. I had grown a beard by then, but our reunion was sweet—and then came the difficult part, proposing our marriage to her family!

Lourdes had me repeat the words over and over, what I was to say to Mama Celia in front of her brothers. When the time came, we sat in a large circle of chairs, and it was harder than doing a *one-eighty* in a box canyon with a tailwind, but somehow I got the words out, and her tears started falling.

Bless her heart, Celia was giving up her eldest daughter to this gringo who would soon fly her away, muy lejos—very far away—and they might never see Lourdes again. I felt like a villain after that, but Mama Celia reluctantly gave us her blessings, and we headed out to get the paperwork done. That is, after a somber meeting with her brothers.

I remember the silent walk down the crude sidewalks of Tierra Blanca to the old cantina, just the men in the family: Paco, the oldest; followed by Pepe, Nacho, Jorge, Beto, David, Daniel, Miguel, and Raul. And the gringo. Arriving in front of the ancient wooden doors, I was taken back in time over a hundred and fifty years. This historic Mexican tavern had forgotten more good times than a weathered collection of *viejos*[71] could piece together.

Gathered 'round a heavy bench-style table along a bullet-riddled adobe wall, Paco ordered beer for the men and sodas for the younger siblings, and tried to put on a cheery face.

In the midst of appearing jovial over our tepid drinks, however, his demeanor took on a hawkish expression. The cantina fell quiet as he described what he would do to me if I ever left his beloved sister: *"I will shoot you—in the gut,"* he said in the clearest Spanish possible, half standing from his chair to lean in my direction and gesture—his right hand in the distinct form of a pistol. There was no smile. *"Do you understand?"* he asked.

"Claro," I answered gently. *Clearly.* Our eyes locked. I smiled at Paco, raised my warm glass of Pacifico, and toasted my future brothers-in-law. *"To Lourdes Maria—Salúd!"*

---

71   Old-timers

Como Se Llama Creek

---

*   *The Customer and a Lesson in Comeuppance*

Running a helicopter operation in the Los Angeles area will net you some interesting phone calls. Western Helicopters' reputation—coupled with a catchy Yellow Pages ad—guaranteed that we would hear from the fellow who just bought a remote mountaintop and wanted to airlift his two-story house up there.

We received calls from a frustrated celebrity aide who needed to land Robert Redford at Pepperdine University *tomorrow*—would we please make it happen?

There was a call from an art dealer who needed a fragile, eighteen hundred-pound obsidian sculpture lifted from a busy beachside street in Malibu over some power lines to a millionaire's veranda—rumored to be owned by Johnny Carson. "Oh, and we'll need a ten-million-dollar liability certificate." *No problema.*

Then there was the forty-story building superintendent who wanted all of his window washing equipment flown from the top down to the busy street below and replaced with a butt-load of new stuff.

The list goes on and on. Over the years, Pete Gillies and I wrote up some far-fetched stuff—but out of these samples, I can assure you the super's job went very well, as did the sculpture, but Pepperdine University does not tolerate helicopters on campus, Robert Redford or no. And the man on the mountain now lives in a humble trailer.

Fortunately for the rest of us, most *Callers-With-Too-Much-Money* are reasonable, and even though they make more in a year than you and I make in ten—they don't profess to know *everything*. Well, there was this *one* gentleman...

Summer was upon southern California like green on a June bug, and I was darned glad to have a phone stuck to my head—instead of out *there*, flopping around in the smoggy sky like my peers were doing. Air-conditioned offices come in handy every now and then.

The gentleman who called that special afternoon sounded like a western cinema cowboy hero or something. Having grown up in Texas, I found his easy-goin' manner soothing and listened raptly as he informed me of his aerial agenda. Turns out he was in the mining business and had an operation underway in northern Mexico. And he saw our ad.

Mr. Got Rocks wanted to rent one of our choppers to fly him, two other guys, and all their baggage down to Como Se Llama *next week*—land at his mine, sling out some ore in sacks, and come on *back*. No big deal. "Got one with an *air* conditioner?" he drawled.

I was soon reciting passages from my *Airman's Guide*, a section called *Baja Traveler*. There was a litany of permits required to fly a USA-based helicopter across the border, commercially.

"Won't be necessary," he replied, much to my amusement. I was trying to be diplomatic when I mentioned the numerous notches on my cyclic grip from a plethora of over-the-border commercial flights. Jobs ranging from spraying illegal crops with Mexican herbicide, air ambulance work, and supporting Baja Racers with fancy camera platforms—filming flying motorcycles and quad-runners. All of this commerce required special permits from the Capitál, ten days in advance.

"Won't be necessary, son," he interjected—as if I hadn't heard him the first time.

Sensing a real denial for the obvious, I switched tactics and went right to the cost of flying his party to the site and back—several thousand dollars—which we would need in advance. "I'll have a cashier's check delivered to you tomorrow morning," he answered, without breaking stride. I sensed that he was good for it, too.

But—as Pete always said—we'd *danced around the fire* long enough. It was time to convince Mr. Got Rocks to set his schedule back several days in order for Mexico's chief of aeronautics in the *Distrito Federal* to process our request. "First I get *permission*, *then* we cross the border," I informed the man, redefining our position.

"You don't know who you're talkin' to," he replied—with no malice in his tone, just a matter-of-fact statement. *"You'll get your check, and I'll take care of the politics. I've got a considerable investment down there, and everybody of import knows me. Just rent me a chopper and let's git goin'."* Soon afterward, he rang off.

Being the director of operations, I didn't make the final decision on problems of this nature, but I did set the paperwork in motion—just in case. The man didn't disappoint me: the next morning, his cashier's check arrived—for the *right* amount, and *right on time*. I took it to the general manager and explained the situation.

After some discussion, the boss gave me the green light to proceed, albeit with shared concern about the permits. Bottom line? We had his money. We were insured, and *additionally* insured. *"There's risk in every venture,"* he reminded me, as he relieved me of the check. (The boss had superior air-conditioning in his office, I couldn't help but notice.)

As Arizona would have it, the heat wave intensified, ripening into a *scorcher*. Which is when the customer showed up. Instead of having me pick him up near his Arizona border-town along the way, he chose to drive his trio over *two hundred miles* through the desert so he could fly right back there in our *non-air-conditioned MD 500D*.

They were all big guys—of course. It took our largest external-load basket to accommodate the sling rigging and their bags, while stuffing the smaller items into every internal crack and corner. Climbing up into the 34° C heat-soaked cockpit, I said good-bye to sweet air-conditioning and lit the wick.

Flying doors-on by necessity, we suffered in silence—flopping slowly along, low-level over the scorched desert, as the piled-high external basket did its best to hold us back.

When we refueled for the second time—at Tucson International Airport near the border—almost five hours had ticked by on the collective-up Hobbs meter. By then, our three VIPs had sweated out all their enthusiasm for *non*-air-conditioned aircraft and had pretty much overpowered their collective deodorant.

Standing bowlegged on the tarmac to allow my flight suit to peel off my partially poached backside, I scanned for shade while suggesting to a wilted version of Mr. Got Rocks that he could probably catch a 737 at yon *International Terminal*—have a couple of cocktails, and *still* beat me to *what-u-call-it*.

Mr. G. didn't need much encouragement. He grabbed his leather briefcase and waved down a cheerful-looking shuttle buggy with fringe on the top.

"We'll meet you there," he announced, gesturing a bit like Douglas MacArthur might have done once back in Dubya Dubya Two. The three Rocks started smiling in earnest as the shady golf cart picked up speed, relishing Nature's evaporative cooling power. A mirage containing the terminal and lounge grew steadily larger, as a young lady who knew exactly how to dress for the heat drove through the oven-like atmosphere.

Como Se Llama was two hours away at my snail-like pace. As hot as it was, the former Hughes 500D was up to the task—if I would be gentle. It was a big relief to unload my pax—a huge chunk of my useful load—and be able to pull off my left front door. It rode just fine in the rear cabin area. Captain Methane could now get some much-needed ventilation.

The road from Tucson to Como Se Llama is depressingly straight. Only a fool would fly any route but *over* the sun-baked two-laned highway, 'cause it goes straight to the destination. They might never find your busted self, way off to one side—if you happened to bust a hose or smack into a tall, meaty cactus.

I considered all the "or-somethings" as I pedaled slowly along. As the OAT gauge's needle went in and out of focus, I debated whether a pilot's familiarity with the *country*, the *people*, and the *language* was such a good thing to have in his resume 'bout now. Maybe I should've convinced that clever Gillies person that this was a perfect flight for *him* to go get some fresh air—or *something*.

He's a hard one to convince, I've noted.

When I called the control tower ten miles north of Como Se Llama, the bilingual tower-guy seemed genuinely surprised to hear from me, although he *must* have known that this was *the Got Rocks Express!* Wasn't long after I hover-parked the bird in front of the main terminal building, a feller on the radio invited me to present my registration and flight plan to *los oficiales*[72] inside.

I relaxed a skosh when Mr. Got Rocks himself met me coming through the door. Those in-flight cocktails converted his breath into something between jet fuel and paint thinner. My confident customer invited me to join him in a meeting on down the hall, with the *oficiale* in question.

Sequestered in a dank vestibule for the appropriate length of time, we waited. Roaches came and roaches went. In due time, a lackey was sent to escort us into the office of the local comandante. Right out of a movie, this guy was.

So here we have *Pancho Villa Reincarnate*, and seated across the old wooden table from him is *Cowboy Got Rocks* and *his* lackey, *Capitán Methane*. Slowly, like Chinese water torture, Pancho came around to the question at hand:

"What is the purpose of your *flight* into *Mexico*, señor?" he addressed the capitán.

The capitán deferred to Mr. Got Rocks, who was becoming a trifle more animated than his former lofty self. Mr. G. *explained* in English, while the comandante *ignored* in Spanish. (Captain Methane thought he heard—through the ancient, iron-barred window—inexperienced mechanics taking his helicopter apart on the apron.) Mr. Got Rocks soon ran out of consonants and reached into his wallet to buy some vowels.

"Why have you flown a commercial helicopter into the interior of Mexico without a permit, señor?" asked the comandante, his eyes staring at me through some expensive-lookin' shades, while trying unsuccessfully to ignore Mr. G's thumbs. They were calibrating an obscenely gratuitous *mordida*[73] from a thick wad of Ben Franklins.

The comandante involuntarily rolled his eyes like a bloated Jackie Gleason character for a second, resisting the impulse to collect the smiling Bens that

---

72   The airport authorities
73   Literally, "the bite." A bribe.

sat basking in the afternoon light from a distant smoky window. The inquisitive commander transmogrified into *Our Faithful Compadre,* as the customer leaned back casually in his chair. He looked askance at the capitán with a haughty expression that begged, *What'd I tell ya?!*

"There is still a problem at the federal level," the comandante politely retreated, as Mr. G. returned abruptly to the dive position. Reaching back into his gold mine, he soon had a small herd of Franklins smiling on top of the old table.

"I will see what I can do—of course," the comandante gushed, barely able to dial the phone number (if he in fact did) but Captain Methane thought he could hear an agitated voice at the other end of the crackling phone line. A few shouted epithets and several no's were overheard, allegedly coming from way down south.

"Did you fly to Como Se Llama with any *passengers* on board, *Capitán?"* The comandante held one hand over the receiver as he relayed the question from Mexico City. The capitán recognized the implication, and truthfully answered to the negative.

There was a pregnant pause, during which Capitan Methane saw for the first time that *deer-in-the-headlights* look on Mr. G's chiseled face, as the comandante set down the phone with one hand and *raked in the green* with another.

"It is fortunate that you came alone, *Capitán.* Now you have *one hour* to go back the way you came or I am under orders to *confiscate* your *helly-copter,"* el comandante said carefully.

Ka-ching!! (No *jail* time? I hesitated to inquire…)

"Pardon *me,* gentlemen," the Captain said, excusing himself as he made for the door with FAA registration in hand, "I've got a *hot desert* to cross."

You could *feel* the impact the comandante's proclamation had on my poor, deflated customer—who was suddenly up Como Se Llama Creek without a helicopter—and not quite as rich as he used to be.

It was, however, a poker hand played with all the gusto of *Cool Hand Luke*—but as for his permit-dodging bravado? Well, history will note that our brash cowboy strode into the toasty sunset that evening without his horse.

Section V:
A Southern California Operation

Flying the Panamints

*   *Precious metal, an incredible vista, and the random heart attack.*

Whether one drives, rides a mule, or flies a helicopter into California's remote Searles Valley for the first time, sooner or later the local *fragrance* hits one's nose and one wonders, *"Who ripped it?"* Since I was alone in the helicopter at the time, I knew the score without having to look around.

I recall with a smile my first good nose-full as I flew by the out-of-this-world-looking Trona Pinnacles into Searles Valley. It was my first commercial helicopter flight to the Panamint Mountains. (I was headed for Ballarat to meet some folks needing a lift to lofty Mormon Peak.) The Pinnacles told me things were going to be different, up ahead.

The abundant sky over the high desert was cobalt blue that sunny day in early May. In stark contrast, Trona's Kerr McGee plant was pumpin' out long, sulfur-colored streams into the atmosphere. They were foul, floating remnants freshly steamed out of the rank white Searles lake bed; deep, slick, gooey mud, times many square miles. The odor one smells is said to be the essence of commerce!

Several tall smokestacks foul the air around Trona on a regular basis. Depending on the relative wind, the aroma is virtually inescapable. You'd think that anyone living here would be miserable under such conditions. You would be wrong.

Never fear, pilgrim—the residents of this proud working community observe the strict discipline of diehard Alaskans—who never mention their ever-present ravenous horde of mosquitoes—by ignoring the rotten egg aroma around Trona and getting on with life. After all, there are countless trainloads of valuable potash and other useful compounds waiting to be exorcised from the muck.

Only on a bad day will the stench reach as far north as Ballarat, which would be good news to the local Ballarat Chamber of Commerce, except there ain't one and ain't likely ever to be one, neither. One look at the old general store pretty much says it all: *We're closed!*

Of the memorable clients who paid four hundred dollars an hour (and up) to be flown around the Panamints, many were geologists. It didn't take long for a backwater pilot to figure out that the Panamints were a popular place to send educated rock hounds.

Many of them wanted to be flown to the same locations, be it the Suitcase Mine, the Homestead, or up through Jackpot or Pleasant Canyon for a look-see. Spotting some rare formations in hard-to-reach places, they had me hover over stark, wild folds in the rock, caused by a tumultuous upheaval in the elements back when all this was molten. Stuff you can read about in dense books, but seldom get to see up close, much less debate it with other experts.

After overhearing many independent knowledgeable sources proclaim the occurrence of quartz, nickel, and gold in the Panamints, you get the idea that ores of these concentrations are indeed rare. It also seems that each new prospector who comes along is interested in digging a little deeper, a little farther than the previous prospector. Discoveries are made that way, as are fortunes lost.

There was little gambling to be done on Mormon Peak, however. At 8,200 feet above sea level, the peak was the ideal location to erect the world's first solar-powered telephone relay station, connecting Death Valley to Slate Ridge and beyond. (As soon as we got busy and built it.)

The outfit that did the early stages of construction (the excavation) was MicroFlect, out of Oregon. I flew a crew of three and numerous loads from a dusty landing zone (LZ) near Ballarat to Mormon Peak that day in 1981. The loads were either hauled internally or in sling nets. These loads consisted of power generators, air hoses and compressors, gasoline, food, water, and radios.

Days later, the holes for the foundation and antenna were dug and the site was ready for concrete. The problem was locating a ready-mix unit from Las Vegas who would send a truck all the way to Ballarat, but they were eventually found.

A deal was finally struck with an adventurous outfit to have them drive a big mixer unit as far up the slope east of Ballarat as possible into Pleasant Canyon. Once there, the driver would wait for orders to start mixing the cement and water.

A Lama helicopter was flown in from Provo, Utah to help with the concrete phase, as the MD500 I had arrived in didn't have the eight hundred horses required to lift a full bucket of "mud" and hover with it at 8,200 feet. Pete Gillies' Lama made the work look easy.

The SA-315B Lama has one of the best views of any helicopter. From the right seat of an open cockpit, the three-hundred-sixty-degree, seventy-five-mile view in every direction from Mormon Peak can make a grown man feel like a tiny speck—even if he's a hardheaded old fart. (Which Pete ain't!)

The on-site mixer gave Pete the three-hour window he needed to fly ten yards of fresh concrete to the site in a quarter-yard aluminum concrete bucket. Ten yards? Up and down, many times! It's all part of the job, and I know Pete relished the roller-coaster ride to and from.

The building panels, antennae, and solar equipment that houses the repeater and heavy-duty batteries followed after the concrete hardened. The LZ serving the site was kept small to conserve the many old piñon pine that grow so well on high. I became a fan of piñon nuts, which were abundant that year. I got down on my knees and stuffed a sandwich bag full the first moment I had some down time up top.

On subsequent flights, we flew personnel and equipment from Death Valley's Furnace Creek Airport to the distant peak. These were the final loads of gear needed to put the new repeater into service, and by the end of the workday, the sun was charging the Mormon Peak telephone repeater's brand-new batteries.

On the return flight to Death Valley, a camouflaged swing-wing F111 bomber suddenly flew underneath me headed south at a blistering pace, missing me by five hundred feet, but catching me flat-footed and off guard! The airspace in the Panamints area is "joint-use," meaning military aircraft may be involved in training, so the word is *heads up!*

This brings us, happy readers—a few years later—to the middle of the afternoon on what could have been your average Panamints helicopter job, parked near Ballarat. Your humble pilot is snoozing away on a flimsy lawn chair in his sweaty flight suit; ditto Craig Wooton, the fuel truck driver, snoring away in the fuel truck.

Flies pester our sweating hides, but we are hesitant to stir, lest we sweat even more. The dusty helicopter sits baking in the hundred-degree sun, parked on the crusty Panamints dry lake bed nearby. Shade is at a premium out here.

I dropped the customers off at the Suitcase Mine hours ago. They left instructions to retrieve them around 4:30, another two hours, easy. They were content to dig for "color," tiny specks of gold. This is the lazy portion of the afternoon that we had promised to ourselves: some quiet time to catch up on the sleep we didn't get at the Pioneer Point Motel the night before. But we won't go there.

Dozing back to sleep, I forgot about the heat, the flies, and that ever-scanning Navy radar facility just west of the dry lake bed, the one you drive past to reach Ballarat from Highway 178. They knew exactly where we were. They could observe every takeoff and landing we made in our slow-moving helicopter. They never talked to us, just directed their supersonic fighters around us when they were performing low-level work.

Those radar guys had to know we were catching some shuteye. Why else would they vector an F16 to blaze a supersonic path north to south over the lake bed, passing perhaps forty feet directly overhead—giving Craig and me a major heart attack as he rocketed by and the shock wave blew us both out of our Fruit of the Looms. (Now, wasn't that funny, Craig?)

This observation comes from a military veteran who knows full well the value of our military training centers, and I wouldn't dare say a discouraging word about our patriotic Navy personnel. But if I ever get a chance to return to the Panamints in a time machine, I would set it for a time before the smokestacks and jets impacted the incredible expanse and deafening silence one can still experience, once the rotors stop.

The Beam or the Bike?

---

* *How to wreck a helicopter without starting it up.*

The chief pilot and senior flight instructor would likely prefer that I skip this story. It wasn't *their* fault that a prized turbine helicopter was substantially damaged that morning, after all. They were just pushing the darned thing!

The director of maintenance sent the shop foreman to Operations bright and early one fine spring day, requesting two warm bodies to help snap on the ground handling wheels (GHWs) and push a freshly repaired Hughes 500C out the hangar door. Don—the young foreman—seemed to be in a hurry.

As it turned out, Bob and Pete had a few minutes to spare for our friendly maintenance department. Besides, getting the 500C back in service solved many of our scheduling problems.

And as luck would have it, I was on the phone when Don asked for a hand. Pete dutifully rose and marched down the hall to meet Bob. They headed into the east hangar together like two men on a mission. It was a beautiful day and the sun shone brilliantly, with both twenty by forty-foot steel hangar doors pushed wide open.

The weather was so California-like that one of our naturally handsome helicopter mechanics rode his sleek black motorcycle to work that morning.

The bike—generously festooned with chrome accessories—was freshly detailed.

The naturally handsome mechanic didn't want his sleek machine to sit baking in the hot sun all day, so he rolled on into the open hangar, eased the machine over to a shady spot, and toed the kickstand into position. Fairly common to see a motorcycle parked in that same spot, it was.

Meanwhile—thirty feet away—Pete and Bob had locked their GHWs down to the 500's skids and are ready for Don to join them and guide the helicopter out the spacious hangar door. With volunteers pushing on either side, the easier job of steering the tail was left up to Don, a veteran of many such routine procedures.

All Don had to do was make sure they attained *track-crossing speed* by the time they reached the open doorway. The GHWs were famous for stopping rudely on the steel hangar door tracks if insufficient momentum were attained. That wasn't going to happen on Don's shift! All he had to do was miss that sleek black motorcycle!

"Okay, men!" he called to his pushers. Heads down, they threw themselves into the task.

It was about then that I walked down the hallway toward the hangar. I had just pushed the door open when I heard a gosh-awful *crash* and the sound of tempered aluminum tearing. Without taking another step, I gazed eastward and made out our intrepid trio and a strangely wounded helicopter in the blinding light of day.

The good news was that the black motorcycle was unscathed. Don had missed it by over three feet. However, the helicopter's "V" tail stabilizer had rudely contacted the vertical steel doorjamb of the hangar doorway during the track-crossing maneuver, stopping the elevator dead as the helicopter continued ahead a foot or so.

There was a garish tearing of metal forward of the tail rotor gearbox that resulted in the whole "V" tail assembly coming badly to rest on the hangar floor. No one said a word as Don slowly lowered his ugly piece of tail, allowing it to wallow pathetically at his feet. He slumped off to one side into a depressed squatting position—his hands covering his eyes—as Bob and Pete stood there, debating the wisdom of volunteering.

Realizing the Maintenance Department might need some quiet time, I backed slowly away, retraced my steps to the general manager's door, and broke the bad news to the boss. My timing could have been better: the boss was briefing his boss's son on the new insurance rates when I walked in with my untimely loss report. (They had heard the *awful sound*, too!)

So as not to rub it in, I didn't take any photos of the aftermath, but I can still occasionally hear the terrible tearing sound from that fateful morning. I did have something to be grateful for, though; *I* wasn't pushing the day Don chose between the beam, or the bike.

Stringing the Center Phase

*   *Knitting Through Steel Towers with a Helicopter*

When day dawned on the Arizona desert for the first commercial application of Claude Chapman's new invention, there were four helicopter pilots on hand to give 'er a try.

The challenge was to pass a sockline[74] through the center phase of a new steel 500KV transmission tower with a helicopter strapped to our backs—assisted only by a puller operator on the ground—employing the newly patented mechanical marvel known as the *Center Phase Stringer*. After that, steel towers beckoned for the next one hundred and twenty miles, all the way to the Palo Verde Nuclear Power Plant.

Passing the sockline through the enclosed steel center phase of wood pole "H" structures and steel towers had for many years been done by hand, employing utility crews who faced climbing every tower to persuade the sockline through the old fashioned way.

Helicopters came along and sped up the process, but there still had to be another human being near the center phase. His job was to disconnect and reconnect the sockline in order to pass the line under the bridge and play it down onto the pulley-like traveler and on they went.

---

74   The sockline is also called a fly rope or pilot rope, which is used to pull in the conductor wire later on.

Of course, there had to be quite a horde of climbers on the job in order to keep up with the helicopter. In some areas, union safety rules required a minimum of two men on the bridge for such work, so center phase-related costs kept rising.

A clever invention called the "FlyTrap" came along in the 1970s, promising to reduce the need for hands-on personnel during the stringing. One immediate drawback was that the device had to be installed (and later removed) from every bridgehead in the project.

I shrink from the task of describing how the FlyTrap worked, but it was a complicated, spring-loaded contraption that gave many a helicopter pilot a scare, according to those who have used it. The device was known to whip the sockline on many occasions, causing vertical waves of braided wire rope to whip up near the tips of the helicopter's rotor blades. That'll get your attention!

Enter Claude Chapman, who had worked on and around power lines most of his life.

"The real reason for the needle," Claude told me, "came out of working in such close proximity to the helicopter up in the towers." He realized that the vulnerability of the machine was proportionate to his welfare while hand-threading the perilous sockline. Claude decided "...if I could remove the lineman, it would be a great benefit to the lineman and the company."

The center phase problem was an alluring challenge for an engineer like Claude, and he correctly imagined that the helicopter—using a side puller—would be part of the solution. To solve the dilemma, he began construction on a scale model of the typical electrical transmission tower on top of his kitchen table. With his wife Charlotte kibitzing, Claude toyed for months to perfect a scale model of the multi-hooked, needle-nosed *Stringer* that came to bear his name.

Their efforts finally culminated in 1979, and suddenly inventor Claude Chapman had a new shingle hanging from his little shop: Sock Line Specialists, Inc. was open for business!

Employing a variety of special hooks and a "headache ball" to grab hold and pull the device into various positions, Claude's prototype was ready for its first aerial test. Pilot Charlie Baze from Rocky Mountain Helicopters, of Provo, Utah, had the honors.

Charlie listened to Claude's *how-to* speech and went to work. Flying a Lama, he pulled the device through a few towers, added his input, and it wasn't much later that our squad of four gathered near Quartzite to start threading the Stringer over the highly sensitive and protected desert of southwestern Arizona.

My logbook reminds me that it was a hot August afternoon in 1981 near Vicksburg when our entourage arrived via truck, helicopter, and the bosses' Cessna 182. The following morning we met Claude and a cluster of power company reps out by the helicopter, Western's trusty old Hughes H369HE (500C).

Mr. Chapman had already laid out and assembled his thirty-foot-long Stringer nearby, and we gathered 'round the thing in wonder. It resembled an aluminum irrigation pipe festooned with two pivoting hooks, two stationary hooks, and a tail clip. It weighed in at just under two hundred pounds.

After some preliminary discussions, Chief Pilot Pete Gillies got busy and installed Western's side-puller to the helicopter's rear cargo deck with four hardened bolts, removing the ship's left rear passenger step in the process. (This was done to eliminate the blind spot that the step produces if left in place during long-line work.)

The sockline "Puller" truck sat idling nearby with two giant spools of wire rope, ready for Pete to start yarding eastward. The Puller operator gave Pete an FM radio check, as Claude snapped the terminus of the Puller's sockline into the (swiveling) tail clip of the Stringer.

Clipping the fifty-foot line of the headache ball's upper shackle into the side-puller's cargo hook, Pete had already worked up a mild sweat in the mid-morning desert heat. He pulled himself into the left seat and lit the fire, as the cluster of hard-hatted observers got out their video and still cameras.

(N506WW—or "Wicky-Wicky," as we used to call her—came with the reliable 400 HP version of the Allison gas turbine engine, a favorite for wire-pulling operations in our region. Light, nimble, and powerful, the 500C is a miser with jet fuel compared to its successor, the 420 HP 500D.)

As the rest of us pilots somewhat nervously anticipated our turn, Pete deftly lifted the Stringer into the air by its front pivoting hook and started toward the first steel tower. He soon had the non-pivoting angle hook moored on the bridge of the tower, and asked the Puller operator for "a touch of brake" at that point.

With the Puller's brake applied, the Stringer stayed in the desired position while Pete slacked back and freed up the yellow iron ball from the forward hook. Pete then hovered back over the Stringer and worked the ball into the mid-point hook, which also pivots.

Pete soon observed that—once freed from the bridge—the nose of the Stringer tended to bob and teeter while being hauled around by the center hook. Still—with patience—Pete persuaded the Stringer forward and under the bridge.

Captain Gillies then coaxed the Stringer's ninety-degree hook into a specific steel lattice triangle underneath the bridge, transferring the strain to the tower and allowing him to slack off the center hook, hover back to the forward side of the tower, and connect once again to the forward swivel hook.

Once reconnected, Pete hovered ahead, pulling the length of the Stringer past the awaiting fly-arm of the center-phase traveler. Threading the wire smoothly through the traveler's gate and onto the middle of three giant rollers, the hovering hardware continued eastward, and a new opportunity for helicopters was born.

Almost before we realized it, Pete Gillies had successfully pioneered the Sockline Stringer's first commercial 500KV center phase application! He continued eastward and after deftly knitting his way through yet another tower, Pete "parked" the Stringer on the following tower's bridge and brought the ship back for the next victim.

The next pilot to fly had arrived commercially from San Francisco, on condition—meaning, if he couldn't fly the Stringer, he'd head back north to his old flying job. The New Guy picked up the 500C and headed away from us, looking steady. As soon as he picked Claude's Stringer off the tower's bridge, however—things got a little ugly.

Several minutes later, he stopped what he was attempting to do, parked the Stringer where it was, brought the ship back, and announced—with an obvious sigh of relief—that he was withdrawing his bid to fly on the project, unconditionally.

I had a lot of respect for the man for trying, and as the cluster of hard hats began to twitch and mumble among themselves, I grabbed my olive drab flight helmet and headed for the Hughes.

Once he arrived at *Wicky Wicky*, Captain Methane hesitated to strap himself into the helicopter seat. It wasn't *fear* that was holding him back, it was the *soaking wet seat cushion* awaiting his dry Wranglers that made him shiver as he sucked it up, climbed in, and plopped onto the seat, clicking the four-way harness locked. (It was probably only eighty-five degrees Fahrenheit by then, certainly not hot enough to account for the quantity of perspiration I was suddenly soaking up. Assuming it *was* perspiration!)

I'm pleased to report that my try-out went fairly well, although not as fast as Pete's. For an experienced long-line pilot, the fifty-foot line is a short cable, but the fact that the headache ball doesn't hang straight down from the belly hook will immediately slow him/her down. Instead, the side puller's cargo hook makes the vertical long-line hang in such a way that it contacts the outside edge of the left skid.

Riding along in this fashion, any rocking motion of the helicopter causes the skid tube to nudge the long-line outward, making the ball move unintentionally—resulting in wasted motion. This is the only real drawback to an otherwise workable situation.

After a few minutes, I learned to minimize the ship's rocking motion, disturbing the ball less frequently. This concession got me into and out of the Stringer's pivoting hooks faster. By then, I was an experienced hand at pulling wire horizontally, so once I figured out the headache ball phenomenon, the job seemed vaguely familiar.

(Our fourth pilot was Clair Merryweather, Western Helicopter's president. With little long-line time to his credit in those days and no wire pulling experience, he nonetheless took the task to heart and in due time coaxed the Stringer through the next tower in line, and the demonstration part of the job was over.)

From that day on, Pete and I logged the remainder of the flying. We commonly strung 15,000 feet of sockline and static wire for the electrical contractor (H.P. Foley) every few days—leaving the helicopter parked at strategic spots in the desert while flying pilots to and fro in Clair's 182A fixed wing.

Once we had all the center phases pulled, we'd park the Stringer and pull the outside phases and twin static lines using the side puller. One day's work with the Stringer kept the H.P. Foley clipping crew busy for about five workdays at a time.

On January 22nd, 1982, I had the pleasure of threading the Stringer through the final structure leading into the Palo Verde Nuclear Power Plant.

There were other discoveries to be gleaned from the overall experience, including:

1. The further along the pull went, the easier it was to predict how far past an anchor point to pull the Stringer before you could slack-back, hang the device on the tower, and change hooks. This "improvement" in *feel* comes from the added friction from hundreds of feet of "belly," or where the sockline makes contact with the ground between one tower and the next. The more contact, the better your control—up to a point.
2. We found that the longer, uphill pulls in the project were a power struggle with the 500C. This was solved easily enough by switching to the 500D. (At higher elevations on future projects, we found the SA 315B Lama to be the next step up in articulated rotorcraft pulling-power.)
3. Not all 500KV transmission towers are created equal! Toward the end of the job, I encountered one particular dead-end tower that was beefier than its brothers. The bridge's dimensions were such that it was almost impossible to hang and reattach the Stringer to the common points on the tower. But we managed.
4. On a windy day, I had the misfortune of hanging the center pivot hook of the Stringer in the tower I was pulling up to, entangling the empty hook in the steel lattice in such a way that I couldn't move the Stringer—or the helicopter! Using the FM radio, I persuaded the

foreman to drive his rig over to my location, climb up the leg of the tower, and disentangle the Stringer *before* I ran low on fuel and had to punch it off!

5. We also had a pivot hook or two crack out, something that was easily repaired by keeping a few of Claude's spares on hand.

Footnotes: We lost the use of our 500C about a month into the project. It was a no fly day when N506WW rolled over onto her roof during a late afternoon thunderstorm. She was the Hangar Queen for months before finally returning to service.

Pete Gillies and I shared the Arizona Stringer job throughout. I have to hand it to *The Master*, though—for being a smoother and faster *Stringer* pilot than Captain Methane. Pete was timed pulling the stringer all the way through a tower in just over two minutes more than once, but my average time was closer to three minutes.

I also got the Stringer stuck in a tower during a hard, uphill pull and couldn't budge it loose! Pete happened to be on hand that day, so I had him give it a whirl and he had it freed up in a New York minute. (Humbling!)

Claude also invented the Chapman cargo hook-up system, which allows a helicopter pilot to fly to a location, pick up a load (and relocate it, for example) without needing anyone there to do the hooking and unhooking. This allows for better management of flight time and makes the helicopter more competitive with conventional methods.

I am pleased to report that Claude's design is still in use as of this writing—and is used widely overseas. To Mr. Chapman's lament—there *are* imitation Stringers out there. You know what they say, imitation being *the sincerest form of flattery*. But from what Pete and I have learned—none are better than the *original*.

Mr. Chapman was kind enough to write me concerning this story, adding, "You and Pete were the ones who allowed us to know that we really had something…thanks."

Thank *you*, Claude, for solving the problem and giving helicopter pilots something truly special to work with. You're a crafty fellow!

Section VI:
See Hollywood from the Air

On Camera, Off Camera

"Just how does one get into the movie business?" I inquired.

It was another pleasant Southern California day in 1980. Sitting across from me on Western Helicopter's comfortable couch was none other than Jack Gillette, or J.W. Gillette,[75] depending on which movie he was in. We were having a brief chat before he took off with one of our helicopters under a Dry Lease Rental Agreement for movie work. A big guy, he sat cross-legged and wore that perpetual smug expression on his chiseled face. I was dying to ask him something, and he saw it coming, I'm sure.

Practically everyone knew Jack Gillette from a plethora of Hollywood movies, ranging from *Catch 22* to *Baa Baa Black Sheep* to *Black Sunday*; he was a cinematographer (turned) movie pilot (turned) second unit director, and a member of the DGA.[76] Gillette occasionally rented Western's JetRangers and Hughes 500s to use "on-camera" and "off-camera," the difference being that an off-camera ship was the one with the camera mount; the on-camera ship was in the film.

Gillette was in Rialto to pick up one of our JetRangers. As Western's director of operations, it was my job to schedule the ship's availability and make sure the contract was letter-perfect and the ship was ready to

75   The author is employing an alias here.
76   Directors Guild of America

fly when he strolled in: clean, fueled, and sometimes sporting a custom Spraylat "peel-off" paint job.

Western, and our parent company, Rocky Mountain Helicopters, had long supplied helicopters for such films as *Birds of Prey*, *Capricorn One*, *The Gauntlet*, *Close Encounters of the Third Kind*, and *Blue Thunder*, to name a few. Plus numerous TV productions, including *Air Wolf*, *Matt Houston*, and *CHiPs*.

Prior to my arrival at Western, more than one of our pilots had flown in a movie for Jack. Karl Wickman, for example, piloted a Hughes 500C in *Capricorn One* under Gillette's direction and practically overnight became a full-time movie pilot, living the good life and (almost) never looking back. Rumors of his success were most interesting.

Get rich flying helicopters? On camera? I had never considered the possibility. My lovely Mexican wife came from proud but humble stock, as did I. She knew that getting rich was not all that important to me. Since my first flight, my focus in life had been the mere *adventure*, the *experience* of piloting helicopters in exotic locations. But SAG[77] pilots made more money than directors of operations, and little Robert needed new shoes. I was intrigued, so I innocently asked Gillette,

"Just how does a pilot *get* into the movie business, Jack?"

It was as if he had been waiting for that one, and he pounced: "If you're not *already* in, you're not *getting* in."

The smug look on his unfriendly face turned kind of sinister; a string of elastic spittle connected his upper and lower lip. Despite his rudeness, I acted nonchalant, then gave him my very best *screw-you-too-pal* smile and handed over the contract to be signed. Following him out to the helicopter and seeing him off, I was beginning to despise one of my *customers* and his *In-Your-Face-West-Coast* attitude.

It was February of 1980 when I took over the Operations job at Western. At the ripe old age of thirty-five, it was my first desk job following fifteen years of enviable flying experiences. My wife and I had traveled all over Wyoming, Utah, Idaho, and Arizona, chasing some choice assignments.

---

77   Screen Actors Guild. Membership is essential to work on productions paying scale actor's wages.

But Lovely Lourdes was becoming weary of trailer life by then, and getting no help from little Robert, who was into his *terrible twos* and equally bored with the thirty-five by eight-foot box we called "home."

Although I was inclined to leave those stuck-to-a-desk jobs to the "blow-dry" pilots I'd come across over the years, I was gently persuaded to give it a try by a splendid hombre who became my close friend, Peter H. Gillies. Pete had relieved me several times on the Mt. Whitney Ranger District fire contract (flying a Lama) and, later, started me on my first power line construction job. Our wives and kids got along famously.

Pete was Western's chief pilot, and over the past year or so, I had learned to respect him as a superb pilot and an all-around great guy. The handsome son of a former Grumman Vice President of Flight Test Engineering, his mother was a legendary WAF[78] B-29 pilot. This guy was born to fly! Pete could do it all, and to this day he is as loyal to Western Helicopters as Audie Murphy was to his WWII platoon in the face of all them Nazis.

(Back to the filming stuff!)

I've loved photography since I was a kid. My mom recognized my passion and bought me my first camera, a Polaroid "Instant," while I was in high school. Money was tight in those days, but I earned $1.10 per hour flipping burgers in Las Cruces to support my motorcycle and photography addictions. My right-sided brain and I spent a small fortune photographing friends, pets, mountain vistas, and my beloved motorcycles—toting that Polaroid all over New Mexico.

I briefly played "director" with a second-hand 8mm movie camera until my draft notice arrived, personally autographed by Lyndon B. Johnson, in January of 1966. I was soon wearing Army green. My motorcycle racing and filming days were put aside while I learned to be a soldier, a cryptographer, and a combat chopper pilot.

Back from the 'Nam, I signed up to complete my last year of military duty at White Sands Missile Range, New Mexico. This was not far from my old hometown of Las Cruces, but my new "home" was at Holloman Air Force Base, near Alamogordo. The Base turned out to be a great assignment, as I had written about Robert Goddard, "Father of American Rocketry," in my youth.

78   Women in the Air Force

The Army sent choppers all over Goddard's old missile range in support of some interesting (and some secret) engineering, space exploration, and weapons development. My favorite was the famous seven-mile-long High Speed Sled Track, made popular by the old TV series *Man and the Challenge*. Some of the many tests conducted there were essential to the development of jet-fighter ejection seats, and the physical limitations of the human body to accelerate and decelerate. And lucky me, the Air Force used Army choppers to film the tests!

My first off-camera movie work was accomplished in an old Hiller OH-23D *Raven*. I'd meet the generic Air Force cameraman at Holloman's Air Operations Directorate, pop off the doors, strap him and his boxy looking ultra-slow motion movie camera inside, and off we'd go to the Sled Track, just a minute or two northwest of the airstrip.

My favorite missions involved shooting the fastest vehicles, which could reach Mach Seven! Not that you could actually see something scorching along at that speed, but watching those liquid fuel sleds go from a standstill at the south end of the track to a *blur* of shock waves headed north was an unforgettable thrill!

Compared to the solid fuel sleds—which took off fast but didn't attain Mach Seven—the liquid fuel jobs started very slowly, with an eerie green cloud of exhaust gas. But before you could say *Alamogordo,* that darned sled was *gone*—smashed into thousands of tiny red-hot pieces, and buried in a big white gypsum sand dune off the north end of the track, seven miles away. Blink, and you missed it!

"Don't *never, ever* fly through the *green cloud,* Chief," the Air Force photographer advised me, and waited for me to acknowledge. There always was a hidden element of danger in those missions. I believed him, but I wasn't afraid. Poisonous gas? *Captain Methane* was born for this line of work!

I got to see and film all kinds of great stuff at White Sands: Sprint and Hawk missile launches, the first radar-guided Gatling guns, the first Maverick (TV-guided) missiles, Trinity Site, stuff like that. What an interesting place to work!

My last military off-camera assignment came in early 1971 when I went to Yuma Proving Grounds, Arizona, and filmed some of the first TOW[79]

79   Tube launched, Optically and Wire guided Missiles

missiles being fired from Lockheed's experimental Cheyenne ornithopter. Flying parallel to the two-hundred-plus-knot wonder, we bounced along in an old Huey at one hundred twenty knots while the beauty plugged a moving target over two miles away. (*Bull's-eye,* we verified moments later!)

After my release from the Army, and a brief *restauranteuring* detour, I ended up working for Evergreen Helicopters out of McMinnville, Oregon in 1974.

The very first day at Evergreen, new employees were escorted into a theater and shown several breathtaking, professionally produced "trailers" of their huge fleet of helicopters at work around the world: erecting steel towers, harvesting timber, exploring for oil, fighting fires, and saving lives. Very impressive! I just had to inquire of the pretty secretary who turned on the lights, "Who shot the footage?"

She informed me that Del Smith always sought out a professional cinematographer from Los Angeles by the name of Doug Allen.

"The best!" she professed, and who would argue?!

As it turned out, I met Doug Allen in Fairbanks, Alaska a few months later. I was piloting one of Evergreen's Bell 205-A1s on a BLM[80] fire contract when Doug appeared one morning, hoping to film us taking off to a fire. I was pessimistic about our chances of being launched, because the weather was damp and things had been very slow.

But some guys have all the luck, because as soon as he tightened his Arriflex camera down on the heavy wooden tripod, a wailing siren split the air and a dozen Alaskan Indian firefighters leapt into action. Being fleet-footed in those days, I was first in my seat and had the chopper in the air within seventy seconds, making one of my smoothest takeoffs ever—straight away from Doug's point of view. My first on-camera experience!

I saw the footage months later, long after Doug had complimented me on a *flawless* lift-off. I realized I could "crank it up a notch" when the cameras were rolling—flying very smoothly—which made the work more fun.

---

80   Bureau of Land Management

つつつへ

(Shift seven years ahead, to Rialto): "Professor" Art Scholl suddenly darkened my Operations doorway—unannounced—and clasping his hands together as if to suggest *Let's Make a Deal*, he exclaimed,

"Dorcey! Have I got a deal for you!" The flamboyant former National Aerobatics Champion and local Fixed Base Operator was putting on an air show at Rialto Municipal Airport, and he came to ask me if I'd ever dropped a car from a helicopter?

Art let on that there was a new "gag" going around the air show circuit: as the crowd gathered, the air show announcer would ask for everyone's attention and read out the license plate of a car that was allegedly parked in a fire zone, and if the owner didn't move it, it would have to be towed.

Well, after an hour or two of these tiresome announcements, everyone is hating the car, so along comes the chopper and hauls it off. But as the car is brought around to "Stage Front," things go screwy. The heavy load appears to get way out of whack and the chopper pilot has to punch it off! It allowed choppers to get in on the fun and it thrilled the audiences. The fans just loved to see stuff get smashed!

I listened as Art explained how an Air Force Huey had dropped the first one recently at a military air show, but his budget wouldn't allow a Huey. He asked if Western could lift a compact-sized car using our Hughes 500D.

"Oh, by the way," he added, "the scene is going to be filmed for a segment of the TV series, *CHiPs*!"

Realizing money was being made and (at the same time) that I had an opportunity to get my SAG card, I clasped my fingers together, mimicking Art's flamboyant entrance, and said,

"Professor, it's time we talked about my SAG card!"

And that's how Wingo broke into the movie business. Now, Art *was* a chopper pilot but he had *zero* external-load or long-line experience. He also needed someone close by with a Hughes 500D, and *voila!* Western had to cough up the $600 SAG application fee. Art, being a DGA member, endorsed me as a helicopter pilot/long-line specialist needed for the gig.

Within days, Art's mechanics produced a junk Opel compact car and removed the engine, transmission, and seats. Even with a fresh bright yellow paint job, it was stripped to just 1,100 pounds, which was *within the ballpark*, as they say.

The 1981 Rialto Air Show took place on a hot, smoggy May weekend. Pete and I calculated that one hundred pounds of Jet-A would do the job: lift out of the yard at Western on cue, dangling thirty feet of steel cable (short enough to keep both ship and car in the camera's viewfinder). Hover over to the car (on-camera), hand the hook to Craig Wooton—who snapped the line onto a heavy nylon strap choked around the Opel's metal roof—and go!

And that's just the way it went at the air show. Once latched onto the Opel, I made a max-power takeoff, dodging several light poles, and flew a circuit around the sheriff's hangar, over to the north side of the airfield, slowly gaining about two hundred feet.

The trick was to coordinate with the air show announcer, who played the role perfectly. As I approached the "red line" (imposed by the FAA for crowd safety) I feigned losing control, got the car swinging around, and suddenly punched the whole thing off. Whereupon, the Opel came screaming out of the blue just across the runway—landing perfectly flat—blowing out all the windows and windshields, and compacting itself down to about two feet. The crowd loved it! Pete met me with a big handshake and a great review after I landed.

And little Robert loved it, too! Afterward, he sat in the ship for an hour, dressed up in my flight gloves and a headset, playing with the controls.

We "killed" the Opel Saturday and a Datsun on Sunday. The scene was incorporated into the *ChiPs* episode titled *Bomb Run*, culminating with the ubiquitous car chase scene, filmed in and around the Rialto airport.

Art was jubilant over my performance at the air show and soon referred more work in Western's direction, including a three-night gig at Disneyland's 25th anniversary party in Anaheim. This was a first, a "PyroSpectacular" event using our Hughes 500D to long-line a huge, flaming set piece, while hovering five hundred feet over Sleeping Beauty's Castle.

Disneyland's producers insisted on two rehearsals. At the onset, they needed all kinds of assurances that we could pull it off. To their credit, they rolled out the red carpet for our families, which made them very nice to work with.

Hanging Bob Sousa's[81] set piece in the right spot required Pete and I to come up with an experimental set-up. First, we snapped a one-hundred-foot long non-twist steel cable into the cargo hook, leading down to a spreader bar supporting the billboard-sized set piece.

To orient the set piece toward the primary audience, we had two very long ropes tied to its bottom corners. The bottom ends of the ropes were controlled by several Disneyland "extras." I calculated the time it would take to climb straight up five hundred feet, and added thirty seconds for a cushion. The extras simply played out the ropes until I reached five hundred feet, at which time they were given the order to "hold fast!" I would then pull just enough power to take out the slack and not levitate the extras.

From that point on, I held everything as motionless as possible and waited for the radio cue from Pete to set it off. A switch wired to the cyclic would send twenty-four volts down the line to a special squib on the set piece, igniting a maze of quick-fuses, and *bingo!*

We employed an illuminated "X" as my ground reference point, and it worked just fine. The set piece lit right on cue, "Disneyland—25 Years" accentuated by a golden "waterfall" pyrotechnic effect, cascaded into the blackness, lighting up the sky behind the castle. A spectacular thing it was, everyone agreed! From my viewpoint, it was so exciting that I had a heck of a time going to sleep that night!

Other high-flying night pyrotechnic events followed: a New Year's celebration at Knott's Berry Farm and a July Fourth spectacular over Long Beach Harbor, this time suspending a huge American flag. The flag was lifted from an offshore jetty and set off over the water during the grand finale, fairly close to the aerial bombshells. We used a drag-chute to make Old Glory trail majestically behind the helicopter.

81   PyroSpectacular's president

There were some magical nighttime "flying saucer" events at the huge *US Festival* in front of 350,000 people. With Sammy Davis, Jr. officiating, I flew a set piece over the Sands Casino in Las Vegas and a flying saucer in Jackson, Mississippi for Tommy ("The Toe") Walker, who orchestrated special attractions at Anaheim Stadium and headed his own production company.

Pete assisted me unselfishly throughout most of these high-profile events but insisted that I fly them myself. A class act, in my opinion, because Pete could have easily handled any of these flying assignments…but there's no "I" in Pete, bless him!

In the *Matt Houston* TV-series pilot movie (originally called *Clint*), Art Scholl did the bulk of the helicopter scenes, flying around downtown Los Angeles in Western's Hughes 300C helicopter and landing at the luxurious ranch where actor Lee Horsley based his make-believe, rich-guy detective agency.

When it came time to film a takeoff between two tall cypress trees with a female stunt-double in the right seat, Art called and asked me to do the gig. Judy Scholl, Art's aviator wife and business partner, drove me to the location in her Porsche. Wearing an absurd brown wig and an ill-fitting suit to stunt-double for Mr. Horsley, I looked fairly ridiculous! But I went along with the gag and after pacing off the distances, the cameras rolled and we split the trees with about fourteen inches to spare on either side of the rotor disc. *Piece of cake!*

Pete and I shared an interesting on-and-off-camera experience filming actor/pilot Christopher Reeve for the *Celebrity Daredevil* special, filmed in May of 1982. A two-day shoot at Rosamond Airport near Mojave, we both flew Hughes 500s equipped with Continental camera mounts.

Mr. Reeve turned out to be as gifted in the air as he was on stage, flying graceful rolls and loops effortlessly around both helicopters in his ultra-modern sailplane, tail number "WK."[82] He did everything exactly as he said he would during the previous night's conference, and he put that sleek little beauty down on a dime in gusting, twenty-knot winds, as the grinning Master of Ceremonies walked over to begin the celebrity interview.

Christopher was gracious enough to sign an autograph for Lourdes. Later, Craig Wooton took our photo, standing side by side next to my chopper. I looked like a shrimp standing next to *Superman!*

82   Mr. Reeve volunteered that "WK" stood for White Knuckles!

Meanwhile, Art Scholl's cinematic talents and flying skills were in great demand. He soared like a scalded hornet in his custom Super Chipmunk as a star air show attraction, and had more movie work than he could handle. He also leased our choppers and Cessna TU-206E for movies and was always a friend and a good customer.

And Jack Gillette even warmed up about half a degree when I ferried an aircraft to his Second Unit set in downtown Los Angeles during the filming of the movie *Blue Thunder*. I was watching from the sidelines when he suddenly motioned to me and said, "Come on, I might as well show you how this is done."

Gillette had me stand behind him out of camera range as the *Blue Thunder* helicopter (an Aerospatiale Gazelle with a ton of Hollywood crap bolted onto it) was chased by the bad-guy helicopter (our Hughes 500D) low-level through the Dorothy Chandler Pavilion, the 500's fake machine guns flaming away.

The day ended dramatically when, in a subsequent scene, our Hughes 500 blew an engine during the continuation of the chase scene. As I watched from street level, Karl Wickman—the *bad guy*—was still chasing the *hero*. Both ships were weaving around one LA skyscraper after another when Wickman's Allison 250-C20B gas turbine engine suddenly cratered, leaving a billowing white (engine oil) smoke trail as it dived for an empty parking lot.

Gillette was piloting the off-camera JetRanger at the time, and observing the action from curbside, I thought at first the gag was part of the script; but no! Wickman did an outstanding job, autorotating dead-stick and just missing a chain-link fence. I ran a city block to the scene and shook Karl's hand, thanking him for not smashing up our wounded helicopter!

Later that evening, we trailered the wounded ship back to Rialto. Upon tear-down, Maintenance Chief Bill Dvorak determined that the engine had lost an internal oil seal, followed by second stage bearing failure. Gillette put the pressure on us to get it fixed, and the ship was back in action a few days later.

After filming continued, Wickman got another good scare in a low-level chase scene. Zipping along through a narrow alleyway, the script called for explosions to take place just ahead of the helicopter, sending up chunks of cork (simulating rocks) along with a lot of smoke—temporarily blinding Wickman! He flew blindly through the smoke and broke into clear air, "just in time!"

Turns out the ship was damaged by several "hits" on the main rotor blades. It was a wrap for the 500D. Post-flight inspection revealed that several rotor blades had suffered damage; one or two were beyond repair. Karl called me that afternoon and was not a happy camper. He described being scared stiff going through the smoke and shocked at the damage caused by the simulated rock strikes.

As the Second Unit portion of *Blue Thunder* finished up, one of Los Angeles' "Big-3" TV networks aired a prime-time interview with Gillette at Piper Tech, LAPD's new police helicopter base and temporary backdrop for some of the scenes in the movie. The downtown aerial filming had created quite a buzz among both the populace and the media, so it was a great time for public relations to start building up interest in ticket sales.

More than once the pretty female reporter opened the door for Gillette to be an instant film-stud hero. Both Pete Gillies and I watched from separate locations as the live interview aired, but we couldn't believe that he stuck to his *bored-to-death-can-hardly-wait-until-this-is-over*-character. Were those lips of his actually sticking together again?

Then he just had to add, "Well, we get paid a lot of money to do this," in response to her polite inquiry. Pete summed it up succinctly when I called to ask if he had seen the interview: "Yuuuuck!" was all he had to say.

Gillette hard-balled Western over the cost of repairing the 500D for several days, creating ill will over the damage caused by the studio's special effects crew. He never admitted any responsibility himself, and I got the impression he was incapable of doing so.

Then came my own day of reckoning, July 23, 1982. In a nighttime Vietnam-era war scene, I was hovering on-camera over a village in *Twilight Zone: The Movie*. We also had a cameraman on a tether filming the set from the left skid. Several mis-timed explosions crippled the ship and sent it spinning out of control, killing actor Vic Morrow and two child actors. The accident is detailed in the following chapter, "The Twilight Zone."

After this highly publicized tragedy, nothing would ever be the same for me or anyone involved in the terrible helicopter accident. Regardless of who was at fault, three lives were lost, and the dreams of many were forever shattered.

As my legal problems ground on and on, there was another serious incident involving one of Gillette's Second Unit special effect crews. The name of the production escapes me, but Art Scholl was piloting a fast-flying Army OV-1 *Mohawk*. Rarely seen in movies, Army pilots dubbed the two-seater *Widow Maker,* for its propensity to roll out of control on takeoff, should one engine wheeze.

The action took place on a set in the high desert near Rancho Mirage. The script called for Art to fly the aircraft over a large special effects explosion, a charge which would propel copious sacks of "Fuller's Earth"[83] into the air, simulating a powerful bomb going off.

But, according to Judy Scholl, the surface charge was set off too early, and the scene had to be re-shot. One little problem, though. The crew had only brought along enough Fuller's Earth for one shot! Gillette told them to prepare another one, so the crew started digging, substituting regular dirt!

This time, the blast was properly timed, but the "dirt" contained rocks, and one flew up and smashed the OV-1's thick "bullet-proof" windshield and caused other damage. Judy told me later that Art was really shook up about the near-disaster. Gillette allegedly summed it up by calling the special effects guy "a flake." Judy later said it was a "nightmare" to arbitrate the high cost of repairing the Mohawk with the aircraft's unhappy owner.

Making movies finally took the life of Professor Scholl. On a sunny day in 1985, Art was piloting his Pitts S2 biplane over the ocean west of Carlsbad, California. Filming inverted spins with an onboard 16mm camera for the upcoming movie *Top Gun,* Art was wearing a parachute and had done several takes.

Art was spinning away, being closely watched by Chuck Wentworth, Art's safety pilot in a nearby twin-engine airplane. As the maneuver brought

---

83   Hollywood's favorite brand of clean dirt.

the little Pitts dangerously low, Chuck radioed, *"Three thousand feet!"* a warning for Art to pull out of the spin.

Art responded, *"I've got a problem."*

Chuck repeated the low-altitude warning: *"Two thousand feet!"*

"I've got a real problem!" were Art's last words. The S2 never pulled out of the spin, pancaking inverted into the Pacific Ocean. A search and rescue mission was launched by the Navy, who found only small pieces of the fabric-covered airplane. His widow, Judy, called off the search after several hours. I stood at her office door the next morning, and gave her a tearful hug. Many followed over the days ahead.

As a tribute from his flying buddies, Jack Gillette put together an impressive formation of WWII aircraft for the final salute to the professor. Gillette, piloting a blue Corsair, led the thundering procession of old warbirds that flew "down and dirty" for the Rialto Municipal Airport fly-by in front of Judy, friends, and family.

Coordinating with a grim-sounding Gillette over the airport's advisory frequency, I followed up in N1090Z, the last ship of the gaggle, Western's Hughes 300C. It was the same helicopter that Art made famous in the *Matt Houston* series.

At seventy knots, it seemed to take forever to fly low level down the length of the runway, as we said good-bye to one of the greatest pilots of all time—on camera, or off.[84]

---

84   Rialto Municipal Airport—Miro Field—is today known as Art Scholl Memorial
     Airport.

The Twilight Zone

PROLOGUE

One thing I learned the first time I strapped a helicopter onto my back: if you're an adrenaline junkie, and fairly fearless, you'll enjoy the work. Shoot a full-on, power-off autorotation to a postage stamp in a small helicopter and you'll know what I'm talking about. There's nothing quite like it. When you get good at it, you can do it in the dark of night with the landing light turned off, something career chopper pilots should demonstrate every year—with confidence—to stay qualified.

The life of a high-profile helicopter pilot can be exciting and rewarding, but when things go horribly wrong and your flying machine cuts down three people on camera, there's no making it go away. It never goes away. And if you let it get to you, it will drive you insane.

I've been pounding the keys for years to document my otherwise wonderful voyage on this huge, wobbly old planet—forty years of defying gravity. Retelling the *Twilight Zone* movie accident is a literary punch in the gut for me, something that took several days sequestered in an isolated hotel room to grind out.

I keep promising myself I won't go back, but I know *it* will come to *me*, regardless.

> "It's a hell of a thing to kill a man...
> To take away all he's ever been,
> All he's going to be."[85]

SUPERCUTS FLASHBACK

Rialto, California: September 1986—There was a line at the local Supercuts family hair salon. Resigned to a long wait, I parked myself in a sunlit chair and surveyed the ubiquitous magazine selection. A new *Time* magazine lay atop the pile, an issue dated September 15. Picking it up, I started flipping through the glossy sheets, from the last page forward; an old habit from reading *LIFE* magazine as a kid.

I thought I was home free until reaching page 28: *Twilight Zone: the Trial* was in the journalistic crosshairs again. Pictured in full color above the article was the on-camera helicopter, N87701, hovering amid the fireballs.

Dare I read another one? Hundreds, if not thousands, of sad, berating articles preceded this one. Looking around, no one appeared to recognize me, an ordinary-looking guy in need of a haircut. I glanced down again at the page...

Western Helicopters' olive drab UH-1B hovered low over the Vietnam jungle village movie set, its rotorwash creating gale-force winds. Gasoline fireballs erupted near the rotor blades. Shot at 2:20 in the cool morning of July 23rd, 1982, Director John Landis' vision-turned-apocalypse was frozen in time, just short of its crazy descent into hell.

After four long years of hearings and pre-trial testimony, it was the first time I'd been labeled a *stuntman*. I had always considered myself a *pilot*. But anyone who saw the deleted helicopter crash scene from *Twilight Zone: the Movie* will never forget it, shocking as it was. A stunt gone insane.

There were quite a few stunt people on the set that evening, as it turned out. At least, it would appear so, after the media wrote it up: cameramen,

---

85   Clint Eastwood's character *Will Munny's* quote from the western movie, *The Unfor-given*.

grips, caterers, special effect technicians, focus pullers, child actors, a unit production manager, and one pilot, to name a few.

THE ACCIDENT

As I guided the Huey into position for the final shot, veteran actor Vic Morrow stood at my two o'clock, beyond the rotor's arc, with child actors Myca Dinh Le and Renee Chen clutched in his encircling arms. They were brightly illuminated by the ship's powerful NightSun spotlight, focused by Production Manager Dan Allingham from the helicopter's left front seat.

Three million candlepower lit up the trio with an eerie wobbling luminescence. Vic was straining, looking toward the river, and listening for our machine gun fire; his call to action. Two stuntmen in the rear of the Huey manned the M60s, waiting for us to echo the *"FIRE"* cue.

I took up a bearing on a bamboo structure forty-five degrees to my right and down forty-five degrees, locking in our prearranged position by keeping two focal points aligned.[86] Director John Landis spoke calmly into the handheld portable VHF radio, *"Lower, lower, lower."*

I complied slowly, switching to alternative focal points in order to hold our position just off the shoreline. Then came Landis' call for action, *"Fire—Fire—Fire!"* at which point our machine gunners opened up and three explosions occurred along the cliff to our right, in the prescribed tempo: thousand-*one,* thousand-*two,* thousand-*three...*

As the fireballs heated up the night, Vic charged into the water with the children, moving north toward the opposite shoreline. Pulling a touch more power, I introduced left pedal, starting the rehearsed nose-left turn, and eased the cyclic forward. Dan followed Vic with the light.

It was then that special effects technician Jim Camomile, for reasons known only to himself and God, raked one electrified nail across several others that were wired to multiple gasoline firebombs intolerably close to the low-hovering helicopter, sending the chopper and one-hundred-odd moviemakers and onlookers into living hell. And three vibrant human beings to their shocking deaths.

---

86 A technique sharpened from years of flying USFS Firefighter Rappel Teams into small clearings in tall timber.

Despite everything that was done in the name of safety, Vic, Renee, and Myca were gone forever, cut down by the unforgiving main rotor blades as our out-of-control, tail-rotorless Huey spun several times and crashed hard onto its left side in the Santa Clara River—mercifully cloaking the horror of the finality in a surreal geyser of water.

Although it happened over twenty-five years ago, I recall the night with disturbing clarity. I can smell the heavy gasoline and adhesive cement vapors and feel the thump-thump-thump of the Huey's rotor blades. As the fourth and fifth explosions detonated, shock waves and rapidly expanding air lifted the ship up and rocked us to the left. Allingham exclaimed over the intercom, "It's too much, let's get out of here!"

But simultaneously a wicked *shudder-clunk* traveled through the pedals to my boots, and I recall that the ship started spinning left.[87] I saw only alternating fireballs and blackness, fireballs, blackness, the cyclic going wild between my legs. Suddenly I caught sight of a bush near the shoreline, the only reference point I had to work with. I struggled to keep the ship level and cushion our impact as she came down on her own at full power, hitting hard in a left bank.

Suspended in midair from the right-hand pilot's seat, I slapped at the ship's power switches, released my belts, and dropped down awkwardly toward Dan Allingham, stepping on him in the process. Apologizing, I squatted down and beat out his overhead greenhouse window with my hands to create an exit.

We were quickly pulled out through the jagged plastic hole into the frigid water by frantic rescuers. Someone yelled at us to head for the shoreline. One last passenger was partially trapped by the shifting camera cases and ammo boxes; they almost had him free.

Illuminated by the flaming movie set behind us, firemen in hip-waders sprayed frantically with their hoses; the rubber cement-fueled flames were resisting the deluge.

Thrashing to the shore, I turned to see that the helicopter's turbine engine was still running! Wading back, I found the main fuel switch still on, and cursed my haste. I shut the engine off and returned to the north shoreline in shock, but unaware of the awful truth.

87   The helicopter actually spun to the right; experts later testified that other pilots had the same illusion with tail rotor failures.

Cameraman Steve Lydecker, a big fellow, walked over to me.

"Don't worry, Dorcey, I got the whole thing on film." Steve had been manning the principal Chapman Crane's Arriflex camera and had narrowly escaped being struck by the helicopter's tail rotor and other flying debris. I stood facing the chaos, my fractured Huey's mast tilted downward into the cold, dark water.

"What the hell happened?" I mumbled through chattering teeth. An urgent voice from the nearby *Escape From New York* movie set pleaded, "Go home, everybody! Please go home!"

I stumbled over the partial remains of the chopper's tail rotor at my feet. Looking up, Lydecker was gone.

Frogs began singing, croaking again, as they had been all night long between takes. Behind me, a terrible wailing was coming from the dense riparian tree line. An Asian woman was sobbing incoherently; someone was pleading with her, restraining her…

Out of the darkness from the wreckage waded Craig Wooton, my friend and fuel truck driver for Western. He had found the ship's soggy logbooks and my ruined Instamatic camera, and brought them to me. Craig had been catnapping in the Jet-A tanker, and (fortunately for him) did not witness the catastrophe. But he heard all the explosions and the terrible crash and came running.

"Where's Vic and the kids?" I asked Craig, noticing Director Landis and a couple of his aides searching the dark, swirling water, just downstream from the mast. Craig's eyes met mine with a painful expression and he said, "They're gone Dorce. The blades got 'em."

I felt my knees buckle and I reached for a nearby folding chair. Thinking stopped. Denial and resignation followed. **NO!** In total despair, I summoned the Divine: "Oh my God. Dear God, help us all!" I prayed through bleeding fingers.

Soon paramedics arrived and began first aid. Roger Smith, the onboard cameraman, had been tethered to the helicopter for a hand-held shot of the action. He miraculously survived the spinning crash but was starting to feel pain here and there. We were both aching from whiplash and were fitted with neck braces, and treated for cuts and scrapes.

Western's helicopter mechanic, Harry Ferguson, appeared at my side and was trying to find the right words. He then asked me what he should do. I urged him to get to a phone as soon as possible. "Call Clair.[88] Wake him up, he'll need to know right away."

Four of the chopper's six-man crew were loaded into an ambulance. Dan Allingham came along. He appeared to be in somber meditation. Randall Robinson (an onboard cameraman and Roger's helper) and Roger were trying to thank me for getting them down alive. Their kind words were of little help in the face of disaster. McClarty and Endoso, the stuntmen who had manned the M60 machine guns, had both declined medical attention and quickly left the set.

My three-year-old son, Robert, was kneeling with Lourdes in front of the TV set in our Rialto home. Awakened at 04:30 by the terrible news, both were glued to the television news bulletin.

"There's Daddy!" He was the first to recognize me.

Our stretchers were hauled past a waiting news cameraman into Henry Mayo Newhall Hospital, Valencia. It was just after dawn. Harry's call to Clair had set off a chain of phone calls to Western's employees to inform them of the accident.

After the X-rays and physical examination were over, I found a pay phone and made the call to Western's chief pilot and my good friend, Pete Gillies. Pete usually backed me up on the more exotic helicopter gigs we fielded. Operations had been deluged with work, and Pete was holding down the fort when we took off for Indian Dunes two days before. It was a sad, brief conversation. I managed only to say, "Pete, they blew us out of the sky, and three people are dead."

Craig Wooton drove me back to Indian Dunes to meet with the authorities and secure Western's helicopter.

Looking back on that decision, I should have just gone home. I hadn't slept in close to twenty-four hours. I was exhausted when I appeared at

88   Clair T Merryweather, Western Helicopter's president.

the crash site and agreed to meet with Investigator Don Llorente of the NTSB.[89] I felt compelled to give a statement to the authorities on scene, make sure the ship was being looked after, and only then, go home.

I didn't count on the coroner being there, tending to the deceased. Countless nightmares were fueled with one glance. I would regret it forever.

Some of my "preliminary statements" would be used against me again and again for the next six years. At the time, I thought I had summed it up pretty well, but I had a lot to learn.

Wingo was about to get a rude education. Investigators and malicious prosecutors would attack each and every word. They would demand that I account for every second of the last several days: every conversation, every safety meeting, and every observation.

They were motivated in part by families of the deceased, photos of the victims, burned and busted helicopter rotors, a "missing" UH-1B Operator's Manual,[90] bogus statements from "witnesses," empty beer cans bobbing around in the wreckage, pursuit of fame, and greed.

My love affair with flying had come to this. The *what-ifs* began to haunt me: *What if* Lourdes and I had never moved to the big city—passed up the operations job? In my helicopter-adventurer past, I always signed up for the remote assignments: Alaska, Peru, Mexico, and rural America. I avoided big cities in general, for years, and smoggy Los Angeles in particular.

What if I had passed on the SAG card, ignoring my passion for photography, the lucrative movie business? *What if* I had stuck with precision long-line construction, fighting fires, and saving lives? (*What if* I had chopped the throttle?) But that's not the way life works. In America, you pursue your dream. Mine had just turned into a never-ending nightmare.

IN THE SPOTLIGHT

The telephone calls poured in: my mother and father from Oklahoma, where they had retired; my brother James from Austin, Texas, and Jon

---

89   National Transportation Safety Board
90   The manual was inadvertently left on the desk of Western's director of mainte-
     nance, Bill Dvorak.

from Ramstein Air Force Base in Germany; my sister, Joy, came while Lourdes was re-doctoring my scrapes and bruises. The ship's cyclic had done a number between my legs when the Huey crashed. The phone kept ringing and ringing.

Following all the uproar and conjecture about the alleged illegal hiring of the children, filming at an hour that children should not have been allowed to work, using children in a hazardous scene, and Jack Tice's assertion that "the pilot flew a *zigzag course*" on the final take, my reputation was suddenly on the line.

Jack Gillette was among the first to call me after I left the set in an ambulance, went through the ordeal at the hospital, and finally arrived home exhausted. Naturally, he wanted to know what had happened. I told him, "They blew the set out from under us." I was wasted. Grief-stricken, I didn't feel like talking to anyone. Gillette never called me (directly) again.

Art Scholl paid me a personal visit at Western to ask questions, but by then the attorneys had gotten to me, and I was instructed not to talk about the accident. Art distanced himself from me after that, and the smile was gone when I met him here and there at the airport or around town.

It was a very sad and defensive time. Good friends appeared to offer their sympathy and their help while others simply disappeared. The vultures would continue to circle for *six long years.*

I began to hear damning reports from one network, magazine, newspaper or another. Chuck Tamboro was allegedly quoted in *Esquire,* words to the effect that my *"inexperience"* had contributed to the accident.

Good ol' Chuck. We provided a helicopter to Tamboro and John Gamble for a *240 Robert* TV episode. I had once flown with Chuck in an off-camera JetRanger to the set of *Up in Smoke,* a Cheech and Chong movie, and rode around Burbank with him in his Mercedes.

Before the accident, we would on occasion phone each other about our various and sundry aerial experiences. The last time Tamboro called, he was excited over having his first talking part in an *Incredible Hulk* television episode, which meant he made more money and better residuals. After my crash, Chuck never called to ask about me, and never has since.

It seemed at times there was a clamor to blast either Director John Landis or myself. Karl Wickman told me that Landis was his "favorite child director," having had a helicopter part in *The Blues Brothers*. Others asserted they "wouldn't have flown the scene without a stunt coordinator," (including John Gamble, Jack Gillette, and Art Scholl). When Pete telephoned Ross Reynolds (a movie pilot featured in *The Stunt Man*) for his help in preparing my defense, Ross put him off. "I can't help him, I can only hurt him," he told Pete.

Gillette testified at the NTSB hearing, saying several damning things; that our contracted price to do the work was "cheap." My communications set-up was "lousy." He testified that he wouldn't have hovered "lower" as Landis directed. He would have "taken his helicopter and gone home" after the first scene involving fireballs. And so on.

Over the course of six years, they truly tried to stick it to me—one of five *Twilight Zone* defendants. The Los Angeles Grand Jury handed down its ruling that the defendants should go on trial. Soon, the charges against us went from *civil* to *criminal*. Eugene Trope became my new attorney.

Suddenly I was being fingerprinted and my "mug shot" taken as John Landis, George Folsey, Jr., and Dan Allingham strode into the room for the same reason. The crushing, ridiculous paparazzi outside the corridors outnumbered us ten to one, an incredible zoo.

"How's it going, Dorcey?" Allingham glibly asked as the trio walked by. I hadn't seen the man since the accident. He, who singled me out for the role as chopper pilot, and allegedly conspired with Landis and Folsey about the children.

"*Not too damned good,*" was my short answer, as the deputy rolled my blackened fingers onto the blotter. It was not one of my better days.

Although I deduced by then that my alleged "inexperience" helped the producers in their plan to film the children without permits (practically guaranteeing a scandal at the least), I had also witnessed Landis' emotional collapse at the hospital the morning of the accident, and I knew his soul was torn.

I am convinced the call John made at 4 a.m. that morning over the hospital's public telephone was to Steven Spielberg. The phone was in a hallway just outside the thin curtain of my ER examination room, and John went totally to pieces. Not since the war have I heard a man in such agony. "We've killed them, we've killed them!" he sobbed, until he was breathless.

The empty cement walls around us echoed with his wailing. Several of his family had gathered there; all were in the depths of sorrow. Craig Wooton was with me in the examination room, and we just looked at each other as the howling and tears compounded the overwhelming grief we all felt.

John Landis changed after the tragedy. The long hair was soon gone, the trademark smirk and brash mouth tended to stay zipped in public. The black horn-rimmed glasses were replaced by modest, round wire frames. He donned identical, conservative black suits, day after day.

Deep Roots

Moral support from my family was complete. A show of unity kept me going in the deluge of criminal indictments, charges of careless and reckless operation of an aircraft, violation of the minimum safe altitude rules set forth in Part 91 of the Code of Federal Regulations, child endangerment, and a few more.

I owned one "suit" at the time, a forty-dollar Lee Rider polyester pants suit that I bought in '77 in Medford, Oregon for my wedding to Lourdes. After having to dress up for the restaurant job, I hated wearing suits, but suddenly I had to cope with the five-day-a-week courtroom fiasco.

Acquiring the proper attire for the courtroom would cost me, though. A company-wide twenty percent pay cut had taken its toll. Lourdes came to the aid of my wardrobe with a credit card. She came back from "a big sale" with three suits. Enough to get me through the ordeal?

My father suddenly fell ill in the spring of 1986 and underwent exploratory surgery. The next day he was told he had a month to live; the victim of swift-moving pancreatic cancer. We all took the news hard.

In the Fifties, when Grandpa and Grandma Burch were on death's bed, Mom and Dad packed us kids up in the '56 Plymouth and headed east. I wanted to do the same with my family, but we were financially levered to the max. There was no money for the five of us to fly east. Dejected, I packed a bag for the solitary trek to Ardmore, Oklahoma.

My brother Jon drove to meet my flight at DFW Airport, followed by a stormy three-hour drive north on I-35. We met up with brother James and sister Joy at Mom and Dad's place on southwest "G" Street. Blanche met us at the door and led us to where Dad lay resting on a hospital bed in the guestroom.

The early-morning April sun burst through the little home's east windows, and an angelic glow graced Blanche's hand-crocheted white lace curtains. Dad had weakly summoned help to use the bedside potty-chair, a function that his tired body would soon shut down. The gravity of our gathering was lifted by a sudden cool breeze, rustling through the curtains. The gossamer fabric waltzed briefly, aglow with the blinding Oklahoma sunshine.

Until recently, Dad had kept up with my legal proceedings. He read the fine print in the Ardmore daily paper through his magnified reading lamp, and he always had a good question or two about the case as it crept along,[91] now in its fourth year of "preliminaries." At this somber time, however, we didn't broach the subject. We all knew he would be gone months before jury selection began. I deeply regretted that Dad would miss the outcome of the trial.

J.B. was just getting used to retirement. He must have felt there were many more years ahead to enjoy. Then the strange illness: weakness, persistent diarrhea, and a relentless bloating sensation. His charismatic young doctor would soon tell him that his pancreatic cancer was inoperable. Mom told me that Dad was angry at first, but it was just like the man when he bravely confronted the reality of putting his affairs in order.

The doctor granted Dad's wish to spend his last days at home. Wingos, Burches, and Parkers gathered daily from miles around. Long-lost relatives, grandchildren, and great grandchildren filled the old house. Dad appeared to appreciate every gesture.

During my first moments alone with Dad, he was able to talk briefly. I told him the long-awaited trial was coming, and I reassured him I'd never be found guilty. Dad had been proud of my military service and helicopter career, and he appeared to be at peace.

We took turns at his bedside, administering prescribed doses of morphine into his IV. In his conscious moments, J.B. struggled through the ordeal as

91   Jon wrote once from Albuquerque: *"I've seen faster glaciers!"*

his body progressively shut down and his core temperature slowly cooled. Mother and Jon were especially brave and attentive throughout his final days. I felt overcome and useless.

A few long days and nights later, I sat for the last time on the side of his bed—the rest of the family watching from the doorway as I tried to say good-bye to my heavily sedated, sleeping father. With a lump in my throat, my voice failed me, but J.B. seemed to sense my presence and opened those familiar green eyes. With a look of love, and a reassuring smile, he turned his head back to the pillow and went to sleep. That was Dad's last conscious moment. He passed on a few hours later.

LIFE GOES ON

Dad died in April, 1986, and Jon Alan was born December 11th. Our second son's birth was about the only thing we had to look forward to during the trial. Daddy was right there with Lourdes, Lamaze classes and all. What was so special about Jon's birth was that it was so quick and easy, compared to Mommy's first delivery.

Lovely Lourdes was wheeled into the delivery room, already dilated to ten centimeters, and anxious to start pushing. Three nurses clad in latex gloves and little green masks stood at the ready, but *no doctor!* He was on the way, someone said, but no Mercedes. Lourdes really wanted her doctor, so to ease her concerns, I said,

"Honey, these nurses can deliver little Jon-Jon any time you're ready; they've done it hundreds of times, so if you're ready, let's see our baby."

And just then the good doctor made a hasty entrance, scrubbed up, and donned his latex gloves. Plucking a razor-sharp scalpel off the white towel, he applied a precise slice in a strategic location of my sweetie's anatomy to speed things along, and....***ZIP!*** Out slid a softly sobbing blue version of baby Jon, who suddenly turned radiant pink before my teary eyes, as the first rush of oxygenated blood reached his brand-new skin!

When Jon was gently placed on Lourdes' tummy, a year of stress fell off my darling. Looking angelic, she gratefully proclaimed Jon as her *"regalo de Dios."*[92] He was healthy in every respect, and we were just about as

92   Gift from God.

happy as people get. Afterward, I drove around town in the Coupe de Ville playing the Beatles' "(Today is Your) Birthday" over and over, fairly loud, too!

Soon, Lourdes' wonderful mother Celia Medina arrived from Culiacán, Sinaloa, Mexico to sit with Jon while Lourdes returned to work and I went back to court. A widowed mother with thirteen grown children, "Mama Celia" had lots of family to watch over her little home in Mexico while she came to see her new grandson; her first trip to *los Estados Unidos*.

Within days following her arrival, however, Celia fell seriously ill and off we went to the hospital. The lucky lady was suffering an inflamed appendix, and a timely operation saved her, *gracias a Dios*!

We were so relieved that she was going to be okay, but poor Celia was feeling terrible about coming to help and now *this*. Our good doctor knew the score when he undertook the surgery: no health insurance for Mama Celia. So when it came time to take Celia home, things were looking grim.

Just then, a very thoughtful friend asked me how I'd be taking care of the bill, and all I could say was, "Well, I'm going down to the hospital and hand them a check for a hundred dollars and promise to pay the rest when I can. I haven't figured out anything beyond that and bringing Celia home."

And to my disbelief, the man said, "I'd appreciate it if you would let me take care of the bill, as a gift to you and your family." I was speechless, because the amount of money was considerable, and the gesture was divine.

William Gargaro, a distinguished Los Angeles malpractice attorney introduced to us by Harland Braun, had participated in my preparation to take the stand. We became friends, and one day he volunteered to counsel us concerning a terrible affliction Mama Celia experienced on numerous occasions: she would begin gasping for air, and would scare herself and everyone around half to death before it would finally subside. The local clinics in Sinaloa could find nothing physically wrong with her.

In one short interview, with Lourdes translating, Mr. Gargaro correctly identified her affliction by an imposing Latin name. In layman's terms, it was a rare psychological disorder in which the patient is so overcome with helplessness that their throat constricts as if the whole world is choking them to death. Knowing this, the healing could begin.

There were other angels. After Celia returned to her home in Culiacán, Joan Sprinkle, a close neighbor, voluntarily took over Jon's nanny vacancy at our house. They were best buddies by the time the trial was over. A lot of love was given with no thought of compensation. On the crest of such gifts we made it through the worst of times.

THE TRIAL BEGINS

The preliminary court processes were interminable; the criminal trial itself had taken four years to get underway, in September 1986, and it was to last ten long months. It seemed like everyone in Los Angeles was called as a witness for the prosecution, spearheaded by a petitie, ambitious, feisty little woman named Lea Purwin D'Agostino, who couldn't seem to get enough of the cameras. She became the object of some of my nastiest courtroom cartoons.

When the long-awaited trial reached the jury-selection stage, our defense strategy was to *protect Dorcey Wingo*, and see what develops. We didn't know for sure if we would soon be flinging arrows at other defendants, or not.

I was uncomfortable being in close proximity to my co-defendants. Here I was, a small-town, Scotch-Irish, Oklahoma-Cherokee Indian, Christian-Protestant, blue-collar-ex-burger-flipper, former military chopper driver, surrounded by flamboyant, wealthy Jewish Hollywood types in a vast, smoggy metropolis pretty much owned by foreigners. *Unfamiliar territory.*

We would gather daily at the Los Angeles Criminal Court House basement cafeteria. Meeting in the secluded northeast corner with attorneys at our sides, we sat in two or three groups: Landis and company in one group, Trope and Wingo, and so forth. We spoke with the others when our eyes met, but that was the extent of our contact.

My distinguished attorney, Eugene Trope, and I normally sipped cafeteria coffee in thick white ceramic cups over a review of that day's forecasted testimony, and the daily comics page. We'd then herd our group together and take the shaky, crowded elevators to the 15th floor—half a dozen Jewish attorneys with one Roman Catholic, Braun, leading the way.

A lot of Yiddish was tossed around in the months that followed, all with perfect accents. One exchange in the foyer between Lea D'Agostino and Landis made the papers: Lea calling Landis a *"rotseyekh,"* Yiddish for *murderer*. Sensational antics in my opinion, just what the restless media was starving for.

At times our wives would attend, but Lourdes Maria worked full time at the Rialto School District. We needed her paycheck to help cover the bills. John's devoted wife, Deborah Landis, was always at his side; likewise Belinda at George Folsey's. Paul Stewart and Dan Allingham almost always came to court alone, although Dan had been engaged at the time of the accident.

My attorney, Eugene, positioned himself between the other four defendants and me at this stage of the trial. Seating arrangements in front of the judge became an increasingly complex problem as the prosecutors, court stenographer, five defendants, and their multiple attorneys were spread out across the courtroom along various lengths of tables. Eugene neither discouraged me from nor compelled me to sit with the other defendants; we weren't rolling out the red carpet, either.

There was at first a great debate over having a camera in the courtroom. After lengthy arguments for and against, Judge Roger Boren allowed the collective media to station a professional model Ikegami video camera in the left rear corner of the courtroom. Optical and microphone cables were bundled and gaffer-taped along the wall, down to the floor, under the doors, and into the hallway, where a gang of reporters maintained a constant vigil. The trial would be televised to the whole freakin' planet.

Just down the hall from us, an infamous case involving a family accused of molesting their daycare charges took second billing. Between the media and the alleged sex offenders, the fifteenth-floor hallway could get slimy.

Personally, I felt there was no way a jury of my peers would find me guilty of any of my alleged crimes. If I was wrong, a second-degree manslaughter conviction awaited me. The reality of a criminal trial was, at times, hard to separate from the media-induced *Hollywood on Trial* that dominated headlines and evening reports around Los Angeles.

Cooped up in packed courtrooms, the prominent odor of dry-cleaned suits reminded me how much I missed my cherished remote cabin in Oregon—her cedar-scented mountain air, the West Fork babbling along throughout the night...a reminder that those days were gone, and the criminal trial was no illusion.

Landis' new attorney was James F. Neal, a famous trial lawyer from Tennessee. Neal was hired to head Landis' defense team, allegedly retaining Harland Braun as Jim's co-counsel. Harland didn't see it that way, and instead took over George Folsey's defense, when attorney Roger Rosen had to step down while undergoing a divorce.

Jim Neal had gained international notoriety helping prosecute the sensational Watergate proceedings during President Nixon's administration. Landis chose Neal after interviewing a short list of top trial attorneys. Neal convinced John that he could be successfully defended, and went right to work.

Looking back, I think it was critical that Harland Braun stayed on the defense team. He was a brilliant trial lawyer and knew the complicated case as well as anyone. Although Harland tended to get excited and shoot off his mouth, the guy was a piece of work, a pleasure to watch.

I felt sorry for the poor court stenographers, though. Judge Boren's stenographer pool was among the best, but from what I've seen, there is not a court stenographer alive who can keep up with Harland Braun when he's *delivering!* They would be begging for mercy within minutes!

Harland was hard to contain. One foible that I observed was in response to a reporter's question: "What would he (Braun) be doing after the Twilight Zone Trial was over?"

"Oh, I'll go find more *scum* and represent them!" Braun responded. His current client, defendant George Folsey, Jr., was not amused! Had it not been near the end of the trial, Harland might have been fired again!

To his credit, Mr. Braun introduced convincing evidence to show the helicopter's tail rotor failed because it delaminated in a fireball—not from being struck by a "glue can lid," as Don Llorente once suggested, and not by "flying bamboo," as D'Agostino would assert.

The trial was going to take at least four months, by one early estimate. Since the special effects people (all but Stewart) had been given immunity for their testimonies, I believed the District Attorney had let one or two of them off the hook. Pretrial testimonies had long been public and it seemed to me there was little left to divulge in the way of new information. But with Lea slinging her mud, over one hundred witnesses would take the stand!

During all this, Pete Gillies and I ran Operations at Western as best we could. Having his director of operations under the gun and absent so often put extra pressure on the man I call "My Hero." Late one evening I was staring at the busy scheduling board, lost in my thoughts. Pete, who knows me perhaps better than anyone on the planet, came up to me and put his strong hands on my weary shoulders. There was that confident look pouring freely out of those steely blue eyes of his, as he said most comfortingly, "Don't worry, Dorce. They'll have to *lie* to defend themselves." And I stopped worrying at that point. What a guy!

But I personally—and the people who loved me—wanted to hear a certain Fire Safety Officer Jack Tice try to explain to the jury his damning statements to the press (on July 28, 1982) that "the helicopter came in too *late*, too *low*, and too *slow*," and that I had flown "a *zigzag course*." Was he making this crap up to try and take the heat off himself? *Inquiring minds wanted to know!*

We especially wanted to hear a certain special effects technician explain his actions on the set that terrible morning. How he concluded that it was safe to set off all the remaining firebombs under his control—in one quick stroke of his hand—before the helicopter (with six people on board) reached a safe point across the river.

And I wondered what "expert witness" would be testifying against me in this case. During the grand jury proceedings and the six-week pretrial hearings, movie pilot John Gamble had testified for the prosecution. As time wore on, Gamble began to fade, and we learned that Jack Gillette had been subpoenaed.

Eugene suggested I let Jack know he didn't necessarily have to testify, just because he had received a subpoena. While I wasn't really worried about Gillette, he had nonetheless been avoiding me for some time. Jack uncharacteristically failed to answer two phone messages I left at his office near Carlsbad, suggesting we have lunch. (Eugene explained that making calls of this nature was a fairly common defense tactic to "test the water" before the trial got underway.)

Jury selection took part during July and most of August 1986, but finally a jury of twelve plus four reserves was selected from a pool of over one hundred and fifty citizens. All defendants had to be present during this arduous procedure, and the days were long, hot, and frustrating. The media was everywhere.

After the courtroom camera was installed, the lens was trained on John Landis most of the time. Not far into one session, I heard John call my name. Looking over my shoulder, he was inviting me to join him; an empty seat was to his left. I leaned over and whispered to Eugene, and although the suggestion raised his eyebrows, he simply said,

"I don't see why not. Be careful."

I hesitated a minute, stood up, and slid into the empty seat. Facing forward, I focused on the proceedings and resumed taking notes. I literally wrote or sketched the length of the trial. As did Landis. Our new seating arrangement raised a few eyebrows in the courtroom, and did not go unnoticed by the prosecution.

A moment or so after I had taken the seat beside him, John leaned over and whispered in his baritone voice. He explained that he was using me as a "block," in cinematic terms, putting yours truly between himself and the camera behind and to our left. The camera-person had had a direct shot; now *my* head was in the way.

Realizing his motive, I started to get up and move back to my former seat, but then I thought: *Screw 'em. Let them think Landis and I are friendly. Let's just see what happens.* I felt that the whole legal procedure was a farce, from the grand jury forward, especially my criminal indictment. Had I not made any statements at the scene for the NTSB, I probably could have gotten immunity (like the special effects people) by being circumspect, but it didn't turn out that way, and now we were all getting screwed. *Let's shake the som'bitches up.*

As I said, John was constantly writing during the proceedings, unless he was sitting straight up in his chair while sizing up the judge, jury, or witness. One exception to that was in making Casting Director Marci Liroff step over his outstretched wingtip shoes after her testimony for the prosecution. She had to walk past us to get to the swinging door and back into the audience.

As she stopped to give John time to move his big feet, he deliberately left them in the aisle. She was not very tall—and her tight skirt made knee bending a real effort. She clucked at him, stepping awkwardly over his crossed legs, and (obviously pissed off) out through the gallery and into the hallway she went. I don't think Landis cared for her testimony, and he was not above letting her know.

Every morning, as the judge called for order and we took our seats, John would break out a yellow legal pad and start writing in his unique, easy-to-read script, "Dear Deborah," jotting down his personal thoughts for his tall, long-tressed mate. Perhaps it was just something he did to focus. This was his routine for the full ten months.

The trial began on September 3rd, and it became clear that prosecutor D'Agostino was going to play to the cameras as if she was up for an Oscar. The silly "Queen Bee" pendants that she blatantly exhibited on one shoulder with each and every costume was a reminder to me that not all was right with the little woman who used to work in a Hollywood studio office.

(I drew a cartoon of her scratching her beehive hairdo absentmindedly with a pencil—suddenly looking up, startled—then running away, shrieking in panic as the swarm of bees she disturbed pursues her. Landis liked that one!)

Tom Budds, a Los Angeles County deputy sheriff, was at Lea's side most of the trial. Assigned to the case for some time, he sat there stone-faced, but I sensed he grew weary of D'Agostino's antics early on. Once the trial got underway, John moved next to Jim Neal, and I sat on one side or another of Mr. Trope—usually next to Sgt. Budds—and I wondered...other than the Lea problem...why he was so glum all the time. Even at this trial, there were moments of levity, but he seemed to be in pain over something.

I soon learned that his only son—a toddler—had drowned accidentally in the family pool while under his care, before the trial began. He was overwrought with parental guilt, and his marriage had fallen apart. I caught his attention outside the courtroom one afternoon, alone, and expressed my sincere condolences.

To my surprise, tears came to his eyes, and—looking around—he volunteered to me that the District Attorney might cut me a deal later in the trial so I could testify against Landis. I kept this revelation very quiet, sharing it only with Eugene Trope. I appreciated Tom's honesty, but the more I thought about it, it angered me that the DA would put me through all this crap as a defendant and then try and use me to screw the others!

So that's what was going on in my head, and Eugene gently counseled me on the implications of socializing with John and the other defendants openly. But it was the only way I could deal with the daily bull, the anguish and the loss of freedom set off by an insanely expensive witch-hunt.

In late September, testimony given by the parents who lost their children was very hard for everyone, especially them. It was heartbreaking for anyone who was on the set to hear again. There are no words…

Lea kept the grim photos of the deceased on her office wall; anyone who paid a visit was in for a shock. Although I never saw the photos myself, I think it was sick to display them. But she wanted the whole world to see them; that was her *shtick*.

A truly strange thing happened early in the trial. Eugene explained to me that he had been asked to meet with Judge Boren and Prosecutor D'Agostino *in quarters,* the judge's chambers, after the daily proceedings. I was not invited to attend.

Mr. Trope seemed to be only slightly amused by the outcome, which he later shared with me: D'Agostino had suggested to the judge, in so many words, that Dorcey Wingo was not being adequately represented! It was a whopper of an insult to Eugene, whose response to Lea's taunt was, "Judge, the road has been long, and the miles many. But I've never heard nor seen anything such as this!" After some discussion, the matter was sealed, but not forgotten. Eugene had been insulted before the judge, yet another reason to question Lea's tactics.

FOR THE DEFENSE

My wife and I were soon engaging in conversations outside the courtroom with John and Deborah and George and Belinda. Logically, invitations followed to join them for the daily hour-and-a-half court recess/lunch break in one nearby Los Angeles restaurant or another, if not the cafeteria, again.

The judge had instructed all concerned that we defendants were prohibited from speaking to or dining near any of the jurors, so we'd either join up in a corner of the cafeteria or jump in John's big white nine-passenger van with tinted windows, and drive to Chinatown or one of several other neat places to eat. We also hit a walk-thru Mexican food stand, a dandy that I had discovered over on 6th Street called The Los Angeles Restaurant. *Sabróso!*

Landis frequently ordered up a feast, always handled the bill, and he fed a large group every day, two or three times a day. The group often included John's mother, his personal attorney, Joel Baer, and his devoted personal secretary, Sharon. I found John and Deborah to be very generous to those around them, and staff loyalty was genuine in return.

More often than not, I dined with Eugene, who had his own favorite places around town, and he was excellent company. Eugene drove in style; his white Rolls-Royce *Silver Cloud* had little trouble attracting a parking spot. I can still smell that wonderful leather upholstery and the feel of the magic-carpet ride. He chose the Mercedes for long trips. Eugene explained that most automotive mechanics didn't know the first thing about working on a new Rolls.

A former WWII U.S. Army infantry officer, Eugene had fought in the bloody liberation of Anzio, Italy. In one battle, he was the sole surviving lieutenant. Mr. Trope always had something to converse about, if not my defense.

Eugene always picked up the tab. He also graciously paid my daily six-dollar downtown Los Angeles parking bill for me. His Universal City law firm, Trope and Trope, may have included the bill for "conference lunches" to Western Helicopter's insurance company, USAIG. By the time the trial was over, I'm sure all of this amounted to a fortune!

Without going into all of the sordid details of Lea's many antics and the immediate backlash of calling prosecution star witness Donna Shuman to the stand—these are available in more than one book written about the Twilight Zone Trial[93]—I was determined to deal with the trial day by day, not looking too far ahead.

The long commute, one hundred and twenty-six miles per day, the loss of essential flight pay while I was on trial, and the extra expenses that came with all that driving, dry-cleaning, and stress took its toll. My sharp Okie vision began fading on me, and I had to start wearing a pair of government-issue granny glasses that my brother Jon (an Air Force lieutenant colonel at the time) loaned me, to read through a growing mountain of depositions in the case.

One cloudy afternoon, I got into a rare pissing contest with my boss, Clair Merryweather, over who should provide the gas for my long commute. Times were equally hard for Western, and my personal finances were never leaner. There was never any doubt in my mind that he and Jim Burr[94] supported me in the legal matter, but my absence was playing hell with our ability to run a profitable operation.

Clair was watching out for the Company. He eventually testified on my behalf—effectively and sincerely—at the trial. He was great. And I think the jury respected his endorsement of my competence as a high-profile helicopter pilot.

I drove my own wheels back and forth to LA, an old '69 Cadillac Coupe DeVille that Lourdes and I picked up used for $1,500. It was powered by a 472 C.I.D. V-8 that sucked *mass quantities* of 88 octane. But it was a grand, roomy, long-haul machine. I usually played tapes on the long commute, Merle Haggard or The Stones, distracting my troubled mind from the jabbering news radio on the way to court.

(Clair finally acquiesced about providing the gas, but being the master accountant that he was, I was tasked with a detailed monthly expense and gasoline consumption report.)

The elevators at the Criminal Courts building were old and unreliable. If the judges had had to depend on them, they would have been replaced

93 *Outrageous Conduct* by Stephen Farber & Mark Green.
94 CEO for Rocky Mountain Helicopters (Western Helicopters' parent company).

many years ago, but judges had their own private elevators on the other side of the building, so we never saw them coming or going. Almost daily we heard the public elevator alarms going off as another nervous box full of suits would lurch to a halt and someone would nail the panic button.

So this brave chopper pilot started taking the stairs, and although fifteen stories took some getting used to, I soon had John joining me for the exercise. Sitting all day long wasn't keeping us in shape, but two trips up and down the long flight of stairs every day woke up all our muscles and gave our hearts and lungs a brief workout. We frequently beat the elevators to the fifteenth floor!

It was on these daily workouts that I began to notice John's dedication to Judaism. Occasionally we would come upon offensive stickers plastered on the walls and doors in the stairwell: hate mail from skinheads.

"There's another one." John would stop climbing the stairs long enough to curse the acts of racists, while working his fingernails under the edge of a sticker and peeling it off the wall: JEWS LIE—THE HOLOCAUST NEVER HAPPENED!! read that particular message.

Some were worse: swastikas, N-word stickers; someone was spreading vile messages around the courthouse, but we never came face to face with them. I commended John's acts, and between us, we kept the southwest stairwell racist-free up to the fifteenth floor.

➤➤➤➤

The Landises eventually invited us to their home in Beverly Hills, and the Folseys also came, bringing along George Senior. The elderly Mr. Folsey was a famous cinematographer from the early days of film. He had actually shot some of the first aerial movies from a two-seat gyrocopter, and he was a joy to talk to. He enjoyed my tales of helicopter adventures around the planet.

Lourdes and Robert were startled to see a real-looking, life-sized gorilla waiting in the home's *entrada*, the handiwork of makeup artist Rick Baker. John had hired Rick for his realistic work on *American Werewolf in Paris*, and Rick became a Hollywood sensation overnight. The gorilla was a gift of appreciation from Rick to John; once you got past the gorilla, you knew you were in for an interesting visit!

Along one wall in the house was an incredible collection of toy soldiers, complete with cavalry, infantry, and artillery pieces, all meticulously displayed in glass cabinets. Hundreds of the finely detailed, hand-painted metal soldiers were lined up in neat ranks, shelf after shelf. Each piece looked as new as the day it was first handed to little Johnny. But the best part of our visit was listening to John talk about the Marx brothers and Alfred Hitchcock.

Landis would take all the dough if he ever got loose on TV's quiz show, *Jeopardy*, especially if the evening's categories included *Hollywood* or *Cinema*.

John always had a good joke to tell at the drop of a hat. He knew all the Marx brothers' best one-liners, and he understood the secrets of great cinema; the man loved to tell stories and talk about the making of particular scenes in some of the classic movies.

While we were laughing it up in the library, John's daughter Rachel and our son Robert ran from room to room, flirting and teasing, while being chased by Max, their youngest. We had a good time. John and Deborah Landis made us feel almost like family.

George and Belinda Folsey were also a pleasure to be around. We found both to be gracious and sincere. They had a lovely home in Bel Air that we visited once, meeting their children Ryan and Erin. George was a master film editor, and he also was a fine cook. He made pasta noodles from scratch for dinner that evening, a task he obviously relished, while I demonstrated my cocktail-drinking abilities.

Lourdes and Belinda were touring the house, doing girly stuff, so I eventually decided to hustle the kids, who were stabbing away like amateurs on the pool table. I must have had one too many margaritas, though. After selecting a splendid, straight twenty-one-ounce pool cue, I failed miserably trying to duplicate some trick shots on the expansive, regulation billiard table. The kids thought I was pretty funny! (Rats!)

The talk over dinner was of Spain—the Folsey's favorite retreat—with dreams of retiring in northern Spain someday—if the legal crap was ever to come to an end. We dreamed of the return of our freedom over a great bottle of wine, allegedly from Francis Ford Coppella's private stock. Not strained of its natural dregs, it was deep purple, fruity, and intoxicating. The view overlooking Los Angeles from poolside was one to remember; a man could briefly forget all his problems and feel pampered for a while, even if only once.

❧❧❧❧

There was another buzz from the press in late September. Lourdes and I invited the Landises to the 1986 California Speedway Motorcycle Championship in San Bernardino. When I mentioned that the event was coming up, John said he thought that might be fun. He commented that he had seen *Spetters*, a 1980 European movie by Paul Verhoeven about motorcycle racers. Speedway Promoter John LaDoucer, a good friend, was happy to provide free passes for our group.

I had raced novice class "T.T. Track" motorcycles between high school and my draft notice, so I found the roaring, no-brakes spectacle a familiar, stimulating interlude. Professional speedway stars like Bruce Penhall, Mike Bast, "Sudden" Sam Ermolenko, "Flying Mike" Faria, Dubb Farrel, Jim "The Animal" Fishback, the Flying Moran brothers, Bobby Ott, John Sandona, Denny Sigalos, Bobby "Boogaloo" Schwartz, and Gene Woods raced around on their alcohol-powered drag-bikes like crazed leather-clad gladiators on the oval dirt track, while the ever popular veteran track announcer Bruce Flanders provided the play-by-play and color-commentary. The Wingos made every Wednesday night a ritual by attending the San Bernardino Speedway races near the Orange Show Fair Grounds.

The State Championship took place on a Saturday evening. John and Deborah left the kids with Grandma, drove John's Volvo to our Rialto home, then accompanied us to the track. The racing action was hot and heavy that evening, but Bobby Ott—wearing the white leathers—won every heat and took away the trophy. John and Deborah truly seemed to enjoy themselves, and although Bruce Flanders announced John's attendance, nobody bugged us.

A less-than-courteous newspaper reporter asked me days later if Landis went with us "to the *drag* races," and I just said "No" and walked away. They get it right about half the time, I'd noticed, and I wasn't giving out any more information. My firsthand experience told me that many newspapers invent sensational crap out of nothing.

I was learning. It was amazing to see what the big-city LA papers headlined and what they left out. A couple of the reporters I had words with blamed the finished product on their editors. "Sensationalism sells papers," someone once said.

EXPERT WITNESSES

I grew to respect Special Effects Foreman Paul Stewart during the ordeal of the trial. We were alike in that we were both *working* men, and I felt that we both had every reason to expect that Jim Camomile, and others under Paul's direction, would execute their responsibilities in a predictable manner that fateful morning, so I didn't expect any grief from Paul Stewart, then or later.

I also liked his attorney, Arnold Klein. "Arnie" usually looked like he was half-asleep, but he kept up with the top-dollar suits when it came to defending his client. Both were fine fellows, as far as I am concerned. If Paul was guilty of anything, it was the *crime* of believing in his fellow man. *Mea culpa*—I am guilty of the same.

Dan Allingham and I didn't talk much. Dan was the man who came to Rialto back when and hired Western Helicopters for the gig. Now this. I felt a mutual need for space between us, but I couldn't blame him for what happened to the chopper. After all, he was on board the aircraft, part of the crew that night. As for the alleged conspiracy stuff that led up to that morning, Dan has to sort that out with God, George, and John. Personally, I feel Dan was the most religious of anyone in the group.

Dan's attorney, Leonard Levine, was a great guy. What he lacked in stature (he was short, but powerfully built) he made up for in brains, strategy, and delivery. He was a real competitor. Word is, he was once a real threat in the hundred-yard dash. Just watching Leonard in action helped restore my faith in American justice.

I think James Neal distrusted me from the beginning, but he put on a good act. He was always in control, so long as he had an audience and could chomp on a Cuban-style cigar. I liked the way he kept Landis in check with his Tennessee slang and "Johnny Boy" deliveries. A moment I'll always remember was our only one-on-one, and it followed Mr. Neal's concern about John's headliner remark, *"You ain't seen nothin' yet!"*[95]

---

95   The rehearsal flight's unexpected water geysers and hot fireballs had upset me. In

When that remark became a dagger for the prosecution, Neal approached me during a courtroom recess in the packed hallway. Leaning in close as he maneuvered by me, he said softly, "I wish we could *do* something about that remark," without breaking stride, Cuban cigar in tow. I let Eugene know about the exchange, and that's all that ever came of it. Bottom line: Did I think Landis was serious? Of course not. Was the honorable Mr. Neal suggesting something? We'll never know!

And I don't blame Neal for worrying about it, but I wasn't going to withhold the statement from my testimony, regardless. One hundred thousand dollars per month was rumored to be the price to retain Neal and Saunders, a handsome sum that got around town rather quickly.[96]

"Jim" Saunders was a bright star in the proceedings; he was James Neal's right-hand man and legal partner. God gave him a Clark Gable-like appearance, a great mind, and an easy-to-see blue aura. He remained high on my list throughout the trial. I often wonder what he might be up to.

It was hypnotizing, in a grim, slow-motion kind of way, to study the film of the accident and to know it from several angles. George Folsey produced a montage for the defense during the trial to determine the locations of off-camera witnesses and try to pinpoint other pertinent details (such as flying debris, or when the tail-rotor gearbox separated from the helicopter, etc.) and the time interval between blasts. This version had a soundtrack, and was not something we wanted to see or hear more than once.

Yet we had to immerse ourselves in it, know it from six different angles, frame by frame, because Lea had her own montage. She also had an "exhibit" on the courtroom floor, constantly in the jury's eye...a "replica" of the Indian Dunes cliffs and village layout, complete with a model Huey on a stick. Lea would make damning assertions as to the proximity of the helicopter to people on the set, and the defense couldn't take her data at face value.

The first thing I noticed was that the "People's Exhibit" used a UH-1H scale model (with a forty-eight-foot rotor), while N87701 was a UH-1B (with a

---

my own evaluation, John found it difficult to deliver a straight line, even if it made him sound grimly prophetic after the crash.

96   Mr. Neal went on to become Exxon's chief attorney defending the *Valdez* oil tanker disaster.

forty-four-foot rotor). Using an "H" model in the Exhibit put the proximity of the rotor blades closer to people than they actually were. So we had to determine the exact locations of the chopper throughout the rehearsals and two pertinent scenes to establish my flight paths, hover points, and so forth.

It was really pointless, as far as I was concerned. The scene should have gone off as planned, but tragically it did not, and our current attention to detail was necessary because Lea was literally throwing everything at us.

The second week of January, Jack Gillette strode into court with a pretty blonde at his side. It was clear to the defense by then that he was going to serve as the expert movie pilot witness for the prosecution, and his appearance was in accordance with his subpoena, a day or so prior to his actual testimony. Gillette avoided making eye contact with me, but as Lea began establishing his expertise before the court, I became focused on his negative energy, and began writing a note I intended to hand to him before the day was over:

Jack, I thought we got rid of you in "The Gauntlet,"[97] the note started out. I went on to say how disappointed I was that he had shut me out; that I thought he was coming for the publicity. I don't recall what else I may have written, but I was really beginning to dislike this guy. It was clear to me that he was out to do me in.

The court adjourned for the day at the conclusion of Gillette's out-of-jury deposition, and everyone walked out *en masse*. Gillette and the pretty blonde (his wife, it turned out) headed for the elevator, and I was on his heels. As fate would have it, no one else wanted on that elevator, and looking both in the eye, I stepped in through the closing doors at the last second.

The wary couple stood with their backs to the wall and said nothing as the old elevator clunked and groaned nonstop down to the lobby. Standing very still off to Gillette's right, I glared, a folded yellow note clutched in my hand. The hell-bound metal box lurched to a halt, its shiny doors parted suddenly, and Mr. and Mrs. Gillette made for the northwest exit doorway. As Jack reached for the brass door fixture, I called his name.

---

97 In this Clint Eastwood movie, Gillette is the on-camera *bad-guy* chopper pilot who accidentally flies into some power lines.

"Jack, I have something for you." They stopped, turned, and looked a little nervous as I extended my hand. Gillette took the note. And before you could say "shoot howdy," I was through the door and back into the flow with the stars, the panhandlers, and the slime.

What came of the note, I'll never know. But Gillette's subsequent court testimony faulted me, among other things, for not rolling off the ship's throttle at the point of losing anti-torque control. And while it is the standard published procedure for the loss of anti-torque control in a hovering Huey, veteran Army combat pilots had long drilled into younger pilots like me to "keep it flying" while you figured out the problem and dealt with the emergency.

In the chaos and confusion of the critical instant, blinded by explosions and spinning back into blackness, I never reached the point that I *knew* what was wrong with my machine. I fought for control of an out-of-control helicopter—with six souls on board—that was flying in and out of some very large, hot fireballs. Would rolling off the throttle have changed the outcome?[98] Would the six of us in the Huey have been burned alive? A real possibility, and another ugly *what-if*.

Gillette testified on January fourteenth. After Lea had her turn, Eugene cross-examined Jack—and Eugene had done his homework. We had just heard—at great length—Gillette's illustrious movie background, and in acknowledging those accomplishments, Mr. Trope inquired if, in all his experiences, had Gillette ever been issued a flight violation by the Federal Aviation Administration?

A haughty "No" was his answer.

I think the jury lost interest in Gillette's expert testimony shortly afterward, as Eugene approached the bench and produced copies of two citations issued to one Jack Gillette! They charged Gillette with flying restricted aircraft over congested airspace without FAA approval, as required for exhibition aircraft specially equipped with mock-up movie armament and the like. Gillette had just perjured himself. Take a bow, Eugene Trope!

Lea must have worked feverishly during the lunch break to try and repair her expert witness. Two hours later, Gillette was back up on the stand when

---

98 I personally know of two pilots who lost anti-torque control in a hovering Huey and, after spinning a bit, were able to return to controlled flight—making a successful run-on landing several miles away (N103CR).

she asked him if the violations in mention were "more like traffic tickets?" A loud male chorus shouted "Objection, your Honor!" drowning out Gillette's answer, quickly followed by Judge Boren's "Sustained!" I almost felt a little sorry for Gillette at that point. Almost. And I wondered if Lea was still concerned about Dorcey Wingo getting adequate representation?

Working late at Western Helicopters the evening of January 19th, I fielded a surprise phone call from movie pilot Karl Wickman. Karl had declined *my* request for help years earlier, the last time we had talked. The thing was, Gillette had just called him from the set of *Jaws '87*. Gillette felt he shouldn't call me directly, Karl explained, so he asked Karl "to give you a call and ask how *he* (Gillette) *could help*" at this point!

I tried not to sound ungrateful for all that Jack had already *done*, saying to Karl that I'd have to call Eugene first and ask *him*. Eugene was mildly amused by Gillette's fatuous timing, and was blunt in returning his answer: "He's done enough." I was pleased to share this late flip-flop with Clair and Pete, who were also up quite late that night.

With all the ducking and dodging, waffling and backpedaling in the testimonies of Special Effects Technician Jim Camomile and Fire Safety Officer Jack Tice, even the newspaper reporters seemed to notice.

It was hardly worth the long wait. Camomile, who was at the switch on the fateful night, spent three long days on the stand. Squirming under the barrage of intense questioning by five defense attorneys, his ordeal before the jury must have been tough—but thanks to the powers that be, he wasn't facing six years in prison. I am not compelled to reproduce or comment further on their lame responses. But I have their Los Angeles newspaper clippings preserved in a big, dark box for my grandkids to wonder about someday.

Eugene's next great move was to call upon Peter McKernan to testify in my defense as an expert witness movie pilot. The ruggedly good-looking owner of Jet Copters and an on-camera pilot of the popular *Airwolf* TV series, Peter told Eugene he had no problem supporting my approach to the job and the decisions I made throughout the fateful event.

(Peter and my brother, Jon, had both piloted A-1H Skyraiders for the USA, Jon for the Air Force and Peter for the Marines. My A-1G Skyraider ride in Vietnam with then Captain Wingo made me truly appreciate this select group of aviators.)

On the stand, McKernan rebutted D'Agostino's argument that working around helicopters was inherently dangerous, and stated that movie pilots' lives depended on special effect technicians to withhold firing the explosives in their care until the flying machines had left the lethal zone of the pyrotechnics. I think the jury understood. Which probably truly pissed off Lea, Gillette, and her aging child-actor/prosecution witness Jackie Cooper, who fire-branded the defendants while he was on the stand.

McKernan didn't have to come forward, but he did. For standing in the breach and making a difference, I regard Peter as a great guy and a patriot, and I told him so.

THE PILOT TESTIFIES

Eugene was convinced that it would be necessary for me to take the stand and tell my story when the time came. After all, the NTSB and the FAA stiffs were still out there, just beyond this trial…my license was at stake.

He was right, of course. Let's present our side, get it before the jury and into the court's transcripts, along with the jury's verdict. If there was any nut cutting to do after the trial, we could club them over the head with reams of sworn testimony and the "not guilty" verdict from a jury of my peers. (And that's basically what we did.)

The Los Angeles County District Attorney, Gil Garcetti, finally tipped his long-awaited hand on February 3rd. His messenger, Jerry Loeb, secreted Eugene away for a private meeting during lunch. Realizing that my testimony was being prepared by the defense, a hush-hush meeting was held at Eugene's office the evening of February 4th. In attendance were Loeb, Dick Hect (the DA's alleged "rocket scientist"), a Mr. Sondheim, Sgt. Budds, and their stenographer, Kay.

I was pretty pumped up for this meeting after all the **b**ravo **s**ierra, as Army aviators used to call bullshit. Once I was sworn in, I leaned in close to the group seated around the massive table and told the District Attorney's henchmen that I was "pissed!" Berating them for making me go through so many months of crap. And now they were dangling the carrot, a legal maneuver defined as an Eleven Eighteen. I doubt that they heard much else I had to say after that, but I went on with my testimony, and since I didn't come out with anything new to hang on Landis, nothing came of it.

On February 11th, 1987, Lea D'Agostino finally announced, "The prosecution rests."

On the evening of February 17th, the day before Landis was to take the stand, I called John at home and encouraged him to "rub Lea's snout in the dust," a term used so hatefully against the USA by Iran's Ayatollah Khomeini.

Landis was on the stand four long days. D'Agostino began her cross-examination midday on February 19th, and she overplayed her hand right off the bat, offering John a Kleenex to absorb the tears she couldn't see. John delivered his case as well as anyone could have.

The only thing in Landis' testimony that rubbed me the wrong way was stating that, since the accident, he "no longer used helicopters in (his) movies!" As if *that* was the problem! Igor Sikorsky must have rolled over in his grave.

And who would fault Deborah Landis for appealing to me, one day before my turn in the chair, *not* to testify? She came forward, joining Eugene and me at a discreet table during lunch at a popular Los Angeles restaurant, the fancy one across from the Civil Court building. Classic photos of legendary movie stars adorned the walls around us.

Deborah Nadoolman Landis, with a master's degree in textiles and the blood of a distinguished Russian officer pumping in her veins, looked me straight in the eye. I could see her million-dollar lips moving, but behind those dark brown eyes I read, *Don't hurt my John.*

She argued persuasively that John *had* to testify since he was the director and that not everyone thought my taking the stand was a good idea. Clearly she felt I might blow it. Lea would trip me up, make a fool of me. Was I harboring some undisclosed hostility, she must have wanted to ask. Eugene and I listened respectfully, but there was little that John's testimony was going to do to save my license, which was my livelihood. And that was that.

My Air Force brother, Jon, was good enough to be present during my testimony. Brother James had made the trip earlier. The family came together and spread out their support, as much as money would allow. Pilot friend Dudley Hale and celebrity flying reporter Chuck Street[99] also came to lend their support. Having them there was most reassuring.

Finally, on March 18th, I waited nervously for Judge Boren's bailiff, Larry Breazeale, to call me to be sworn in. Seconds away from my taking the stand, Landis smiled and slid me a note: *I know you'll be great! John.*

The first day on the stand was relatively easy, a *curriculum vitae*, coached along by Eugene to establish my background as a chopper pilot and my experiences in Vietnam, big-name events with pyrotechnics, and other high-profile helicopter gigs.

At one point, Eugene had me don my olive drab flight helmet and strap myself into N87701's Huey pilot seat, which was actually dug out of storage for the purpose. I didn't always agree with Eugene that all this was necessary, but he felt he had to establish to the jury that *Wingo was the pilot;* the other guys were the moviemakers.

Long before I took the stand, I broached the subject of agoraphobia with my attorneys. This country boy had an abnormal fear of crowded public places and public speaking. Just the thought made me nervous, something I'd lived with for a long time.

Taking the stand before a live international audience made me nervous, of course. Eugene knew what he was doing, though; my impeccably groomed elder statesman did a fine job of preparing me and keeping me focused. And I just forgot about the TV camera, yonder.

I felt the jury was politely attentive throughout my four days in the hot seat. Their expressions ran from stoic resolve to sympathy to respect. I was especially encouraged by a few brief, friendly smiles and nods from that very special group of people. In them, I saw the light at the end of the tunnel.

When she got her turn, Lea did her best to mock my testimony and my

---

99   "Commander Chuck," the famous Los Angeles flying traffic reporter .

bout with PTSD.[100] She tried just about everything, and she bit and thrashed around like a bulldog whenever she thought she had something.

One of the arrows she shot at me was the suggestion that I had been intimidated by Landis's "dictator-like," profanity-laced manner on the set (therefore I'd do anything he suggested?). I lightheartedly reminded her that after five years in the Army, I'd seen and heard it all! That drew a good laugh from the gallery, and no points for the Queen Bee.

I was confident that this woman would not send me to jail, so I focused on her red aura and how she was applying herself so negatively. It gave me an edge, and it worked. And that was the last time I spoke to Lea.

The Verdict

Eventually, the final argument stage of the trial arrived. I was proud of the whole defense team; our attorneys made convincing counterpoints to Lea's flaming arrows, and I think their confidence in the outcome came shining through.

In her final argument before the jury, Lea Purwin D'Agostino suddenly produced a paper bag containing a large raw potato and a plastic straw. While still trying to make her point about bamboo allegedly doing the damage to the helicopter, she stuck one thumb over the top end of the straw and jabbed the other end into the potato![101] You really had to be there!

Finally, Lea could delay the progress of justice no longer, and near the end of May 1987, the jury was presented with the heavy burden of sorting through ten months of testimony, and coming up with several verdicts for the five defendants. For several days, they patiently deliberated before one another and finally, exhausted, they voted one time. The bailiff was summoned.

---

100 Post Traumatic Stress Disorder: Diagnosed by two separate psychologists, I received months of therapy after the accident through Worker's Compensation. Harvard grad and PhD, Mark Mills testified on my behalf, shedding some light on my nightmares and memory lapses.

101 "The Potato Incident," as it came to be known, spawned another Wingo cartoon of Lea repeating her potato trick while simultaneously shooting herself in the foot. Braun was quoted as chuckling to the press, "We're all wondering what other vegetables she has up her sleeves!"

Lea's "Potato" Theory!

Just before eleven o'clock on May 29th, while I was working on a helicopter lift permit in Trope & Trope's law library, Eugene suddenly appeared, smiling. The jury had reached a verdict! I felt spiritually elevated; something told me that justice was about to set us free!

Lourdes was at work in Rialto—waiting for the word—and soon she and Clair Merryweather were heading west in the company's Caprice to the Criminal Court House. An hour and a half later, we sat close together at the familiar long table one last time as the jury entered the courtroom. Did Lea see the faint smiles on some of their faces? I did!

When the long list of "not guilty" verdicts was being read, not one defendant so much as flinched, except for me. I was so relieved in hearing "not guilty," my head fell forward as if I'd been clubbed. There was an electric levity in the crowded room, waiting to explode. And that's what happened in a civilized kind of way. Six years of grief, and now some sunshine!

As Judge Boren thanked and released the jury, his voice elevated to announce that we were "free to go," as cheers broke out from the gallery, and our relieved group of former defendants and their successful attorneys headed toward a clamoring sea of reporters with floodlights, sent to scoop the long-awaited verdict.

Some of the jurors stayed behind and agreed to meet with the defendants, and field questions from the media. Lourdes and I stood in line to thank them and put our grateful arms around these wonderful citizens, while Lea and her impotent bee made their way down the hall toward prosecutorial obscurity. She wasn't present in the courtroom to hear more than one juror suggest to those interviewing the jury that "a fire official or two" should have been indicted!

The Aftermath

A lawsuit naming the studio, Steven Spielberg, and on down the line to the landowners was filed on my behalf long before the pretrial hearings. I had received a ton of legal advice by then, some suggesting I sue the studio for damages. This was done, but I let my lawyer shoot his legal arrows where he saw fit. Once the trial was out of the way, many days of nasty depositions began. This slimy experience revealed to Lourdes and me the depths to which attorneys can go to undermine one's humanity. And we had to answer all the questions, nasty or not.

Harland Braun and Bill Gargaro helped Lourdes and me through our complete tour of the legal sewer system; both were excellent when it became our turn to attack. Harland was really looking forward to taking my personal injury suit to the jury; first because he felt our case was so solid, and second, he loved the courtroom action. But Lourdes and I agreed we'd seen enough of the Los Angeles courts for one lifetime, and we're not greedy. A settlement was reached out of court, and we went on with our lives.

The terms of settlement included no admission of guilt and no release of the dollar amount. We were able to pay off most of our bills and put away some toward the boys' educations. I was beginning to think maybe there'd be enough left over for that Harley I'd always wanted.

But I had promised our friends and neighbors that, when it was all over, I'd throw them a heck of a party. On August 6th, 1988, we did just that. Since our place in Rialto lacked the required space, our good friends John and Judith Cromwell allowed us the run of their Topanga Canyon estate for a two-day shindig.

THE TWILIGHT ZONE ❧

The celebration party was fully catered: a rambling feast, complete with a wet bar and valet parking. A fine gathering of old friends responded, some from as far away as Vermont. We got moderately *schnockered*. And that's where my Harley money went. I have no regrets.

♪♪♪

It would be another year before Eugene finally negotiated a settlement with the NTSB and the FAA. Together, they withdrew their fangs from my neck in exchange for a thirty-day suspension of my beleaguered license. I had hoped for exoneration, but Eugene had been negotiating all this time for virtually no fee. The government's attorneys could go on forever, I supposed. We all needed a long rest, so I capitulated.

A month later, the FAA's regional attorney sent me what I thought was a truly corny letter when returning my license, words to the effect that I would *hopefully fly right from now on*. That letter was wadded into a tight little ball of paper and slammed into the trashcan.

A Movie Pilot Drops By...

*   *Years later: Loose ends*

GUESS WHO'S COMING FOR LUNCH?

A few years after the trial ended, I just happened to land Hiser Helicopter's sharp-looking MD500D near a popular seaside airport café, right at lunchtime. It was a fine day; yours truly and two utility patrolmen were performing the countywide power line patrol. The rather exclusive beachside airstrip we landed at is home to many fixed-base operators, including—you guessed it—Jack Gillette.

We used to frequent the café over the years, and more than once I had run into Gillette there, in better times. He was what you'd call a *regular* there. And there he was, sitting at the counter by the cash register, sipping coffee.

This was the first time I'd seen the guy since he perjured himself at the Criminal Court House, and I was kinda hopin' he wouldn't be around, if you know what I mean.

Looking a bit older, heavier, and grayer, Gillette appeared to be as surprised to see me as I was him. But of course, he tried not to react to my sudden appearance. Walking past him as I directed my customers toward the only empty booth, I put on an insincere smile and—without looking at him—announced, *Jack Gillette!*

My patrolmen were big fellows, so there was no room for me at their small booth. I insisted they go ahead and order as I looked all around the busy place for another empty seat. But there were only two, and both were barstools next to Gillette! I said loud enough for him to hear, "Well, I ain't sittin' *there!*"

Gillette sat cradling his coffee cup, staring straight ahead...as I stood there looking for another seat. I was hungry, though, and we didn't have much time to waste. Reluctantly, I took the far right bar stool, leaving an empty seat between us—and pulled a menu out of the holder.

I realized my keen dislike for this pilot hadn't gone away, yet sitting five feet away from him, I found myself answering a casual question about our line patrol mission. Before I knew it, Gillette and I were engaged in an edgy conversation about (God rest his soul) Vic Morrow!

Ironically, I had just seen an old (1974) movie of Vic's in my motel room the night before, one of many in which Gillette had flown an on-camera JetRanger. *Dirty Mary and Crazy Larry* was the title. Gillette didn't go out of his way to be friendly, and I would have rather pounded my fingernails with a twenty-ounce framing hammer than sit and socialize with a man who tried to send me to jail. Eventually he left, and I was able to start digesting what had hit my stomach and turned to bile.

(Short) Flight of the Columbia

I've long been an aficionado of *The Pacific Flyer*, an aviation-oriented paper published in Oceanside, California, by Wayman Dunlop. This colorful rag is mostly about the fixed-wing world of General Aviation (the privately owned aircraft of America) but Wayman also features articles and photos from the world of helicopters, and never disappoints when putting out a paper.

There are always lovely photos of vintage aircraft and sometimes there are lovely ladies wearing *butt floss* posing alongside them. Wayman even ran a couple of cartoons of mine in the late eighties or early nineties, and paid me for the use of them. I rarely failed to search out a free copy of *The Flyer* whenever I visited an airport. Pete Gillies would sometimes drive over to our house with the latest issue, where we would have our monthly meetings in the shade of my garage.

I was reading the one Pete brought over the day before—flipping past the pages of a certain late Nineties Spring Edition, and lo and behold! Right off the bat I detected a short newsy article describing an aircraft accident that involved my old pal, Jack Gillette.

He and a passenger had taken off from Palomar Airport in a WWII-era XLJ-1 *Columbia*, a single-engine radial amphibian, and in my opinion, one of the homeliest things that Grumman ever designed. (Tough to fly, too—from what I've read and heard.)

Following ten years of detailed rebuilding, Gillette took the bird aloft with a passenger, R.W. Martin's shop manager. Over-flying Camp Pendleton Marine Base, the Wright C9HD engine failed and Gillette was faced with a dead-stick emergency landing near Red Beach.

The article went on to say that Gillette tried to glide to a small paved strip, but the aircraft's main gear, wing float, and the forward portion of the hull were snapped off as the plane fell short and flipped inverted. Several nearby Marines came running, and eventually took a hammer to the old bird as leaking fuel added to a stressful rescue situation. Both Gillette and his passenger escaped with minor injuries. *Words to that effect.*

And that got me thinking how peculiar it is how a guy's mind can go to town on that kind of stimulation, because my first thought was—if it had been me coming to the rescue—what would I have done? Would I have run blindly to their aid and pulled them to safety? Of course I would have. Well, I'd certainly help the passenger out, first. What if there had been a *fire?* (There are those nasty "what-ifs" again!)

The Dream

His Teeth Were On Fire, But I Couldn't Let Fly!

We all have weird dreams from time to time, and I confess, my subconscious and I have been out there and back. The hardest part is remembering what the heck I was dreaming after I wake up. Or making any sense of it. But after The Movie Pilot, I had no problem recalling the sordid details...

I was lost. They teach you as Army aviators that you're never *lost*, just temporarily *disoriented*. I wasn't flying, though; I was stumbling along through tall chaparral and mesquite; their unforgiving thorns had torn my Nomex flight suit to sweaty shreds. A thirst like *no tomorrow*. I must have gone down or something, but I remembered no mission, no ship. I also needed to *go*, but I couldn't make myself stop; I was searching desperately for something.

It was miles to high ground, where I had a better chance of locating myself. Yet something was oddly familiar about the baked desert in which I was standing. The angle of the sun told me it was early afternoon and that I was facing west. Stark vertical granite rose several thousand feet in front of me like organ pipes. Vast stretches of white gypsum dunes played out on the southeastern horizon.

White sand? If that was what I thought it was, then about twenty miles north—beyond that gap in the mountains—those black lava flows had to be Oscura, an obscure military base with a small landing strip near the notorious Trinity Site!

Hell, I'm not lost! I'm in south-central New Mexico! This is where I played out my last year in the service as a young chopper pilot! I beady-eyed the gap in the mountains ahead, struggling to recall its name. My brain strained to go back thirty years: flying overhead for the first time with a tall retired Army pilot by the name of "Po," in an old Army Otter. Mr. Potoliccio was the first to point it out to me: *Mockingbird Pass!!*

I couldn't help but shout out "Mockingbird Pass!!" which echoed harshly off the bedroom walls, waking Lourdes and your dream guide to boot. The lovely Mexicana raised up a few degrees, mumbled *"Weeen-go!"* and rolled away from me.

Recalling my dream re-immersion training from the master—Carlos Castaneda—I closed my eyes and slipped back into subconsciousness before yielding to my silly bladder, or losing my place in yet another mysterious dream.

Looking back the way I had been walking, that was Pole Line Road. Nothing but poles and dirt, stretching on forever to the south, eventually coming to Highway 70. Over Organ Pass to the west was my old hometown, Las Cruces!

I had no idea why I was stumbling around inside White Sands Missile Range, nor why I was walking toward Trinity Site, where in 1945 the first atomic fission device turned night into day and desert sand into glass beads for half a mile around.

I scooped up a handful of dirt and the sand cooperated by transforming into wondrous marbled b-b's in my palm. As I poured them out, they fell away noisily, tinkling off the toes of my dirty $19.00 Wal-Mart hiking boots. I felt another strong spasm; time to water the daisies!

I could make out the tall black marker made of lava and the chain-link fence, designating *Ground Zero*. I sensed a deep hurt in the Earth. My Cherokee ancestors were rolling over in their graves, disturbing the Okies buried all around them.

The swelling in my bladder almost immobilized me, but I could find no relief; something was driving me on. I was bent over in frustration.

The desperate sound of an old warplane's huge four-bladed Hamilton Standard prop suddenly split the dead quiet of the desert and ricocheted tenfold off the Organ pipes.

I scanned and quickly zeroed in on a blue-winged dot, low in the sky. It just cleared the sharp ridge to the west, and it was trailing smoke! Something had gone south on the big Wright R2800; flames were flowing aft through the cooling fins and burning out the cowling, no doubt giving the F4U Corsair pilot living *hell!*

One thing was certain; that big WWII beauty was comin' down, and its lone pilot didn't have long to make it happen. Down to fifty feet and turning in my direction, the big motor chugged one last time and died. Her graceful gull wings clipped off several tall century plant stalks, and suddenly the whole enchilada stalled and fell heavily from twenty feet onto the rolling sand dunes right in front of me!

I dived for cover as the *thud* sent a shock wave rippling through the earth, and I doubled up with another severe bladder spasm. Getting back on my feet, I ran headlong into the dust and flames, knowing I was the pilot's only chance for survival.

Sizing things up as I ran, I could see that the bird had fallen hard gear-down, rupturing the fuel cells loaded with high-octane 130/145 AvGas. I could smell the volatile vapor as I sprinted around a splendid, mid-sized barrel cactus; the dry wild rice around its base was ablaze.

I leapt onto the Corsair's left wing; it was bent forward around a thick tangle of chaparral. The Plexiglas canopy was gone, but the smoking figure of the pilot was stuck, waving me on like Oz's frantic *Scarecrow*: his sleeves filled with straw were on fire!

I had strained myself leaping onto the wing and almost lost the only fluid I had at my disposal with which to extinguish the flames to save the victim, but I held off. Reaching down into the cockpit, I shoved my right arm behind and around the big man, pulling upward. His cries of pain amplified my strength and determination.

We struggled and burned together for what seemed an eternity, but it was no use! He was pinned by stacks of flaming movie scripts and a cockpit full of gold Krugerrands; a testimony to excessiveness was blocking his salvation.

It was at that moment, as I strained to pull him out of the Krugerrands, that I beheld the hand-sewn label inside the fancy shirt's collar. A pricey Rodeo Drive tailor had embroidered his name and attached the label with silk threads, which were also beginning to smoke. "Small world, Jack," I let slip...

I relaxed my grip on the smoldering movie pilot and stood erect, feeling fresh blisters rise up on my hands as I stepped back from the heat. The sizzling lips of my former antagonist curled like bacon below his smoky Ray Bans, grimacing over his flaming dentures.

I purposefully zipped down my smoking, shredded flight suit and grabbed the elusive one-eyed trouser snake. I calculated elevation, crosswind, and range, and let fly. Just as the quenching stream arched high enough to reach the cockpit, cracking the crystal lens of his red-hot Rolex, I did a crisp military about-face, and thoroughly hosed the flaming wild rice around the poor barrel cactus!

Dreams of this intensity end suddenly, I discovered, and a little later that sunny morning my wife returned to our bedroom from the kitchen with a steaming cup of java. She gave me an understanding smirk, as I patted smooth the fresh, clean king-sized sheets, pulling them up and over our fluffy pillows.

Section VII:
All in a Day's Work

A Little Help from "Hose B"

* *Cool runnings and a skosh more power, for free!*

My finely feathered friends out in the middle of Montana might act *gut-shot* to hear it, but it won't be long before million-square-foot warehouses start springing up in their bucolic pastures—so get ready.

And helicopter entrepreneurs *rejoice*, because each megaplex needs an aerial crane to install literally hundreds of air conditioners on every one of them. As *Mom and Pop* are plowed under by Target and Wal-Mart, helicopter opportunities arise from their demise.

The wave of humanity encroaches, and here comes someone's chance to employ their aerial skills, setting countless air conditioners (or *air handlers*, as they're known in the vernacular) onto delicate rooftop curbs—work that would otherwise have to be done by humongous, pavement-crushing cranes. It's another no brainer—'cause everyone knows that choppers are much faster, quite a bit cheaper, and a lot more fun!

The standard air handler is shaped somewhat like a pickup camper shell and weighs about four hundred pounds. It is essentially a big four-bladed fan powered by a beefy electric motor. Long-lines are necessary between the helicopter and the load to minimize rotor downwash onto the unit's aerodynamic shell.

In the lifting process, the new units are pre-positioned into long rows in an adjacent parking lot/staging area. Coordinating the lift work requires air-to-ground radios, and things quickly get interesting when the pilot flies his long line and rigging to two ground riggers waiting patiently in the parking lot. Crowd lines are roped off and out come the camcorders!

The riggers nimbly position the rigging's two six-foot metal bars on matching "Y" cables under the edges of the air handler's top. The pilot observes their work from fifty feet or so overhead and responds to one man's hand signals as the load is readied for levitation to the roof crew. Once he gets the go signal, the pilot lifts upward—the steel bars pull up and inward, securing the load for quick delivery. (When *dropped* from about thirty feet in the air, they make quite an *impression* on a new warehouse roof, and anyone standing nearby!)

It no doubt irritated our competition to no end when my outfit won that bid for the work in Fontana a few years back. They probably felt a *lot* better after hearing my hardworking Hughes 300C dropped not *one*, but *two* units out of the hundred and ten that the job called for. They both hit the roof within a few feet of each other, just inside the warehouse's perimeter.

Yes, the Murphy-prone *manual release lever* had reared its ugly head, as my old pal Pete Gillies would lament. We had both been bitten over time, learning the hard way about loosening that darned manual cargo hook release lever's cable to the point of *sloppiness*, or it will command the hook to drop its load, with just the right application of forward cyclic! ("*Kaa-ching...*" followed by the more *expensive* "GGGRRUNCH!")

You can imagine the disappointment, after helicoptering in an A&P mechanic to re-check everything, when the *second* air handler smote the roof before the departing mechanic had cleared our airspace. The customer assured us the damaged roof would be quickly repaired, but I declared a *safety stand-down* at that point, and rescheduled the job. Time to think about the problem; solve it, test it—and finish up the following weekend.

Pete's right eyelid began to spasm involuntarily[102] as I explained what <u>happened on the</u> Target job. Instead of slapping me with his big, fat 133

---

102   This is Nature's way of signaling the speaker that Pete's *Bullshit Threshold* has just been exceeded.

Manual,[103] he gently recounted a story I'd managed to forget over the years. Pete's very own mishap involving the same model helicopter.

Fortunately, all Peter dropped was a chunk of wrecked aircraft that he was slinging from the crash site. No harm, no foul, in his case—but his lesson about maintaining some *slack* in the hook's manual release was forgotten over the years as I spoiled myself with larger, turbine-powered helicopters. Pete's cautionary lesson about the *Mattel Messerschmitt* had moved to an area of the Captain's brain where *good info* turns to *plaque*.

So what on earth has "Hose B" to do with this little story, you should be wondering by now? Answer: The ensuing week passed and our stellar Saturday morning econo-lift team arrived on the job with the very same Hughes 300C. Within minutes, we were dripping with sweat. It was hot! There was not a breath of wind to speak of.

An unseasonable heat wave threatened to further *screw* our already screwed-up project. With twenty-something units to go, the stripped-down little helicopter was suddenly pulling its guts out—I barely succeeded in lifting a four-hundred-pound unit to roof level. A gentle breeze helped once on top, but the dead-air staging area was another matter.

Our elevation was only 1,100 feet, but I had lost over two inches of manifold pressure since sunrise, due to the climb in density altitude. As the sun's angle increased, so did the OAT.[104] The freshly patched roof's metal drip-line glared, adding *eyestrain* to our bitch list. Sweaty frowns were observed on the roof—and in the hot, dusty staging area.

Yes, dust was *also* becoming a problem—so in a moment of pure frustration, we let the *Bug Smasher* idle while one of the ground crew wranglers (dare we call *Jose, Hose A?*) began to spray the sweltering, dusty LZ with the contractor's burly water hose.

And then it happened!

Sitting hunched over in the hot little mix-master, I could immediately feel the cooling effect of Jose's Hose B! Miraculously, he had temporarily improved our *weather*. A cool, gentle breeze was born. The other wrangler grabbed

---

103 A highly detailed "External Load Manual" required by the Federal Aviation Administration for hook-equipped helicopters.

104 Outside Air Temperature

another hose and cracked open another valve. The two gleefully sprayed their hydrogen/oxygen mixtures everywhere and with passion, cheered on by their sweltering work-mates and one refreshed aviator.

My story ends *happily*, fellow throttle twisters—Jose's "Hose B" saved the day. Evaporation had lowered the OAT five degrees Fahrenheit! With the cooler temps and the breeze came an increase of over two inches in manifold pressure, and my little Lycoming engine was suddenly ready to *kick some butt!*

The remainder of the air handlers went up with ease. Frowns turned to smiles, and hose water turned into ice-cold beer. A handsome check was handed over—and I vowed to pass this tale along someday—you never know when *changing the weather* might pay off.

Comes a Lineman

*   *A Big Fella, Packin' a Mean Lunch.*

As my father was laid to rest in the small cemetery at Hennepin, Oklahoma, I was a thousand miles away, patrolling power lines in San Diego County, doing my best to keep my mind on the dangerous job and live to collect another paycheck.

"Gabby," the power utility's elder patrolman, was sound asleep in the seat to my right. Accustomed to his periodic departure from the alert, all-seeing honcho, I hovered methodically from pole to pole, looking for the cause of an outage on the 69KV line near Julian. Gabby could pass for *Santa,* were it not for the utility's uniform shirt he was obliged to wear under his white beard.

Dark horn-rimmed sunglasses ajar, mouth agape, his long white whiskers flagellated in the windy open door of the Hughes 500D. I studied the tautly strung conductors and glass insulators for clues. The computer in San Diego calculated that the lines had relayed near this location, so there should be a smoking gun.

The answer came into view at the next corner, a "dead-end" pole. A skimpy pile of bloody-black feathers marked the remains of a turkey vulture at the base of the fifty-foot pole.

Gabby was jolted awake by the cessation of motion. Predictably, he became animated and then went into a dramatic pointing and gesticulating routine, as if it were *me* who was napping.

"Hold 'er here a second!" he thundered over the intercom. "Hawh! Just as I thought!" Clearing the sleep from his throat, he continued, "Stupid buzzard landed on the cross-arm and stretched out his wings, a fusible link! Let's go sit down by that café, yonder, and I'll call it in! Get some goddamn pie, too!"

A YEAR OR SO LATER...

Flying from the left seat of our trusty MD500D helicopter, the terrain rose and fell ahead of us like a roller coaster at Six Flags. Countless "figure four" power poles floated slowly by at our three o'clock, testimony to our down-low-and-slow flight regimen, inspecting each structure—and the wires strung between them—for any number of problems: ballistic damage, cracked load-bearing arms, foreign objects (kite string, Mylar balloons, etc.), lightning strikes, fire damage, bonding wire problems, et cetera, et cetera, *ad nauseum.*

(If you're up on your Latin, let them last two words serve as a preview of things to come, as we were not only inspecting one of the trickier stretches of 69KV power lines in eastern San Diego County, we were also training the fellow in the right rear seat to be an aerial power line inspector.)

Usually it was just "Gabby" and me, since he'd had his inspector's job a very long time—and he didn't plan to retire (or die) any time soon. But somehow the young buck in back had impressed somebody important and—*voila*—he wound up as the guy-in-back of our five-seat helicopter, on one of the nicest weather days we could possibly ask for. (The summer sun was startin' to climb, though.)

Heading up the hill from the electrical substation where we picked "Ralph" up, there was nary a bobble from the wind nor the pilot. Being my usual smooth self, I took pride in hovering smartly along, then rotating around to the right as the next pole got close—putting Gabby and Ralph in the *box seats* so they could discern buzzard crap from lightning strike. An aerial ballet, out-of-ground effect, surrounded by wires.

Peter H. Gillies taught Captain Methane the helicopter pole inspection technique around three decades ago, and together we'd spoiled most of the inspectors from Tijuana to Fresno. Gabby seldom had to say a word; with just a wiggle from the hairy index finger of his left hand, I knew to go back for something that caught his eye. And Gabby loved showing off his *remote control* to the new guy.

Ralph didn't talk much, but when he did I could tell he was enjoying himself immensely. This was a sight better job than he was used to: bouncing along in a one-ton patrol truck, craning his neck underneath some monstrous 500KV power lines; a job that could get old in a hurry.

About thirty minutes into the patrol, I caught a whiff of an unfamiliar odor. Even with the left door off, my Okie nose sniffed it out, all twirled up between some jet fuel fumes, valley piñon, and a touch of sage. Gabby looked my way—his seat was breezy but he had also detected the curious odor.

"You eatin' lunch already, Ralph?" Gabby giggled over his David Clark headset.

"Yeah, sorry guys," Ralph confessed with a mouthful. "Mama-san packed me a *killer* barbeque beef sandwich and I just couldn't wait no longer." So *that's* what smelled so good. Gabby grinned, knowing our trainee had a good woman to pack his favorite lunch and send him off to work every morning; a prerequisite for this line of work.

We had a full bag of jet fuel, which would take us to the fuel truck rendezvous site way out by Campo in another hour and a half. That's where we would stretch our legs and eat our lunches. This particular leg made for but a quarter of our long patrol day, but we'd have accomplished a heck of a lot by the time we dropped Ralph off at his truck. I had to admit—this sure beat hammering the phone back at the office.

The sun shone brightly on our rolling hills and them poles kept on a-comin'. Gabby had me waggin' a little to the right, a little to the left, a hard right at the top of the next ridge. The route was quite familiar but never the same twice. Gabby poked his plastic wind-vent outward with his right index finger as the ambient temperature rose and more ventilation was required.

Then I saw that dangerous left hand of his moving toward the (red) fuel shutoff knob and shot him a knowing glance. He returned the look and smiled ever so slightly as his big ham of a hand settled on the *blue* knob—just to the right of the *red* one—and pulled the fresh air vent full on. He'd learned that critical cockpit lesson from another pilot not long ago, almost flaming out Mr. Allison by pulling the (red) fuel shutoff knob by mistake. And I'm sure he didn't need me reminding him of it with his trainee listening in.

Up and down, rotate, rotate, rotate, up and down. The poles in this stretch looked really ancient and weather-beaten. Lots of cracked wood on the figure-fours. Gabby relayed the comments to Ralph, who wrote down the *squawks* on his clipboard as we hovered slowly onward.

Sweat was breaking out on Gabby's forehead as we started up the next steep incline, and I was doubly glad to have my door off. But something had happened since the time I looked briefly out my left door at a darting rabbit and back to check the gauges.

There was a strong odor—again. Not like the last time, though. *And Lo!* There were spots before my eyes—make that on the *windscreen* ahead—and lots of curious little things dangling from the instrument illumination posts all of a sudden.

Drops of some strange fluid were trickling down the altimeter and airspeed indicator, headin' for the Wulfsberg. *What the heck?* Craning my neck to the right for a gander at Gabby, his eyes darted my way but he faced straight ahead; Gabby knew something that I didn't. The strange odor was Ralph's lunch, making an *encore!*

Ralph (not his real name) had kept it a secret about his becoming increasingly airsick back yonder, right up until the time his sandwich sprang forth: through the open, shoulder-high partition between him and his supervisor and *onward* to the instrument panel. What they call *projectile vomiting*, in the gastronomic vernacular. Gabby was wearing quite a load on back of his head—hence the lack of motion in the normally animated man in the right front seat.

"Sorry, fellas," came Ralph's apology, *"...thought I could hold it."*

And a few (rather *long*) minutes later, Western's white fuel tanker never looked more inviting at the base of the next hill, where I was able to shut the machinery off and vacate the premises—while Gabby supervised his trainee in the fine art of *wiping out the cockpit*.

Picking Up the Pieces

*   A Graphic Tale Involving Aluminum Things That Smash Into Clouds

The mother of the family made it farther up the hill than anyone in the twin-engine airplane. Had you been standing beside me on the crest of that rolling ridge, you could have read the heartbreak and disappointment on her battered, ashen face. Her once stylish hair was wildly grotesque, blood-caked.

Only a day ago their pilot announced that he was beginning the descent for John Wayne Airport, near their destination—Disneyland. The pilot— the holder of an Airline Transport Rating—had been inexplicably "scud running," and flew them through a low cloud layer straight into a rising ridge of granite. "CFIT—*Controlled Flight Into Terrain*"; the Feds have a name for everything.

The plane—on a VFR flight plan from Las Vegas—had been overdue many hours, and then the call came to Hiser Helicopters in Corona. The wreckage had been located by a media chopper just south of town. Operations responded with their five-seat MD500D helicopter to fly the coroner and members of the NTSB to the rugged, remote location.

The mother sat upright in her seat. Testimony to the strength of her seat belts, her torso was securely strapped in place. She had been ejected through the front end of the chartered Cessna 402, one of many in a terrible surge of humanity as the aluminum craft came to a sudden stop at *two hundred plus*. Her family, her policeman-hero husband, seven children, and the pilot were left in a terrible display.

The deceased had shed her limbs as she hurled through the exploding wreckage, wildly tumbling up the incline; freakishly coming to rest upright. She was facing away from the sorrow behind her, but straight at the mountain that crushed her family's dream—a celebration at Disneyland after winning millions of dollars they would never spend.

…These morbid things I vividly recall from the grim, three-day mission to recover the bodies and pick up the pieces of the fragmented airplane. Nightmare material.

There were others, before them and after. The work of retrieving the dead was usually already done before a hardworking guy named Al Head would call our twenty-four-hour number. It's less traumatic to help load the nets with scrap metal, shattered engines, and upholstery after the coroner's crew has mopped it up; but we've learned that those guys are not perfect. Things get left behind and *rubber gloves* is the name of the game.

Al wound up with most of the salvage work around our part of the state, and in responding to his call, we would put a crew together. We'd usually dispatch a fuel support truck to the end of the road, loaded with special rigging. Experienced long-line pilots would fly out to meet Al's party and set them down close to the situation. We have cleaned up many on the magnetic mountains that ring greater Los Angeles.

Much to the lament of the insurance companies, the local mountains seem to turn into magnets when clouds pack around them. Perfectly fine people check out early in these tragic mishaps, owing to pilot error more often than not.

The deserts north, east, and south of Los Angeles offer clear skies with fifty miles' visibility or more. As pilots approach the Cajon or Whitewater Pass, however, clouds frequently obscure the mountains. That usually turns the most cautious around, but not all.

They auger in in singles and twins, air tankers and air ambulances, sailplanes and biplanes. They are piloted by amateurs, professionals, politicians, air tanker pilots, homebuilt pilots, doctors, and lawyers by the score.

You can almost imagine their last cognizant thoughts. "Too much trouble to file for *Instrument Flight*. The clouds look thinner over that way. Let's probe around a little." Bad flying decisions killed most of them. *Controlled flight into the terrain* more often than not. There's that term again.

Not all of these mishaps end tragically. Now and then an airplane or helicopter will end up nestled in the trees, or a tiny Swift will crash-land in a boulder-strewn ravine with minor injuries. (That Swift pilot survived; his unfortunate wingman got vertigo and spiraled into the rocks below the canyon.)

One lucky fellow was forced by Mother Nature to land his classic Cessna 140 at the round-peaked 10,000-foot summit of Mount Baldy, only to have the little tail dragger freeze into the ice before he could salvage it. At least his Guardian Angel can catch up on some needed rest.

Back in the old days, when we arrived at the scene of a non-survivable accident, rubber gloves were something you gave little thought to. Then came HIV. Almost overnight the crash kits had to pack dozens of pairs of latex gloves; even the older hands began donning them.

On these kinds of jobs, it's best to be the lift pilot who hauls the nets away. It's the cleanest part of the job, and the stuff of nightmares is left unseen. Like when I hoisted out the nose section of that Cessna 402 and we found why none of the passengers we hauled out had any feet...they were all jammed under the instrument panel. What a sight.

I write this as a tribute to those I have had the honor to retrieve — with my personal gratitude for showing this pilot the errors that were made, thereby saving me more than once along the way.

Lightning Fire at Flooter Rock

* *The flames were creeping toward the helicopter, and we knew the score...*

Your average third grader knows that helicopter pilots drop big buckets of water on wildfires from above. It is a well-kept secret, however, that pilots have been known to park their flying machines, grab fire tools and take up positions on the fire line! The top guys at the Bureau of Indian Affairs (BIA) might be surprised to learn this, but it does happen - especially if the fire is headed for the helicopter. In which case, they would probably approve!

I dipped my first heli-bucket on a fire in Alaska back in the early Seventies and fought fires on and off seasonally for the next thirty-plus years. I have a collection of OAS[105] cards *this thick;* they are tough-to-earn, demonstrated skill endorsements that made me proud to be part of the program. Our areas of responsibility were well defined; my yellow-shirted friends have their jobs and I have mine. But when the fertilizer hit the fan, we were all <u>firefighters</u>, period.

---

105   Office of Aircraft Services – the Federal agency that oversees the certification of pilots for fire duty.

In my mid-forties at the time of this incident, I wasn't in what you would call *prime physical condition*. My sinewy, ground-pounding friends, however, worked out to stay in shape, including - but not limited to - their daily morning run paralleling the seven-thousand-foot runway at Window Rock Airport.

I didn't envy the fact that they got good and sweaty every morning before donning their familiar yellow flame-resistant shirts, with *BIA Forestry* stenciled on the back. Weight lifting and stretching exercises usually followed, as I watched admiringly from the shade of a nearby tree.

Eventually the daily exercising was finished, which meant we could turn our attention to foursquare, horseshoes, hackey-sack, and pellet-rifle target practice. Between shots, we looked longingly at our MD 500D out standing in the sun, yonder; all dressed up with no where to go.

After a few weeks of this mind-numbing routine, the crew became a small, competitive assemblage of muscle-bound *ringers* and expert marksmen. *Firefighters?* Oh yeah, we do that, too. But not lately. We passed the remainder of our time jealously debating the wildfire reports from the other forests, as we had none of our own to fight.

We began yearning in earnest that some alert, dark-eyed yellow-shirted Navajo - vigilantly manning one of several tall, tiny, Fire Lookouts overseeing the Reservation - would key his or her radio for cryin' out loud and put our *gung-ho* Helitack crew *to work!*

After all, thunderstorms had rumbled across *The Rez* ten long days before, spawning several reports of cloud-to-ground lightning activity. After so many days, though, there was almost no hope that a lightning-struck pine top could still be smoldering.

"Fluted Rock" Fire Lookout suddenly interrupted our radio's boring weather report. The young observer had sighted a smoking treetop, less than a mile due south of his lookout. It was as if our prayers had been answered! In minutes, our five-bladed aeronautical Jeep was buzzing over the taxiway, laboring with the weight of two Indian firefighters, forty gallons of jet-fuel, our initial-attack gear, and yours truly, Captain Methane.

Cutting across the active runway straight into the feeble breeze, we slipped into translational lift. Up through the warm Arizona atmosphere our little ship augered, leveling off finally at seven thousand, five hundred feet. Our track took us westbound over Highway 264 toward Fluted Rock. We were to patrol for any new smokes along the way.

A *fluted rock* – I should explain – has numerous vertical cracks or rib-like rocks along its perimeter. The one ahead of us was made of black lava, and – eons ago - it rose up nice and level like a freshly flipped sourdough pancake, and stayed that way.

Flooter Rock, as the Natives say it, is just about large enough to play baseball on, and - with its forty-one-foot tall, 1930-era *Aeromotor* tower - topped by a seven foot by seven foot metal box – *voila!* You've got one *sturdy* fire lookout! (Or, *lightning rod*, depending on whom you ask.)

The shiny old tower appeared on the horizon after passing Cross Canyon, where we turned north and caught our first glimpse of the enemy: a prominent plume of white smoke!

Descending to a more strategic altitude, I held the aircraft in a gentle clockwise turn to enable Delbert Henderson, my right-seat Navajo Helitack Foreman, an opportunity to size things up. After a couple of slow *three-sixties*, he began transmitting his fire report to Dispatch.

"Dispatch, Six-six-foxtrot, circling the Flooter Rock Fire. Estimate one-tenth of an acre, puttin' up a column of gray smoke. Burnin' in medium pine and heavy duff. Smokin' treetop and fire around the

base; probable lightning strike. We're preparin' to land and put a line around it. Request an Engine and hand crew backup. No water close-by for the helicopter bucket, over."

I loved the way Delbert pronounced *Flooter Rock*, but his closing comment was something a *gung-ho* pilot never wants to hear: *no bucket*. He was right, of course. I got to use a bucket only *once* in three fire seasons over the Navajo Nation. What we really needed was a nice, deep, strategically placed stock tank for an event like this. But no such luck.

Fast forward: The helicopter has been shut down a *reasonable* distance from the flames, but due to the lack of an LZ, we had to park within one hundred feet of the fire....something I did with reluctance. The fire was creeping slowly at the time, however - and Delbert didn't look nervous to me.

Time was of the essence, though; the fire tools were quickly removed from the helicopter's external basket. Delbert grabbed his packset radio and a shovel while "Deadeye" Lyle pulled out a Pulaski, and they darted off on the double.

Delbert wasn't kidding when he reported *"heavy duff"* fueling the fire. I verified by scanning all around the flying machine: there was a deep carpet of pine needles - punctuated with old rotten logs and limbs – and it was crackling dry; primed for ignition.

My Navajo pals left a *McLeod* for the Captain. That's a heavy-duty hoe-and-rake combination on the end of a sturdy wooden handle. Not that I planned on charging the fire line any time soon. Heck, Delbert and Lyle could handle this. It might insult them to even *suggest* they needed help.

Watching them drag fallen limbs and logs out of the way, and flail at the fire line, I had renewed confidence. It's over eight thousand feet above sea level here, but they're both in shape from physical conditioning, while I've been walking around leisurely here and there, getting soft around the middle. They'll holler at me if they need anything. Time to dig out the camera!

I had time for exactly two snaps of the shutter when a light northerly breeze started to *stir the bucket*, as they say. The flames began to leap ahead, and Navajos with raised voices could be heard, hollering for *Captain Methane!* Grabbing the McLeod, my cowboy boots made crunch-snap-crunching sounds as I dashed for Delbert and Deadeye.

As I came stomping up to Delbert, he pointed through the acrid smoke to a void in the fire line where he wanted me to start pulling the debris away from the approaching flames. Deadeye was twenty feet to my left and Delbert about thirty or more to my right; both were heads-down as they flailed, dug and scratched to expose the mineral soil underneath, and they were breathing heavily.

The flames were menacing. Wincing from the smoke, I tried to ignore them, though they felt hot on my knuckles though my thin leather flight gloves. Drawing a clear breath of air from behind me, I held it in and raked hard toward my boots with the McLeod, moving backward now instead of sideward as we planned. My McLeod was filling up with pine needles; the incessant flames threatened to set the tool ablaze!

Lyle took another assessment and moved my way, seeing that I was *in the bite*. Delbert soon did the same and we had three guys digging like men possessed, stopping only to gasp some air and check to see how close to the helicopter the advancing fire was getting (too close for comfort!).

The way the flames were growing, I had my own reservations (pun intended) about cranking that Allison engine up any time soon. I'd surely lay waste to the hard-won fire line and spread wildfire like the devil when I pulled power to lift off. You're darned if you do, but who'd forgive me if the ship burned up?

Fast forward through ten more minutes of devilish fire fighting and double guessing ourselves. My limp arms are supposed to be moving in and out, up and down; but the McLeod's mass has overcome my flaccid biceps. Signals go from my brain to my exhausted arms, where they are met with indifference. My labored breathing sounds like the old iron hand-pump on Grandma Burch's water well.

Nonetheless, Lyle, Delbert and I stood victorious, caked in ash and sweating heavily near the fire line. Our broad, professional-looking line checked the advance of hell toward the helicopter. We had gambled and won.

It was a quite a relief to our tired little trio when the Engine and hand crew arrived on scene, bringing in some fresh faces and strong arms – not to mention fire hoses and many gallons of water. Now, if my frozen grip would only *let go* of the wooden handle, I'd gladly trade it for a cyclic and a collective pitch about now!

Section VIII:
So You Want to Be a Heli-Logger?

The Velcro Lizard

We've all heard or read about people who commute long distances to work. I never envied these folks nor their dreary hours behind the wheel! And I certainly never dreamed I'd be commuting 1,300 miles to work, and enjoying the heck out of it!

It all began when I landed a job *teaching logs to fly* in western Montana. For eight years, I commuted by airliner back and forth every month to my southern California home. I never considered alternative transportation. Saving those air miles! Most chopper pilots are comfortable with airliners, I'll wager.

Then came October of '99. I'm standing in yet another long line at yet another crowded airport and it hit me: This isn't *fun* anymore! The airline routine was no longer the *feel good* way of getting back and forth to work!

Being the adventurous sort of guy that I am, I decided to bid the airlines "adios," buy a good used American-made car, and *drive* from Rialto to St. Regis instead. (My wife and children thought I'd gone *certified*.)

Practically overnight, I joined the ranks of the Long Distance Blue Road Commuters Club—an *excellent* decision.

The long lines are gone, the travel anxiety to boot! I now roll on *my* schedule, sit in *my* assigned seat, sip a (bottled) mocha or cold soda when *I* choose, tuned to *my* music of choice. And when the need arises, I pull over. True freedom is redefined on America's "blue roads." The vistas along my commute are extraordinary, a freelance photographer's delight!

The *dessert* of my desert commute goes through Nevada, *the Silver State*. It takes ten hours to motor the length of Nevada, and to help the miles fly by, I've stocked up on the Classics, Pink Floyd, and Rock & Roll. I've also become a fan of a distant NPR station, broadcasting from on high, overlooking "*Lost Wages.*"

Curiously, I find myself cruising along, suddenly aware that the stereo has been turned off for *hours*! I'm tuned instead to the humming of my comfortable machine as it rolls along a great American highway. The freelance writer in me emerges. I have time to think, air ideas out, or stare at the incredible blue sky. I should have done this years ago!

I've long been an admirer of wide-open spaces, and *this* is what is rightly called America's Outback! I came to know this vast desert wilderness as a young pilot, pursuing fires or hauling geologists around for hire. I learned to mimic the desert fox: hide from the oppressive midday heat; make my moves in the cooler hours; conserve water; waste no motion.

On the longer, straighter stretches of my commute, I have come to know a particularly remote Nevada highway a little *too* well: it lies between Tonopah and Ely, and rarely does one see another vehicle during the 168-mile stretch.

The route is smooth and a lonely sign says "SPEED LIMIT 70," which is just what *cruise control* was made for. Once dialed in, my eyes are free to feast: the surrounding snowcapped mountains contrast starkly against burnt volcanic cones and rambling sage ranch land. Distant mountain passes break up the otherwise straight road that bisects them. The desert air at this altitude tends to be very still; the silence—intoxicating.

So explain to me why so many critters along this stretch of highway don't seem to see, or even hear The Captain's speedy approach?! Although he drives with headlights on, from road level his sled emerges suddenly out of a shimmering mirage.

Alas, I am sad to report that along my favorite road, there is a dark side: things die! Birds on the wing fly low-level at high speed in opposition to the road and ricochet off the car's sleek bonnet, as if they were blind. A red-tail hawk sits right on the highway stripe, eating nothing; day-dreaming—and as I smoke the power disc brakes, he crouches, grabbing two great red wings-full of air, and vaults over the roof as I skid by just under his talons. Close call!

Tiny shrews, extra-large stinkbugs, handsome brown tarantulas: poor little things that you mustn't swerve to avoid. I've dispatched more than I care to recall. Then came The Lizard.

On that mysterious June morning, I zipped once again down my *favorite* highway, absorbed in Schubert's Piano Sonata D.845 when just ahead of me, stage left, dashed a humongous leopard lizard, the likes of which I have not seen since I was a young lad in Las Cruces!

He had to measure eighteen inches from his whip-like tail to his leathery snout, and he moved with dazzling speed over the sizzling surface, only to stop—facing me—directly in front of my right front P185/75R14 TOYO Premium Touring radial! Frozen for an instant, he tilted his head and did a couple of those cute lizard push-ups!

A faint *thump-thump*, and I continued on my way with the impunity one has in such circumstances. (I muttered an oath under my breath. "*Poor lizard!*")

Now this part, gentle readers, you may have trouble believing, but all of us Long Distance Blue Road Surfers owe it to the Lizard in remembrance of the style with which he took his lumps: as I reluctantly verified the mayhem in the rearview mirror...not really wanting to see what I had just rubbed out...to my disbelief I observed a defiant figure spring up—belatedly— from the scorched tar. Wavering drunk-like—yet tall and defiant in the rush of air that followed my speeding conveyance.

No, my Outback Brothers and Sisters, our racy reptile would dash around the desert no longer, but I recognized the *pose* his sudden-fried skin had manifested: a Velcro Lizard, emulating Bruce Lee, balanced tiptoe on one arched foot, daring me to *come back, and try that crap again!*

As if by reflex, I backed off the gas and reached for the ever-present digital camera in the seat next to me...

No...no...not this time. I've learned from experience: they always look better in the mirror than they do close up. I reluctantly fingered the cruise control's *resume* button and disappeared once again into the shimmering mirage.

Too Close to the Trough

*   *Beware the Tsunamis of Winter*

My crusty old logbook was useful in recalling the wintry morning when I learned the real meaning of the word trough. I'm referring to the weather kind of trough—not the kind Dad had on the farm outside of Longmont, though. That one was for the pigs.

It used to fascinate me as a kid to watch hungry hogs feed, but I learned you have to climb on the fence and get up close to the trough or you'll miss out on all the action. In being close to the trough, however, you are also in danger of being eaten alive, a chewed-up old hog farmer told me once.

Turns out, if you happen to be flying a chopper when a trough comes through, you're *too close* to the trough once again—and the thought of being eaten alive might cross your mind.

Raking away the cobwebs of time, my meandering Okie-fied brain remembers well that second day of February in *Double Ought One*, when I augered Lorena (our outfit's UH-1H) out of the Little Joe quarry and headed toward Two-Mile Canyon in western Montana—with long-line a-dangling. Five rowdy hookers and a few other bad actors fought off the cold awaiting her arrival—a white Huey helicopter, which was soon to disappear into a winter storm.

The weatherman hadn't beat around the bush at all that morning; we knew an *Arctic Clipper* was forecasted to cross the Idaho/Montana border some time after daybreak—which meant a short work day, if he was right. But we considered ourselves to be *stand-up* heli-loggers—we were gonna give it a *go*, by golly.

It had been that kind of winter for us loggers: down for weather, back up until the mud got too deep, then down for mud until it froze hard, then down for low ceilings again. Paydays were a mite disappointing. The boss was hangin' around more, too—frettin' about production and payroll, while we peeled the frozen covers off our flying machine, waging our daily race with the rising sun.

"Hopefully, it'll blow over and we can keep logging," the boss mumbled under his turned-up collar as I pinned up the latest colorful weather-map printout he brought in from his toasty truck. In the jittery glow of the maintenance trailer's fluorescent lights, the weather map highlighted one of those menacing "Ls."

Another rapidly moving cold front was symbolized by a trough that drops down out of the Bering Sea and races across Western Canada, bringing to us year-round Montana *wind loggers* the minions of wintry hell. This was indeed the suitable playground for thickheaded fleshy creatures to butt heads with Mother Nature.

Every man-jack on the line that day wanted the forecast to be wrong, and I heard all about it on the radio. "We've logged in blizzards before!" someone suggested.

"Suzy needs new shoes," came a more reasonable voice over the FM. "*Lace 'em up!*" taunted Pie-cut. It was clear that *the girls* were hungry— and in denial.

Under the first horizontal rays of dawn, I banked left into Two-Mile Canyon and eyeballed the darkness to the northwest. Was it moving this way? I had my sensors on *extra vigilant* for a fast-movin' snow cloud or distant treetops all bent over, my signal to backtrack down the canyon to the quarry before JC closed the curtains. *The girls* would be unhappy, of course—but we'd still have a helicopter come tomorrow.

My log book shows "0.7" total flight time for the second of February. You can take off 0.3 for the ferry to and from, so my actual logging time that morning was just enough to get my first round of hookers sweaty beneath their orange hard hats and multiple-layered garments. That was when the *trough* busted through the trees on the high ridgeline to our west, dropped down the face of the slope, and came roller-ballin' in our direction.

Doug had just thrown several choker eyes onto my remote hook's load beam when someone at the log landing radioed something about "a storm cloud comin' this way." Holding a steady hover at the end of my 185-foot synthetic long-line, I craned my neck around in the left bubble to get a gander at this untimely visitor—as Doug yelled, "Clear!"

There were 160-foot-tall standing larch trees all around, restricting me from turning Lorena's nose down-slope and into the wind—the best way for the ship to take her punishment—so I made a quick decision and pulled power, knowing that I needed something attached to the ground to hang on to. Doug's turns were heavy, snow-laden timbers and I guessed that they'd resist forty pounds of torque without breaking loose.

Applying pitch, the choked-up butts and tops of several logs lifted partially out of the snow as I concentrated on the dark mass of green limbs underneath them, my only visual reference in the forest of white below to help me avoid the oncoming rush of vertigo when the first wave of blinding snow hit.

Taking a blast up the tail like that made me feel momentarily like an old schoolmarm caught outside, goin' to the privy in a Norther—hanging on to a fence post with one long, bony arm, my long black skirt held tightly in the other hand while my white pantaloons flap wildly in the frigid wind—tall larch trees bending over in unison as the blast raced up and over the hill facing me.

"That's all for me, fellas!" I announced, finally pickling Doug's partially hoisted turn as a brief clearing appeared behind the first wave. The valley beckoned downhill to my left, inviting me to drop on down—bring my long-line and head for the quarry. The second wave was seconds away, and it looked twice as nasty!

"Wh—where' ya goin'?" came Ted's comical inquiry, as the ship rock-and-rolled amid some rude gusts and rapidly changing conditions.

"*Waaaaa,*" I heard Doug cry, imitating a bawlin' baby bear—the howling wind buffeting his hand-mike.

"You guys are about to get buried!" I replied. "I suggest you either head for your rigs or build yourself a big fire!" the Captain kibitzed, while struggling to keep the ship upright and the swinging long-line out of his tail feathers.

Swallowing a lump in my throat, I knew we had once again strayed a little too close to the trough. A logging pilot makes a lot of decisions in a day's work; some are more important than others. As for February 2nd, I decided to try and please everyone, and we all got showed who's boss.

Despite what she had thrown at us, we were evidently going to survive the effort: I listened raptly as the guys described the second wave clobbering them. Now *they* knew what a trough was! They barely made it out that morning—it snowed like there was no tomorrow, and we were *down*, once again.

Hook Riders Anonymous

With little prodding, my 1970s subconscious musters up a surly Jim Morrison singing a helicopter pilot's version of The Door's legendary "Riders on the Storm." As the thunder track starts rolling, enter the drums, Ray Manzarek tickles the keyboard…raindrops splashing…more thunder…

> *Riders on my hook.*
> *Riders on my hook.*
> *I can't bear to look,*
> *My ass the Feds will cook,*
> *There's riders on my hook.*

Whichever helicopter pilot it was that gave the first ground-pounder a ride on his long-line was sticking his neck out like a turtle. Same goes for the second. And the third, and so on… Yep, there's more than one.

Having been in the shoes of the former (but not the latter) I envision a veritable sea of double-breasted attorneys stretching to the far horizon, all clambering to attach themselves to either side of the lawsuit: a chopper pilot whose impromptu long-line "passenger" was injured (or worse) while skirting the rules of the sky.

For those fortunate many who remain sheltered from the unabridged Code of Federal Regulations (CFRs), you need to know that there is a slew of tedious rules overseen by the Federal Aviation Administration (FAA) governing what (and who) can be legally suspended from a helicopter, whether by hoist, trapeze, Billy Pew net, long-line, etc.

Without going into a full-blown course on the subject, forgive me if I just throw out here that there are many law-enforcement agencies and emergency rescue teams who practice with humans suspended beneath hovering helicopters for hours on end. Legally, I suspect. Then again, law enforcement agencies don't answer to the FAA.

We've all seen dramatic TV rescues of various victims clinging to listing ships, giant (burning) construction cranes, etc., most of which were performed by professionals trained in helicopter rescue work. Some of these machines were single-engine helicopters; twin-engined models add critical redundancy. Practicing to be ready for the real thing is essential, but there is also a risk in the rehearsal process. Gravity is so unforgiving of malfunction or lack of precision in these situations.

Chances are, these agencies foresaw that emergency external load work would someday be essential, and they satisfied the local FAA Flight Standards District Office (FSDO) by way of a manual detailing things like standardized procedures. Once the manual is submitted, approval by the FSDO clears the way for the hoisting of human flesh, at the operator's discretion.

I'll wager "Cowboy" couldn't have cared less about the CFRs, as he unloaded the last canvas bag of blasting powder from the expanded metal basket one hundred feet below my French helicopter. Without missing a beat, he hopped over the basket's rail, landing squarely in the center of the steel cage. One gloved hand gripped his Motorola portable; the other clung to the overhead iron bar, which was welded to the basket. (Which was attached by a long, wire rope to the jet-powered helicopter hovering above him.)

Facing the lush river valley to the northwest, he keyed his radio's mike, saying only one word: "Recorder." He then set the radio down, yanked off the big blue rubber band gathering his long, blond hair up behind his head, and held on with both hands as the Lama started upward—the basket following obediently.

It was a three-minute ride from the Powder Crew's location to the Recorder over the river drainage, within view of one of Wyoming's most alluring mountain ranges. This bountiful forest was thought to be harboring a share of America's future oil independence deep under her crust.

The French seismic crew that I was supporting hired scores of tough, hard-working guys like Cowboy to gather geological data while the summer sun shined. Our monthly "shot-bonus" checks reflected the fact that we were the most productive surface seismic crew under the Denver Office's supervision. If the overhead knew about any hook rides, they kept quiet about it.

Riding the hook—although the practice was never publicly acknowledged and never discussed over the radio—was one way to help increase productivity, save daylight and Hobbs meter time. Safety aside.

So basket rides were nothing new when I arrived on the scene, but Cowboy had held off for weeks before he decided he could trust his new pilot. That was the day he hopped into the basket.

Galloping along at a leisurely clip, I flew about four hundred feet above the river as we made our way northward, fully aware that should my right thumb so much as touch the little red button on the control stick, Cowboy would fall away like a big, blond stone.

Or the belly hook could malfunction. Or the engine could fail. The more I thought about it, the more reasons there were not to be doing what we were doing.

With my right door off, there was a strong scent of cedar in the pleasant afternoon breeze. Cowboy glanced momentarily upward, a broad white smile on his bearded face as he began lunging from one side to the other—making the basket sway side-to-side!

I caught his drift and began banking a bit harder into the turns I was making. Checking well below me, Cowboy was in hog heaven—banking at forty-five degrees, his long, blond, flying mane making him look like some kind of crazed Seismic Surfer in the rare air above the Uintas. (Which made me the crazed chopper pilot above him, I suspect.)

(More thunder, rain...Morrison continues):

> *It's a thrill to ride the cage,*
> *...a thrill to ride the cage,*
> *Flying mighty high,*
> *We ain't never gonna die,*
> *There's a Rider in the cage...*

Landing Cowboy gingerly at the Recorder moments later to an appreciative audience of three—two heeler dogs and a troubleshooter—I heaved a sigh of relief as they waved an *attaboy* my way and I mentally logged my first "hook ride."

Never again, I promised myself—although it *was* a mighty exciting thing to do!

Over the decades, I've found that logging crews are the most likely of coworkers to request a lift. The very camaraderie that makes a logging pilot and his crew *gel* is the catalyst that can lead to calculated risks.

"Your relief pilot does it all the time," a hooker would taunt, using the ol' *one pilot against the other* ploy. Pressure from the peanut gallery. That's okay. They work very hard and deserve every reasonable consideration, but they don't have a pilot's license to lose.

When the winter snow gets zipper deep and a hooker finishes logging his strip, he is often faced with a tough, three-hour hike (in snowshoes) to reach the top of his next strip. Production will lag until he starts sending out turns again.

The fastest way up the hill is on the end of the long-line, so that would be a good time for the pilot to have onboard an approved FAA External Load Manual that includes the coveted people-hauling Class "D" FAA endorsement. Without the endorsement, one must question his motivation.

But back in the day before all these manuals started appearing on the scene, the beleaguered hooker ("Dirk," in this case) would simply radio his daring pilot: "Show me the way, Captain?" That's the cue for a hook ride!

The first thing we did after hatching such a conspiracy was to radio the log landing. This was done to check for White Hats,[106] who might ruin our day by accidentally observing our expeditious mode of aerial transport.

---

106 Governmental supervisor types who wouldn't likely approve of our *ingenuity.*

A "coast is clear" radio call from the lead chaser or woods boss gave the pilot the discretion to proceed; and before you knew it, ol' Dirk would be way up at the top of his strip, ropin' logs; buoyed by a fresh adrenaline rush, and grinnin' like he had teeth.

One might wonder, with such occasional aerial improvisation going on over the years, was there ever a mishap doing this stuff? Fog enshrouds my long-term memory like a thick cap of virgin sheep's wool, but seems to me a few episodes might deserve some dishonorable mention...

"Jeffro" was being shown around in the forest just south of Alberton, Montana a ways by a very experienced Huey pilot. The pilot skillfully flew his 150-foot long-line over and down through the thick stand of trees where Jeffro stood patiently waiting.

Jeff grabbed the braided synthetic line above his head with both hands, sat down on the remote hook's sturdy rubber cone, crossed his legs, and hooked one boot over the other...for safety. (*Ahem.*) Off he fluttered, vertically.

The pilot, however, was sort of in a hurry and was multitasking big-time: hovering along in the Huey, he checked the critical gauges and then scanned the steep, rocky mountainside, trying to find where Jeffro's new strip started. But by taking his eyes off Jeffro momentarily, he inadvertently flew the poor guy into a vertical rock wall!

Not *too* hard, but hard enough that Jeffro had to be lowered to the ground at the base of the rock wall to take assessment..."until the bells quit ringing," he was heard to say. (That was Jeffro's last hook ride with *that* pilot, by the way.)

"Willy" was hooking a mean strip along the Little Joe River near Saint Regis one summer afternoon. We were short-handed, which upped the stress level. The terrain was quite steep, and when Willy reached a rocky thicket of dense brush, he knew he'd have to move a couple hundred feet further up the hill—past the impenetrable brush—to his next wood.

I responded to Willy's request to *show (him) the way* up the hill. However, there was something strange going on when I hovered over Willy with my 185-foot long-line. As he got seated and crossed his legs, I began to feel a bit dizzy.

Fighting the illusion of my flickering rotor blades in the adjacent shadows, I dialed in maximum VertRef[107] concentration to lift him straight up, trying to not drag him uphill through the very brush he was at war with.

Trying to. The weird dizziness I felt was unusual, but turns out this happened only over Willy's predicament. (Kryptonite?!) After making two brief, shoddy attempts to lift him straight up, I only succeeded in pulling him uphill ten feet through the nasty brush.

"Real nice," he growled over the portable, as I gave up and lowered the hook, allowing him to roll off the cone and back down the hill to where he started.

"I'll walk—if it's all the same to you," he mumbled over the radio after my apology for practically tearing his shirt off in the harsh brush. (Had I not regularly flown well for Willy over the years and beat him convincingly in eight-ball, that might have been his last hook ride with me.)

There was a heli-logging show going on near Clinton, Montana and I was flying "H" model Hueys for a Washington-based outfit and loving nearly every minute of it. The Unit had a plethora of big logs. The log landing was close by, and the wind was usually spot-on perfect. We shoulda known something was about to happen.

"Timber" called me over to relocate him and his Husqvarna chainsaw way up the hill to buck some hooters that one of the sawyers had skipped. After dropping him off at the big buckers, I picked up a two-log turn from Byron and hauled the bonus over to the log landing. After setting the logs down, I opted to swing the butts a few feet closer to the choker chasers. It'll just take a second, I rationalized—and they won't have so far to run to retrieve the choker. It's a teamwork thing.

As my green and red eyeballs gazed downward in amazement, the <u>helicopter's cargo</u> hook—allegedly secured to the main transmission—fell

107 Vertical reference work. Utilizing long-lines to relocate objects over rough terrain or water.

like a greased warthog, long-line and all—smacking the earth at terminal velocity just a few feet away from the chasers, who were staring back at me in shock!

Cause: the tough, metal alloy tube linking the hook to the transmission had fatigue-twisted and failed.[108] After this happened, Timber—and the rest of the crew—took a hiatus from hook rides for quite some time after that. And who would blame them?

Ted and Mark were big on hook rides: they were two tall, swaggering hookers who loved their heli-logging. One day that we worked together on Sunshine Mountain, it was almost too hot to fly. By the end of the day, everyone down yonder was caked in dirt and pitch, soaked in sweat, and ready for a cold shower. Ready to the point of requesting that I show them the way down the steep slope, please, Captain Methane.

They had worked so hard and done so well in the August heat that I figured—*what the heck*. In a rare double-ride, they stood facing each other, their corked boots biting down on the hook's circular steel perimeter ring, and held on to the long-line (and each other) as I started upward and away from the mountainside.

It was a one-minute hook ride to the log landing along the Little Joe River Road, but I sailed by the place one normally sets hookers down, keeping them ten feet in the air as I continued down-slope to a deep, rushing, ice-cold dip site in the Little Joe itself!

Seeing that they were about to get dipped, sweaty Ted keyed his radio excitedly and shouted, "Yeah, Baby!" practically daring me to do the deed. But I held them right there like the professional I am while I reconsidered doing damage to two expensive company radios. (At least I was thinking of something.) Reluctantly, I levitated them slowly back to the road and set them gently down. They were so disappointed in their captain!

"Dougie" got the hook ride of his life the following winter when we

---

108 The operator, to his credit, replaced all his Huey cargo hooks with a six-thousand-pound after-market logging version that stood up to the rigors of logging much better than the standard military hook.

struggled to heli-log in the face of numerous snowstorms coming out of Canada. The roads were so bad that the hookers parked their chained-up 4X4 rigs at the log landing and rode Doug's snowmobile from there to the top of the ridge.

We had a productive day, finishing up the high strip and moving downstream toward the St. Regis River when the next wave of snow hit. We thought we were gonna beat it to the barn, but one last thing had yet to be done: fly Dougie back up the hill to retrieve his snowmobile! Once Doug was on the hook, I flipped the engine anti-ice on and gave the bubble a good wipe with my left flight-mitten. Wet snow began to fall in earnest.

I can't adequately paint the image that Dougie became as I flew slowly ahead, staying close enough to the trees so I could keep visual reference with Mother Earth and yet not drag Doug through any treetops. Going fast was not an option.

Doug had turned lumpy and white one minute into the two-minute flight. He looked like a frozen mountain climber, dangling from his icy rope, and had ceased joking about it over his radio. (Freezing lips, he told me later!)

Getting a visual on the partially buried snow machine was a small reward for sticking both our necks way out, but attempting to retrieve the snow machine any later in the day would have been a lost cause.

Doug rolled off the freezing hook's cone into the snow as I set him slowly down. He peeled his mittens off the long-line, radioing to me as I buzzed off into the blizzard, "Thanks, Captain—I hope she'll start now." (She did.)

〽〽〽

One might wonder why a guy would bring all this subterfuge to light after so many years, but there is a method to my madness: I'm here to suggest that we may not really need all these alleged hook rides to perform our unique kind of work. In the interest of safety.

But, knowing that a crisis can happen in a heartbeat, develop a manual—with the cooperation and support of all your overhead managers, field workers, and the FAA. If everyone can't agree that hook riding can be done with an acceptable risk, I'd let it go.

It's just a job, after all. Until someone gets hurt and needs help fast; tall, blazing infernos with panic-stricken people on the roof; or an unconscious logger who's been struck by a falling snag. Help must arrive in minutes, and with precision.

I'm not saying that every single-engine helicopter (or pilot) can be signed off for this high-risk kind of work, but if properly done—with training and step-by-step procedures—one will have set up a valuable emergency response tool that is likely to save someone in real trouble.

Within Reach of the Hose

Lolo, Montana can be found in most U.S. history books – tucked away in the diaries of Lewis and Clark – for it was through Lolo Pass the famous explorers wound their way up and over the Bitterroots, into eastern Idaho and points west. In those days, the lofty mountain pass was known only to a few high-country American Indians.

Not far down the hill on the Montana side of things is the renowned hot springs by the same name, where many a traveler have dropped their heavy packs and yielded to the blissful sulfur-scented water that steams forth from between the rocks.

Just a mite farther down the hill, one can easily miss the Lolo Work Center, a Forest Service camp with several shady places where forestry workers sometimes camp while engaged in the business of logging. Nothing fancy—but to our band of heli-loggers, it was home for a spell.

Our loggin' outfit had relocated there in April of '97, having come to heli-log a passel of freshly cut units of timber close by—and a blow-down unit that would prompt every man-jack on the crew to cuss a blue streak every time the name *Smith Creek* came up. A nasty thunderstorm the year before had spawned some renegade microbursts that ravaged the mountainsides yonder. Harvesting the tangled-up mess of lodgepole pine logs was part of the "deal" our buyer made with the USFS. ('Course, he didn't have to work there!)

As the heavy equipment arrived and the fuel tankers got situated, cutters, hookers, and chasers made camp at the Work Center. Sewer lines were nonexistent. Electrical outlets were few and far between. Power was available, but not in the usual sense of the word. Several trailers were plugged into multi-plugs, which were downstream from some other multi-plugs, and so forth…a sight that would make an electrician twitch and ruminate.

As soon as the men got their rigs leveled and the women and children placated, loggin' got started in earnest. That's when "Mike" came to roost in his bright red Huey, all bushy-tailed and *ready to rip*, as they say.

Fueling up every morning thereafter and between cycles from the smaller of two tankers, Mike yanked and banked on the nearby sale that straddled Lolo Creek. Much of that sale was tangled-up lodgepoles as well, so the helicopter had to work hard to pull the slender interwoven logs free and teach them to fly for the short trip down to the log landing.

Using a one-hundred-fifty-foot long-line, Mike was making hay on a fateful day in May, and had just about flown out his hour-and-twenty-minute fuel cycle. "Last turn," he radioed the hookers, the standard courtesy call to let 'em know this was the time for the heaviest turn in their strip, and then he'd head for the fuel hose.

'Long about here I need to add that most Huey loggers call out *last turn* somewhere around two hundred pounds (roughly thirty gallons) indicated—give or take—depending on (one) *how far away* the tanker was; (two) how *familiar* he was with that particular Huey's fuel quantity indicators; (three) how *brave* he was, and (four) how *lucky* he was feeling at the time. And Mike was (1) *close* (2) *fairly* (3) *brave as anyone* and (4) *feelin' lucky!*

That's probably why he allowed himself to be called back for "one more turn" by a hooker who just couldn't wait ten more minutes. Taking that turn to the log landing, Mike allegedly had one hundred and fifty pounds of Jet-A *in the bag* when "Kelly" seen him a'comin' toward the tanker.

Kelly had been busy all that cycle felling a tree that was within forty feet of the fuel service LZ—too close for comfort. He had dug around the root wad of the stump to the point that Mike could likely pull it the rest of the way out of the ground whenever it was convenient.

Throwing a choker around the stump, Kelly called out to the captain, "Hey, Mike—got time to pull this stump outta the ground for me?" And being the conscientious, agreeable sort that Mike was—and one through four above—he said, "Sure!"

Kelly slapped the eye of the thirty-foot wire-rope choker into Mike's remote hook and cleared quickly away. Captain Mike then rared back for one more of his classic rip-and-tear maneuvers. Which was when Mr. Lycoming's thirsty fuel pumps started sucking air.

The powerful turbine engine abruptly spooled down, as did Mike—strapped into the powerless helicopter's left seat—rapidly consuming the one-hundred-fifty feet between him and terra firma. The big red machine landed hard and level, briefly relighting the wick as the last gallon and a half of gas found its way back into the vapor-sucking pumps. The good news was (one) Mike wasn't hurt, and (two) he landed within reach of the hose. The bad news was (one) the stump hadn't moved, and (two) the helicopter was toast.

More Collective Pitch, Scotty!

*   Hydraulic Failures of the Rude Variety

It would be my hunch that the Huey is about the largest helicopter most of us could be expected to fly with no hydraulics. That's probably why just about every helicopter larger than a UH-1H has dual hydraulics, or some kinda stored-pressurization system that gives us pilots perhaps three movements of the controls before all that altitude, airspeed, and rotor energy comes back to haunt us.

The ease with which a stiff collective pitch control moves (hydraulics off) depends largely upon the precise adjustment of a certain *acorn nut* on the rotor head. When a rebuilt rotor head is installed on the aircraft, it is standard procedure for the maintenance technician to install the main rotor blades, then track and balance everything to within point two IPS[109] on the Chadwick balancer. Afterward, a flight check—with the hydraulics turned off—is necessary to determine if the acorn nut adjustment is set correctly.

Here's what happens when the acorn nut ain't set correctly:

It had been around ten days since my previous ride's turbine engine exploded amid great fanfare. The ringing in my ears had subsided somewhat and I was just beginning to feel comfortable with my replacement Huey. The load of partially burnt Idaho logs I had swinging along under me never did make it

109   Inches Per Second

to the log landing, but at least they had my expensive Mechanical Specialties remote hook and long-line for company when I punched them off from three hundred feet.

I had felt a sharp *lurch* in the controls and heard a frightful *shrieking* sound as the hydraulic pump cavitated, prompting me to reduce power and ditch the external load—as called for in the manual. The customary *Master Caution* light was beaming back at me from its central place on the instrument panel, and the appropriate caution segment light announced *hyd press*—just in case I'd been napping.

Calling out my problem over the logging radio frequency, I stayed on my heading and went through the usual circuit-breaker *slash* control-switch checks and came up on the short end. The pungent odor of military hydraulic fluid reinforced my diagnosis: no fluid—no pressure! My helmet's sweaty earphones filled with choruses of concern from the ground-pounders as to my well-being, then trailed off politely as the plot thickened.

Having force-landed a flaming Huey near the upcoming log landing a few days back, I knew for a fact that there was not a clear place around where I could shoot a running landing, as was called for. Control wise, anything below twenty knots wasn't going to fly.

The steep terrain below me was heavily forested. There was a dirt access road that twisted and turned under tall, scorched sugar pine and burned Douglas fir trees. Hover landing opportunities only—running landings were not an option!

Heading southwest down the hill toward Lake Payette, I eased the power back from eighty knots to make flying the big bird less of a strain. I noticed as I pushed down on the collective pitch lever, it went down about a half-inch— but it would not come back up!

I had flown stiff-controlled Hueys before—and figured this was one of them— but I soon discovered, despite my greatest efforts, I could not regain the pitch! I could only lower it. The power I had dialed in now would not be enough to hover with. I was in descent mode—like it or not.

Fortunately, we were logging 7,000 feet above sea level, at the edge of a steep forested plateau. There was the lake below me, surrounded by roads—but they were heavily traveled and tree-lined. I thought seriously about ditching the ship along the rocky shoreline, but the lake was deep (and *cold*) and the ship would be lost.

Realizing McCall's airport was less than ten miles ahead—at a little over 5,000 feet—I swallowed hard and radioed Scotty—my trusty A&P field mechanic—that I was going to try and make the airport. Signing off, I silently prayed that nothing *else* went south until I reached dry land. Scotty jumped into the company's panel truck and raced down the hill after me.

Owing to the prevailing *severe-clear* weather conditions, the central Idaho airport was already visible. I got busy on the local Unicom frequency, advising McCall traffic that I was inbound from the north with a hydraulics failure, planning on a run-on landing. A friendly fixed-winger's voice came back advising me that the local smoke jumpers had a large, converted four-engined submarine chaser *shut down* on the active runway, a demonstration of some kind. (Can you spell PB4Y?)

Okay, I can make out the giant, high-winged plane from here. That leaves half a runway in front of him and half behind him, but it wouldn't be prudent to slide onto the runway anywhere *near* the BUF.[110] No more headlines for me, thanks!

Deciding I would vie for the parallel taxiway instead, I heard a tail dragger taxi out and radio for advisory. Before he got out his entire message, a loud squeal from a competing transmitter blotted him out. The pattern was heating up, and here I came.

I decided by then that I'd wasted too much time on the taxi-way and re-aimed my red helicopter for the two-ship heliport just east of the active runway, and take my chances. The twin *Hs* were vacant—no airplanes were taxiing by—and I'd be headed right into a ten-knot wind. There would be no go-around.

On a half-mile final, I couldn't have been happier with my glide slope. But since I couldn't pull any collective pitch at the bottom, I knew I was going to have to slam the big red toad down like a toddler with a maxed-out diaper.

I tried not to be too surprised by the pole-and-cable security fence that came into view at quarter-mile final. The would-be arresting-cable ran across my flight path left to right and cut back across at the far end, right to left. The Captain was boxed in!

110 Big Ugly...Airplane?

With my dusty cowboy boots standing on the pedals, straining my abdominals like a ruptured duck behind the thick lap belt—pulling as hard as my weenie-like left arm could possibly pull on the (slightly bent) collective pitch lever—it is indeed a wonder that I didn't bust a gut, right there in the saddle!

The skids weren't quite level when I contacted the pavement, but that's the way the cookie crumbles. My head bobbed as the ship's rear crosstube bottomed out and the ship bounced and pitched forward, sliding twelve more feet before I got the pitch down flat and slid to a smoky stop, parked right on the second H.

I'd have paid good money about then to hear the various glowing comments from the unawares smoke jumpers off to my right, as a few of them craned their necks in my direction—arms folded. *"Chopper pilots! His best landing of the day!"* Ha!

I was glad to get my feet back on the ground after that. No one came out to check on me, neither—guess it looked too *uneventful.*

After shutting down, I checked for damage and made it to the pay phone—dialing up the home office. After explaining why I was calling from the airport, I asked my stressed-out boss in the most sincere way, "Would you blame me if I quit, right here and now?" And he was kind enough to say, "I wouldn't blame you in the least."

While walking back to the ship, Scotty (and the whole, wide-eyed logging crew) drove up in a big cloud of dust. After admiring my parking job, Scotty refilled the hydraulic reservoir and had me fire up the machine. As soon as the oil pressure came up, he started banging on the tranny housing with his flashlight—hollering over the noise, *"I found it!"* and *"Shut 'er down!"*

The cause of my little crisis? A *tiny* little hole in an oil line just underneath the hydraulic pump—it was spurting a laser-like stream of *cherry juice* my direction as I turned to look.

"Well, don't just stand there, Scotty," I quipped. "Fix it! We've got some loggin' to do!"

Neener Nena, Tough as Nails

My stalwart helicopter logging mechanic—a former Marine sergeant whom we'll call "Z-Man"—was seated comfortably behind the wheel of our outfit's Ford service van early one morning near Grace, Idaho. Having just completed a thorough preflight of our frosty Bell UH-1K logging machine, we were busy re-warming our fingers and toes for the kick-off of our heli-logging day when the Crummy pulled in behind us, lights off. Before we knew what hit us, a shovelful of partially frozen *doggy-doo* slammed down on the shiny white hood of the van, right in front of the Marine.

Nena—our logging crew's feisty lead chaser and no one to trifle with—was wielding the shovel. She had appeared unsuspectingly in the early dawn at Z-Man's half-open window while we casually discussed current events, not expecting an ambush.

"How do you like that shit?!" Nena screamed in Z-Man's left ear, loud and shrill enough to give us both a migraine. (At five foot seven, she really got into her anger, you see.)

Several seconds passed before Z-Man countered with a clever comeback, one that was not near as memorable. A few more heated words were exchanged, and having made her point, Nena left. During all that time, though—Nena (or *Neener,* as her friends knew her) did not once back away—nor did she *reload*, thank goodness. We had all the dog poop we needed, thanks just the same.

Minutes later, after the Crummy spun down the greasy jeep road toward the log landing and the ringing in our ears abated, Z-Man sought answers. Why—for example—was the familiar-looking dog crap on the other side of his defrosted windscreen there, and not on Nena's utility trailer, where he had shoveled the stinky stuff just yesterday?

"This is *totally* my fault," I explained to my trusty A&P mechanic and most agreeable coworker. Z-Man had merely been trying to keep the helicopter service landing cleared of *land mines*. He did little more than return said crap to the dog's legal owner. (My mistake was mentioning to Nena that evening what the *problem* was and where she could find "Chief's" doggy-doo. Having had some time to think on it, I guess it wasn't such a good idea. It never dawned on me to warn Z-Man of my diplomatic blunder.)

The main culprit behind the offensive piles was none other than Nena's out-of-control, soon-to-be-neutered male Dalmatian. The flatbed utility trailer was parked next to our grassy helicopter landing, where the dog felt right at home. Get the picture?

Chief routinely sprang from the Crummy when it arrived every morning and seldom took more than ten steps before doing his thing, often within spitting distance of the helicopter. Z-Man—being the regimented hard-striper he was at heart—kept a *tight ship* and would get his hair up every time Chief squatted.

Z-Man knew better than to complain to Nena (or her soft-spoken husband, B-Man) about the dog—since they technically represented *the customer*—and worse: Nena had a reputation for biting people's heads off. So Z-Man got out his shovel and now you know the how the *land mine* wound up on the *Econoline*.

After that, I was more careful what I said around Nena. I flashed back on the time I rode behind her in the Crummy and observed how *butchered* her hair was in the back. I said something profound like, "Jeez, Neener, who cut your hair? It looks like *crap* in the back!"

For some reason, she didn't bite *my* head off by the time I realized my Freudian slip. Little did I know, she cut it herself—when she was pissed—with a dull pair of scissors and no mirror. Not one to fret about her hairdo, that one. Slap a hard hat on her, she's dressed for work!

Born August 20, 1962, Lena Nanette Rochelle was born a *Leo*, if you *parlez* the Zodiac. Leo, as in *the Lion*—appropriate for one of the toughest gals I've ever had the pleasure of working with. How she came to be called Nena, or the particulars about how she and husband Brian came to be married, is a mystery.

How I managed to stay on the good side of Nena is also a mystery to me, because my remote hook was seldom *sweet* in my early logging days. I flew the hook *quickly*, but not very *smoothly*, and was always in a great hurry. I flew like a house afire to keep up with all the other fast pilots out there. *Get fast and stay hot*—that's how you made a living. Nena knew the score and kept an eye out for my raw hook. Regardless, I still managed to injure her at least twice, and I remember both like yesterday…

We were *wind loggin'* north of McCall for Wescor, a burn sale up at seven thousand feet. I was nursing a beat-up, two-piece one-hundred-fifty-foot wire rope long-line that made "hookshots" all the harder. I took to using a whipshot in getting the hook from the just-parked log way over to Nena, where she worked alone across the landing, coiling up them nasty chokers.

A well-timed snapping of the line got the hook to her quickly, where it always landed with a clunk near her right boot. (The steel remote hook weighed over forty pounds.) She'd slap a choker drop into the hook and I'd be gone.

And about the time we both started believing I could do my whipshot all day long and never hit her, I hit her. On the anklebone of that right foot of hers. I saw it clear as day, her all bent over rubbing her ankle, as I flew the ten-drop gently away. Following my sincere apology over the radio, she insisted it was *okay*; but I knew it had to hurt. Nena was *tough*. The next time would be worse.

Things were screwy right off the bat when we moved the logging show to Ennis, Montana. Range cattle were climbing the gravel roads to the high grass when we got there, cow pies everywhere. The only good level spot for my motor home was just off the gravel-and-cow-pie spur road that dove down the hill toward Service. The Crummy would routinely stop there and meet up before dawn for what they called a *tailboard*.

It was still quite dark when the Crummy drove up kinda quick-like, doused its headlights, and screeched to a halt in plain view of the Captain. The right front door flew open and out spilled a couple of warm bodies, including (hooker) Stacey's pregnant wife, who hunkered down and puked loudly in the dim light of the Crummy's interior lamps. "God!" she gasped, as others staggered out, fanning the air around them.

"*Pizza fart,*" came Stacey's belated explanation for what brought on the Crummy's dead-stick landing. His early morning *ripper* behind the wheel made his knocked-up wife toss her pretty cookies. (Turns out, a powerful *strain* was moving through the logging crew that whole week, and performance suffered. The Captain offered encouragement, but kept his distance.)

The hotel the crew was staying at was in Ennis, one hour north on Highway 287. I paid them a cordial visit on our first "off" day. Stacey and "Puck" had young wives with babies in connecting hotel rooms, and their wired, shrieking toddlers had apparently declared war on the old hotel. It was one of those 3-D refresher courses in *The Joys of Bachelorhood*, so I excused myself to go do my laundry.

Built around the north-flowing Madison River, Ennis resides in the high country, one day's ride northwest of Yellowstone, and just southwest of the Lee Metcalf Wilderness. We were loggin' in what's called the *Gravelly Range*. This is officially the *middle* of the middle, in the middle of nowhere. It was good to be alive.

Meanwhile, we had work to do. No sense in re-tellin' anyone with ears that it was going to be hard on the Hueys. The air's thin up there, especially in June. We'd have to work 'em hard to haul seasoned, sixty-five-foot lodgepole pine logs to the 7,000-foot rock bench of a log landing. Once there, the rigid logs would jolt the rigging as they landed hard and snapped the line. (I started missing green timber right off the bat—it flexed.)

The logs were destined for custom-built log homes. The client came now and then to look over our harvest. He knew how to run the loader and was soon picking his choices from the mountainous log deck, tossing any with blemishes or tight spirals in the grain off to one side. The *cull pile* would grow large. Righteous firewood!

Then came June 22nd. We had the landing to ourselves once again and were haulin' logs from close around. Hovering high over the log landing between turns, I spied someone in a plaid shirt I didn't recognize; he was walkin' around on the far side of the log deck. Calling him out to Nena, she replied, "Yeah, he's with me."

The logging crew's kids were out of school and would ride out to the log landing now and then. B-Man and Nena grew up that way, I heard. A family tradition of loggin'. Anyhow, we kept our heads up for snoopy types and any unfamiliar rigs driving up or down the road. (Might be thieves, scopin' you out.) On this day, though—it would be our tired old cargo hook that would bite us. The day went just fine until the last cycle.

At the start of the *spin* cycle, I brought in the first two sixty-five-foot logs on two chokers, and as soon as their butts hit the ground, the rigging slap came. But the cargo hook's *keeper* failed to arrest the energy of the flinging steel shackle, spitting the two-hundred-foot wire-rope long-line out toward Nena—who was standing over someone not involved in logging. Someone in a plaid shirt.

I immediately radioed, "Look out!! Look out!!"

As the rigging fell toward her, Nena looked skyward, giving her a split-second to shove her young ward away and take the impact of the whistling line herself. It was hard to watch.

"*Nena is down!*" I radioed B-Man. "*The line got her. I'm going to land!*"

"*Come get me, first—there's a clearing right here,*" B-Man shot back.

There was a gathering around Nena by the time I set the hooking crew down at the log landing. Climbing out of the left seat, I took a look under "86," as we called the red, surplus Huey. The cargo hook's load beam was hanging partially open. I left that problem for our mechanic "Mike" to sort out and prepared the cabin's deck for a medevac.

B-Man had taken off running for Nena, who was writhing in pain the last I saw her. In minutes he was back, carrying Nena in his arms. No bleeding was evident, but her intense discomfort was plain enough to see. With the helicopter running, no time was wasted loading her onto the cargo deck on top of several sleeping bags.

With B-Man and a young man in a plaid shirt flying along for support, we spiraled upward—northbound for Ennis, as the Crummy spun out in pursuit. Following Wescor's emergency plan, I knew where to find the city's emergency clinic and radioed them our arrival time to get a gurney headed for the LZ.

There was no shortage of attention from the clinic as we touched down. In minutes, Nena was loaded onto the gurney and wheeled away. Since my mechanic was waiting for the ship back at the Service Landing, I secured the cabin for the solo return leg and took off.

After shut down, Mike Gambrill slid his supple self under "86" and took a hold of the cargo hook, flashlight between his teeth. "This hook is *wore-the-heck out!*" he exclaimed, almost swallowing the Maglite.

"I went down to the log landing earlier today and watched the riggin' spank the hook," Mike grumbled. "It wasn't designed for this kind of abuse." I agreed with his assessment and made note of the particulars in a detailed Incident Report. (I made no mention of the youngster in the plaid shirt.)

Hours later I drove back into town to check on our patient, and was very happy to learn Nena had already been discharged! Miraculously, there were no broken bones, but she had taken the full impact of the long-line on her left hip and all down her left leg. She was said to be swollen, bruised, and very sore.

Upon locating Nena's trailer at the RV camp, I knocked and found B-Man and kids gathered around her bed. I was so relieved to see her smile! With her help, I moved the bed sheet aside for a gander at her injury. *Hamburger on a stick.* (Ouch!)

It was to her credit, though, that Nena's muscles were in top physical condition from working hard her whole life. Though battered and bruised, her sturdy leg stood up to the punishment that would have hospitalized most people. Still, it would be awhile before her physical therapy was signed off and she could rejoin us on the log landing.

Not long afterward, Wescor ceased logging with Hueys and let the logging crews go. B-Man and Nena left Wescor and—as I did—hired on with Skyline's operation near the Fourth of July Pass in northern Idaho. By then we had graduated to a synthetic long-line and my hook was *tame*. It was good to be working with Nena again and giving her *sweet hooks* at the dusty log landing.

When the Skyline job was over, B-Man and Nena went home to Kamiah, Idaho to regroup. Later on, I heard that B-Man hired on with a concrete crew and Nena started working at the local café. Knowing her tendency to fly off the handle, more than one of her friends speculated how she might handle a mouthy customer. I learned through the grapevine that that job didn't last very long.

A year or so went by and I was heli-logging with Skyline in St. Regis, Montana when we got word that Nena had been diagnosed with cancer. I was shocked to hear the bad news, especially after seeing what good shape she was in—but cancer it was.

It came as a pleasant surprise one sunny day thereafter when B-Man and Nena stopped by St. Regis to visit their old loggin' buddies. We were off on Saturday, and durned if they didn't drive right into the cozy little KOA where most of us stayed.

Frankly, Nena never looked better. After a friendly hug, I asked about her battle with cancer. She had recently finished a round of chemo, but on her I saw none of the usual signs of frailness or hair loss. Indeed, her straw-colored lioness mane was thick and shone in the afternoon sunlight as we talked about the good ol' days.

When I asked about her chemotherapy, she sighed and admitted that she was truly dreading the next round. I tried my best to cheer her up and gave her my "go get 'em" speech, convinced that anyone as tough and resilient as Nena Wilkins had nothing long term to fear from cancer. I meant it, and I believed it. The Captain was wrong.

Nena left us on June 15, 2004, at the age of forty-two. She was buried next to her grandmother in Kamiah. Nena will long be remembered by her logging friends for her admirable work ethic and her toughness. Add to that long list, one ex-Marine helicopter mechanic and this old logging pilot. Amen!

On Getting Fired...

Captain Methane did *not* get fired for flinging that twelve-dollar Radio Shack digital oven timer out of the hole in his logging helicopter's bubble. The timer was intermittent, ergo undependable. But his stressed-out boss, parked at the Captain's *seven o'clock* in his burly Dodge Ram pickup, didn't know that. Looking back on it now, it must have looked plenty provocative from the viewpoint of a non-rated, small business *entrepreneur* who had paid dearly for everything within view—the troublesome timer, too.

Captain Methane—no stranger to stress—threw that sucker with extra angst to make *sure* it broke. That way, the mechanic would quit trying to "fix" it and hand the piece of crap back to him—as had happened twice already. Cheap (unsealed) timers get corroded internally in the harsh logging environment and turn into junk within a year's exposure, he noticed.

It broke into pieces, all right—and spit out its "AA" battery power source. Seeing it disintegrate and puke its battery out gave him a brief feeling of *revenge*. He was damned tired of it stopping in mid-cycle on him. They flew their loggin' Hueys down to the *fumes* six times a day, so if the fuel gauge—and/or the "low fuel" light—were to go gunnysack, the timer was his only salvation. (It *said* so in the FAA approved Company Logging Manual.)

There's no avoiding it—the *Captain* and *I* are one and the same.

The boss did *not* fire me over my long, reckless (uphill) dirt-and-gravel-showering burnout leaving the Service Landing in my Buick a few days later, but these kinds of events tend to add up. My puny little six-banger's front tires broke loose, churning furiously and peppering the side-panels with rocks. The few hands that were around that day got to see their pilot go temporarily insane. One noticed that he looked *pretty pissed*, that he mashed down real hard on the foot-feed. They got an eyeful, I reckon.

Personally, I thought at the time that I was doing a pretty good job of demonstrating my immense displeasure with a totally unanticipated fire-fighting assignment—far, far away. To cement my fate, my normally reliable relief pilot had *bailed* on me that morning. Something to do with an early morning, high-speed encounter with an elk that all but destroyed his cherished Chevy pickup. He was practically weepy over the damage and wobbled off down the road in a bald-headed funk, looking for a body shop.

It was head-wrench "Big Al" who relayed the boss's decision to shut down our once-happy little logging operation in beautiful western Montana. After all, the price for timber was at an all-time low. Clinton's N.A.F.T.A.[111] had made *imported* timber far more attractive to the few American log mills in the Northwest still in business. Not only was imported timber cheaper, Canadian outfits were giving the log mills up to four months to pay for the logs! Small businesses like ours were left to *fish* or *cut bait*.

Just days before—to make the boss's decision easier—a huge violent thunderstorm blew down most of the timber that was left standing in our current "sale," trapping most of our freshly bucked logs. Our religious boss probably decided it was a sign from above, and he pulled the plug.

The Captain's orders were to pack his bags and head for a stinkin' *project fire*[112] seven flight hours distant—another dry, featureless, dusty damned desert on fire. Who cared that the Captain had just driven 1,300 miles to a nice shady RV park, laid out his crusty sewer pipe all nice and pretty, hooked up his phone line to the freakin' World Wide Web, and stocked his little fridge with a week's worth of fresh groceries?

Who the heck cared?

111 North American Free Trade Agreement
112 A fire which has grown into a massive conflagration.

Nobody but me, pilgrim. However, the remnants of my laid-off logging crew did gather 'round my camper to see me off as I packed my bags again. There stood Pie-Cut, Tex, Johnny-wad, Hooker Doug, and the boys. And that relief-pilot-guy, too—for some reason.

To a man, they were keenly aware that I was *mentally retired*[113] from fighting fires and that I had carefully chosen an employer who—up until now—had lived by that policy. (Gypo[114] logging pilots take a severe pay cut when they trade their remote hook for a water bucket—and I figured I had already done my fair share of fighting fires, thank you just the same.)

I didn't get fired for screaming at Big Al and Hooker Doug that following October in central Idaho when I went *crazy* over radio interference problems. Somebody should have thrown a bucket of cold water on me, and I might not have offended two of my favorite work mates. I didn't know it at the time—but my PTSD was *back*, my blood pressure was *way* up there—and I'd never had much patience for radio problems in the first place. Al would eventually label this little episode *radio madness*, once we got back on speaking terms.

Yes friends, Captain Methane was near *losing it* (again) while his trusty mechanic tried to figure out *why* his super-dependable VHF radio frequency kept getting hammered by a loud squelching sound, in flight. What started as a small annoyance grew into a minute-to-minute ordeal. The strange, overriding noise blocked him from hearing his logging buddies, no matter which frequency they switched to. Production was weeks behind on this sale already, and our distant boss was turning the thumbscrews by remote control.

The ground crew couldn't hear the mysterious noise on their portable radios. Once it started, however, the Captain could no longer hear the hookers giving him critical information (advising him of *riders and slack chokers; I'm over here by this tree; you're on fire*) and other critical safety-related data. Regardless of the pressure frequently put upon gypo pilots to ignore such problems, he couldn't safely continue the way things were. He had to have dependable two-way radio communication—it says so in our *FAA-Approved Logging Manual*.

---

113 As in *burned out!*
114 Gypo – the handle loggers give to small logging operations.

Getting *"mad as a hatter,"*[115] I flew back and forth from Service to the logging strips trying to understand and resolve the problem. We tried the "aux" radio to help troubleshoot: *Rats!* It produced the same results. I kept hearing a maddening noise that sounded just like somebody spray-painting (loudly) with a macho spray gun. It would stop now and then, and I would think, At last! But back it would come, like an aggravating loop recording. Like somebody was jamming us![116]

To make Al's troubleshooting job more difficult, the noise wouldn't manifest itself if *Lorena's* skids were on the ground, but the moment she climbed a couple of hundred feet, there it was! Little did Al and I know, yours truly was about to *Hulk out!*

While I sat smoldering in the left seat, Al had me work the radio with the rotors turning at ground-idle for what seemed like forever—while he pored over the avionics wiring diagram in the heat of day. Then he listened methodically over his headset while wiggling one wire or co-ax cable after another, checking numerous wires around the Huey with his multi-meter.

Finally, after reaching the limit of his military training and civilian experience, Big Al whipped out his cell phone on the spot and called the owner of a certain radio shop in another state. A shop that had caused me a *very serious* problem in the past.[117] So when Al spoke the guy's name, I *snapped.*

Judging by the look on his freckled face, Al could not believe how I was ranting and raving! He was trying to give his radio tech a simple synopsis of the problem, but I was uncharacteristically furious and cussing loud enough for the technician to hear every word I said—over the racket of a Huey at flight idle.

Reaching the meltdown point, I locked down the collective, flipped on the *force trim*, added friction to the cyclic, and yanked my lap-belt open. Leaving the ship idling while I bailed out, I was beyond talking in a civil tone. Within minutes, Big Al, Hooker Doug, and I exchanged some choice,

---

115 Beaver-skin hat makers of old frequently went insane from absorbing mercury, a highly toxic chemical used in the tanning process.
116 We were not alone—a logging pilot two hundred miles away reported the exact same interference.
117 "A Boot Full of Trouble!" First published in *Aviation Maintenance Magazine*—November 2000.

heated words and I shut the helicopter down. I was too damned *mad* to fly, and I finally recognized the fact. I was soon climbing into that dusty old car of mine.

Thank goodness there was a long dirt and gravel road right there for Captain Methane to burn out on, again. He hit seventy mph on the narrow, bumpy, elevated farming road before the little Buick started vaulting and fishtailing. His heavy right foot came off the accelerator; the Captain checked his rage. He was mad enough to *kill*, all right—but in no hurry to *die*.

The Captain realized that an irresistible force was on course toward an immovable object, so he concentrated upon the dilemma once he got back inside his cozy camper. The radio noise problem had to be *grokked*, so he decided to consult his latest pile of H.A.I.[118] *Operations Update* pamphlets to see if *just maybe* there was a hint in there as to what might be going down in the big scheme of things.

And there it was! An easy-to-miss column devoted to informing pilots in the Western USA that the US military was *testing certain equipment* that might *interfere* with GPS navigation. The stuff was coming from selected locations in neighboring states, and interference was anticipated, *especially* at higher elevations! George W. and Tommy Franks were making preparations to kick Saddam's butt, you see—and the rest just fell into place.

Due to the way our ship's VHF radio, GPS and antennae were wired, we needed a rewired adapter plug for the Aux radio and a "private" code programmed into the main unit to block the military's noise. This was determined the next morning after flying the ship three hours cross-country to my *favorite* radio shop. *Sheesh!*

"Socket-head Joe," our overhaul shop's mechanic, met me after *Lorena* landed. Over lunch I asked Joe if Big Al had happened to mention "our little blow-up." Being a good friend of Al's, he didn't exactly say so, but he did ask me pointedly if I'd had my *blood pressure* checked, lately. I thought he was joshing me, of course. What would *hypertension* have to do with losing one's temper?

At least we solved the radio problem. But I knew things would never be the same between Big Al and me. So after the long ferry flight back to the

118 Helicopter Association International

sale, I got eye to eye with the man and told him that he and I "need to get a *divorce*." He was ahead of me on that issue, it turns out.

By Christmas time, I was still hangin' in there, somehow—but good timber sales were not coming our way. Destined for a scattered-out unit in central Washington State, I headed VFR cross-country out of Coeur d'Alene, Idaho one morning. I was flying the familiar, rough riding but allegedly "in-track" *Lorena*—our trusty old UH-1H—westbound into a thirty-knot headwind.

About an hour later—over the little town of Davenport, Washington—I had my first hydraulic failure in years. The sudden noisy *lurch*, bright *Master Caution* light on the panel, and the howling/cavitating hydraulic pump caught me flat-footed.

Although Socket-head and I had previously "dialed-in" the acorn nuts on *Lorena's* rotor-head, she was very hard to handle hydraulics off! Using all the muscle and body English available to me, I managed to get her turned around and headed back to Davenport's quiet little airstrip and into the stiff headwind; the final approach appeared to come in slow motion.

Lorena slid slowly into the soft, gooey mud of the old crop-duster landing strip. At a dead stop, she still read forty knots on the airspeed indicator. After cinching down her wildly rocking rotors, I took a long walk through the mud and endured yet another night in a strange, pink motel room. Our new wrench, "Dusty," arrived eventually, and by morning the repairs were done and we were off again and flying west toward Wenatchee.

It turns out that I would make two more hydraulic-less run-on landings before my two-week work shift was over. We "closed" the Cashmere, Washington airport twice in just over three days, as *Lorena* was marooned on the runway—waiting for parts and/or ground handling wheels.

And sports fans, when the Captain heard his long-time mechanic, Big Al, muttering the next morning about *"this chicken-shit outfit,"* he should have turned in his notice. Being the head wrench, Big Al had never even hinted that something might be rotten in Denmark. Since Al was a Christian at heart, I stood silently by and tried not to believe what I had just heard.

That third hydraulics failure was a *blue-haired bitch.*[119] After radioing my problem and intentions to "Tex," it was a long, stressful ten-minute flight from the logging strips to the airport. That was the closest suitable site in the mountainous valley, but in transitioning to descend over the northerly ravine ahead, I inadvertently let *Lorena* accelerate to one hundred knots... well beyond the recommended hydraulics-off maneuvering speed.

It was all an average-sized guy like me could do—reefing hard aft on the cyclic—literally bending the control stick back into my groin! *Lorena* grunted, whistled, and bucked, but her nose rose slowly, reluctantly inching upward—gradually slowing to eighty knots, and I began to breathe again.

Reaching the freshly snowplowed airstrip, it was all the Captain could manage, wrestling the collective pitch down to10-PSI torque—barely enough to make the empty ship descend. By the time he made the second go-around, he was sweating and breathing hard, and his spindly arms were beginning to shake from the exertion. *Lorena* wanted to float to the very end of the runway, where at last Captain Methane got the skids down and slid to an icy stop.

Later in the evening, Captain Methane detailed these rare, redundant incidents via email to another former Huey captain who lived in Arizona. They had been close friends for over thirty years—but unknown to Captain Methane—his old friend was about to be professionally diagnosed with *Acute Social Anxiety Disorder, Narcissistic Personality Disorder,* and *PTSD!* Having been shot down in Vietnam and badly injured in a JetRanger crash eleven years later, "Spanky" was operating a can or two short of a six-pack.

It turns out that Spanky's cheese had slid further off his cracker than Captain Methane ever thought possible. As Spanky read my troubling words on his flickering Macintosh monitor, he tried hard to recall how many close calls his old friend and former Army-pilot-buddy had lived through. *How many??*

As for the hydraulics phenomenon, each failure originated from the same exact hydraulic line fitting—in a foot-long piece of hydraulic tubing

---

119 A familiar logger's term for a bad experience.

located just under the ship's single hydraulic pump. The repair-work was performed by two different A&P mechanics using two different serviceable lines. Something was shaking that upper connection apart! Three times in the last thirty days—twice in the last ten flight hours. Spanky let it all sink in…

Spanky's eggshell brain sloshed the troublesome info around inside his pointed, shiny skull for a couple of weeks. *What to do with this worrisome data? If I don't do something to stop him, he'll just keep logging—and Captain Methane will be killed!* Spanky worried and fretted, suffering one anxiety attack after another—while popping little pills to help him cope.

Then it happened. Spanky decided to head off Captain Methane at his home before he started back on that long road to Washington. (I had already left, but that didn't matter.) He had lost the battle raging within his loopy gray matter—the lobe that deals with restraint and logic. Spanky picked up the telephone early that Saturday morning and called my wife, who was blissfully ignorant of any such problem, or even *one* emergency landing!

And before you can say "Great Leaping *Lunatics*," he brought Lourdes to tears with his credible forecast that a poorly maintained helicopter would soon kill her ill-fated husband. Having managed to reduce her to a blubbering carbon unit in short order, he convinced her to dig up the logging company's private phone numbers, and he went to work.

Two days later and none the wiser, Captain Methane unpacked his weary bags inside his frosty motor home—parked in a snowbank in eastern Washington. By early evening he had his groceries unloaded and his laptop plugged in. The ISP delivered his e-mail and *up jumped the devil*, in black and white! There was an electronic confession from a madman! A horrifying admission, spelled out in a long, self-deprecating message from Captain Spanky. Words to this effect:

> *I am so sorry! Two days ago I called your wife, thinking you were still at home. When I realized I had missed my chance to persuade you to quit your logging job, I told Lourdes about all of your emergencies and that you apparently have a death wish. She broke down into tears, and I convinced her to give me the private cell phone number for your boss… and the one to reach his wife. I then called them individually and told them*

*that I knew all about your emergencies and **BEGGED** them to **LAY YOU
OFF** before something else breaks and you come falling out of the sky
and are killed by their 'lousy maintenance!' Now I realize that I probably
shouldn't have done so without your okay and I hope you will forgive me
because— after all—I was only **looking out for you**...[etc. etc.]*

Reeling from this incredible revelation, I spewed forth a choice string of
Thai, Hispanic, Army, and logging obscenities at the little screen, just inches
from my disbelieving Okie eyeballs. I then reached for the company cell
phone. The boss and his wife both had Caller ID, so it was no surprise that
neither would pick up the phone.

Leaving each a long, sincere, recorded message, I offered them my
apologies—assuring them that I loved and valued my job and that I just
could not believe that a trusted friend would betray my confidence, intrude
into their business, and take such liberties in the guise of friendship.

To his credit, my boss called me two days later. I quickly brought up the subject,
but he soft-pedaled the fallout of Spanky's upsetting and bizarre phone calls.
He changed the subject, asking about my mom's latest health report.

The boss knew that my ailing, ninety-year-old mother was about to check
out in an Oklahoma rest home, and two days later he arranged for my
relief when Jesus finally came for her. Following a long, bleak, cross-
country drive, I attended her funeral service in Ardmore, Oklahoma.
Financially stretched to the limit, I had no means to take Lourdes or the
kids with me. Within a few days, I was back in eastern Washington to work
yet another logging shift.

A few days later, "Crash"—a considerably drunk timber sawyer (and a
former hooker friend of mine)—stumbled through my camper's doorway
on a snowy evening, and dropped the bomb:

*"They're out to git you, Bingo! Big Al and Hooker Doug. I think they suck.
You're one of the few pilots I like. You're easy on the forest and the chopper.
Jus'h thought you oughta know, pal."* And with that, he vanished into the
swirling snowflakes, and the cold blackness of midnight.

Try as I might to dismiss the echoing words of an inebriated sawyer, I
knew the man well. And because I'd never screamed at him, he was still

my friend. I didn't sleep a wink that night, and almost fell asleep at the controls the next day. Facing them at last, Al and Doug unconvincingly denied the rantings of a drunken woodsman.

Walking on thin ice, I finished my shift—then the ax fell. The boss called it a *lay-off.* He had Dusty help me locate a U-Haul car-towing dolly to trailer my car home. Early the next morning, I was headed south down the long, familiar road in my crusty motor home, the little Buick trailing right behind me.

This "lay-off" thing went on and on. While waiting for the boss to call me back to work, I learned through the grapevine that *Lorena* had been sent to the shop for extensive repairs. Weeks turned into months, all the while the little company continued logging with *Blue Duck,* the other Huey—and *without* Captain Methane, their original, FAA-approved chief pilot and designated external-load pilot. It said so, right there in the Logging Manual! As if that mattered anymore.

So there it is, my fellow logging pals and confidants. The Gypos had had enough of the madman, and his hysterical friend, *Spanky.* And soon enough, I learned that the Logging Manual had been revised, designating a new chief pilot. Captain Methane had been cut loose. Thank you so much, boss—for letting me know.

The Line

After my third hydraulic failure in less than thirty days, I realized that my Huey logging career was either going to kill me or put me in a wheelchair. A long list of dead or crippled logging pilots preceded me, several that I knew personally.[120] A savvy tree faller they called "One-eyed Donnie" summed it up best: "We're in the *hard-on industry*, Wingo. Logging is *hard on machinery* and *people!*"

I knew the risks. The money earned over several danger-filled years had recently paid off my Chapter 13 bankruptcy, but living to finish the book I was working on and see my kids grow up was what really mattered. As timber prices plummeted, I suspected that some worn-out and timed-out parts were staying bolted to the helicopter; yet the wrenches kept signing her off every morning while the boss cracked the whip. The stress finally got to me; good working relationships became a distant memory, and, as described in the previous chapter, I was gone.

Lourdes was happy to welcome her husband home again, but there were no *real* flying jobs for me in the local area. My old friend Pete lamented that there wasn't an opportunity for me at Western Helicopters. His busy little flight school was home to two or three senior certified flight instructors. There was just enough outside lift work for Pete to handle

---

120   See Section IX

with his MD 500D, and I knew there was no budget for another full-time utility pilot.

As our meager savings disappeared, short-term, low-paying flying jobs popped up here and there. A long flight to Chiapas, Mexico to fight fires for two weeks, and seismic work in faraway places kept me busy, but the pay was best described as *entry level*. Returning home for Christmas 2003, were those dark circles I saw under my lover's eyes? I was depressed, and I sensed it was infectious.

My wonderful mother had passed away the previous February. Ninety years old, she had managed her tiny teacher's salary and retirement meticulously. After a few months in the rest home, her money was running out. As her four children circulated a plan to begin picking up her expenses, she checked out—illustrating one last time how things should be done.

At her Valentine's Day funeral service, Blanche's Church of Christ pastor spoke rhetorically of her life and her children—eventually turning to me. As my tears streamed liberally into my suit collar, he admonished me: "You should finish your book!" Even in death, Mother was the motivating matriarch.

Blanche joined our father, James Beauford Wingo, that afternoon in Hennepin's tiny cemetery—before an impressive gathering of friends and family.

Months later, proceeds from the sale of Mom's little house in Ardmore were divided among her children, temporarily silencing our howling debtors. Her final gift also paid for some long delayed repairs on our 1959 vintage home, and got us through one more Christmas.

As New Year's approached, we anxiously awaited the arrival of my long-time literary friend Matt Thurber, his wife, and two daughters. They had flown from Maryland to southern California for a family reunion in Poway. Sadly, his father-in-law (who had just flown in from Guam) became seriously ill. With his untimely hospitalization, Matt had to cancel, and we lost a rare opportunity to discuss the publication of *Wind Loggers*, an anthology of my helicopter tales.

With all the Christmas house lights a-blinking, Lourdes went to visit her sisters and the kids did likewise to their friends, and the Captain slipped into a funk. I decided to drive across the valley to see an old friend. A successful artist, he had no DOT[121] license to lose and was known to self-prescribe an ancient herbal remedy for depression.

His conversation was inspiring, and in short order I was temporarily transformed into a euphoric state of mind—lifting me out of my holiday doldrums. But the remedy left some microscopic metabolites behind in my system: diminutive *smoking guns*.

Returning home, there was a message waiting on the answering machine: an old friend had called while I was out and offered to put me back to work (for a *month*, anyway) four hundred miles away. Though it paid *peanuts*, I was bound by the terms of unemployment to accept, and was soon loading up the trunk for yet another dangerous hiatus away from my family.

Arriving the next day to check out the JetRanger, I was disappointed to see that there was no VertRef[122] bubble on the pilot's door. Here it was, the beginning of January, and I had complained about the lack of a bubble door back in Texas, when it was still November.

I visualized freezing my butt off while flying five hours per day. Resigned to my fate, I bundled up and prepared to negotiate my way around the power line-strewn oil field with a hundred-foot long-line, hauling cargo to the hardworking crews. Alas, I had no cold weather goggles, something I taught my younger pilots to always carry.

As the rising sun hit me square in the face, I headed for the first drop point, following the ship's sophisticated satellite guidance system. Hovering slowly down into a dark valley, a power line came into view as the radio came alive.

"Do you see the power line?" The worker waiting for my cargo near the drop site was correct to inquire, and I assured him: "I've got the power line."

Maneuvering just shy of the two-hundred-foot span of wires, my cockpit display indicated another thirty meters to the invisible "target." Applying power

---

121 Department of Transportation, which governs the Federal Aviation Administration.
122 Vertical Reference—Keeps the cold wind and weather off the pilot while he's looking down.

to raise the load up and over the energized wires, the chilly morning air hit my bifocals and the tears began to flow!

Not the first time, I reminded myself, as I shook my head and blinked hard to regain my focus on the wires. Judging that the load was safely above the span, I eased the cyclic forward. One more blurred look downward, and I was stunned to see the load meet the wires, pushing them a trifle in the direction I was headed.

I immediately applied aft cyclic, but the arcing and sparking had already begun. In microseconds the whole span was aglow and dancing around like Shakira's little butt.

The power line melted, then fell into a smoking heap in the shadows. My heart sank, and as I levitated my blackened load back into the sunlight, I radioed to all within radio range, "Well, *shit*…I just took out the power line! It's on the ground. I'm returning to the staging area."

The customer's honchos soon arrived in their gleaming new pickups as I shut the JetRanger down and faced the music. I described the tear problem, debunked any fault of the ground crew, and told them it was totally my error.

"We're not using the chopper again until you guys get a bubble door on this thing," was the project manager's gruff response.

The senior safety officer, "Alfonso" (not his real name) soon arrived and I handed him a hastily penned Incident Report, underlining *pilot error* at the bottom of the page, next to my signature.

"Takes a *man* to say that," Alfonso said kindly. With an apology, he asked me to follow him back to town for the standard post-accident drug screening exam.

Alfonso met me in his motel room slash office and soon produced a sealed commercial drug-screening kit. From it he extracted a beaker for a urine sample. I went into the lavatory and did my thing while he softly hummed a friendly *Frontera* tune and waited patiently.

The last item to be unwrapped was a MedTox urine receptacle, an innocuous-looking little device which Alfonso laid on the desk in front of us. Using a sterile eyedropper, he carefully transferred three golden drops of Captain-pee onto both channels of the MedTox receptacle. He turned to me and said, "This'll just take a few minutes. I'm real sorry we have to put you through this."

"Not a problem, Alfonso. I understand," I said, wondering now if the high-tech-looking device would discover my indiscretion from New Year's. "I was the anti-drug officer for two different companies," I assured him. "I've written the manuals and have been to the seminars. You're doing it just right."

With this revelation, Alfonso began chatting like an old friend while my pee began producing small lines along the pair of parallel channels in the receptacle. *Lines* were *good. No* lines were *not* good. He continued our conversation, periodically glancing at the unit with a feigned disinterest.

"We'll wait a little longer, these things are sometimes slow," he added. I sat in the hot seat listening to the gentleman—who was about my age—but my mind was on one little line that wasn't coming into view. I was feeling the heat.

Alfonso began describing the problems he was having with his own sons. "The kids, they smoke the *marijuana*," he said softly, like the word made him sick. "It is a big problem. And the *ecstasy*."

I nodded, waiting for the other shoe to drop.

Standing now over the aging test, Alfonso picked it up and strode slowly over to the window, bent over. He was straining to see a line that wasn't there, right next to the THC[123] symbol. He offered me a look.

"My eyes are bad, can you see a line there?"

"I see no line," I answered, handing him back the unit.

"Would you like to do another one? These things are not fool-proof."

"Let's do another one," I suggested, my heart sinking.

More drops from the same beaker were dropped carefully into a new MedTox strip, and within minutes the same results. No line beside "THC."

"Now what?" I asked.

123   THC—the chemical derivative of cannabis.

Alfonso asked softly, "Is it possible you were recently around someone who was smoking *weed*? Second- hand smoke can do this, you know."

I stood up, pacing slowly around the room, my arms crossed in front of me, nodding ever so slightly. I knew what the policy was: Flunk, and you're *gone*.

"I think it's time I packed my bags and headed home, amigo. I'm really in shock about all this, and embarrassed. I'm very sorry for all the trouble."

"You're doing the right thing," he said. "What happens here is confidential. We don't tell any *agencies*. But I'll have to inform your employer, of course."

Collecting my new Professional Helicopter Pilots Association ball cap, I headed slowly up the stairs and began the arduous job of repacking my bags for a long trip home. Giving my boss some time to hear from Alfonso, I emailed Lourdes a brief message before closing up the laptop:

"Things are pretty screwed up here, my darling. Daddy's coming home. I'll try to explain when I get there."

An hour later, with the motor running, the old Buick's orange *Service Engine* light glowing brightly, I made the dreaded (short, apologetic) phone call to my boss. He was as kind (and brief) as anyone could have been under the circumstances.

Tossing the cell phone onto the floorboard, I headed down the long, twisted road to Rialto.

Lorena Bites the Loader

*   *"All good things must come to an end..."*

February 23rd it was, Ought Four. One year to the day after heli-logging's legendary S-61 Captain Griffin "Skip" Fisk crashed and burned in his Sikorsky, leaving all who knew him in a state of shock.

It would be on Skip's anniversary—his widow's birthday—that *Lorena* slashed her last victim: a huge, heavy, track-mounted, yellow steel log loader. One of my favorite A&P mechanics called me the day after she augered in. "Larry" telephoned from Bonner's Ferry, Idaho to let me know my old bird was totaled, and his relief stint near Liberty, Washington was now a moot point.

According to the *Northern Kittitas County Tribune*, her logging pilot would survive. "Shlomo" was conscious and breathing after the accident, and was treated for facial lacerations. He complained of chest and back pain, and was transported to a hospital in Wenatchee.

Ten months had expired since I was "laid off" by my old logging outfit, and frankly, I was surprised that *Lorena* had held up that long. I had sadly forecast her quick demise to a close friend or two, after leaving her in the hands of some *yankers* and *bankers*—determined to haul wood like no logging pilot before them.

Her resurrection began in 1999, starting as a worn-out logging veteran. By August, she was a refurbished, OAS *cardable* and fire-ready UH-1H Bell/Garlick helicopter, with all the whistles and bells a logging pilot could want. Considering *Lorena's* composite blades, tail boom strakes, and a couple of those superior retrofitted transmissions, she was *lean and mean.*

"Don't f_ _ k with Lorena," I jested with the boss while suggesting her new name. "If you do, she'll cut off your [easily severed male anatomical member]!" A religious man, the boss laughed out loud—the first and last time I heard him do so, as "Big Al" transferred the black letter decals onto her cabin's sides—Lorena was finally ready to resume logging.

A mere 1,658 days later, Shlomo had the dubious honor of gliding *Lorena* to her death, but he took a lickin' and was listed in the NTSB report as *serious.* It hadn't been much over a year that his Sikorsky S-61 mysteriously flamed out "with 250 lbs. of fuel indicated *per side,*" one report said. That had to be one *quiet helicopter* for a few seconds. Igor didn't make it back to Service that day, but I hear both pilots walked away.

My vacancy at the old logging outfit created a convenient opening for Shlomo to fill, but switching to Huey loggin' didn't improve his luck. Following *Lorena* to her grave in the log deck had to be a *blue-haired bitch.*

I pondered the Preliminary NTSB report and translated it into my own personal imaginary Huey hologram: *Shlomo is bringing in the load of logs; everything is just peachy. He reefs aft and right on the cyclic and milks in collective pitch as Lorena's vectored thrust brakes and lowers her very last load. In the midst of placing the logs close to the loader, a loud bang is heard as her tail rotor's "slider"*[124] *allegedly fails!*

Under the heavy load, both unhindered tail rotor blades pitch out radically, liberated from their pitch restraints. Spinning near the speed of sound, the blade-tips make contact with the forward pylon that protects the upward-angled forty-two-degree drive shaft, twisting the shaft in half. The attached tail rotor system quickly ceases to rotate and, kinda like Captain Shlomo, is now along for the rude ride to the ground.

---

124 An essential component of the "Ninety Degree" gear box, which transfers tail rotor pedal movement to the tail rotor blades.

Shlomo lowers the collective pitch, following through as Lorena makes two frightful 360-degree turns to the right, long-line attached. At approximately 150 feet over the ground, Shlomo rolls off the throttle and then the main fuel switch, as the 1967-era helicopter wop-wop-wops to her last landing, just behind the loader and next to the log deck.

Lorena's ability to defy gravity is finally exhausted. Her composite main rotor blades smash into the loader's thick, steel engine housing and the uppermost logs in the deck—knocking Shlomo's fillings loose and giving the ground crew a wake-up call they'll never forget.

Logger Doug was hiking nearby at the time and told me later over the phone, "It sure got quiet after the tail rotor quit turnin': just an eerie, droning sound," he recalled. Until Lorena's main rotor blades kissed the loader—then there was Hell on Earth for a few more seconds.

The loader operator had laid the boom down moments prior to the helicopter's approach. He was working on a redundant hose-fitting problem at the grapple end of things when *Lorena* made like the *Huey from Hell* above him, slicing her way down to clobber his loader! Nearby, the chasers and knot-bumpers *beat feet*, wasting no time to dart behind the nearest tree/truck/boulder for the impending impact of their aerial crane.

Courtesy of USFS

The accident occurred around a quarter to one in the afternoon. After seeing Shlomo off to the hospital and notifying the authorities, repairs were started on the loader to make it operable. They would need the loader to place *Lorena* on a flatbed trailer, and once she was out of the way, the log deck could be loaded onto log trucks. After it snowed a bit.

A few days later I had to call up my old boss. Some of the totals on my W2 form didn't quite jibe with my calculations, and I was trying to file my 2003 return. It had been many months since I'd spoken with the boss, and I wasn't sure he'd be helpful. Answering the phone, there was no hint of any old differences. The boss was more than helpful in resolving the numbers on the W2 form and—logically—*Lorena* came into the conversation. "Yeah, she's gone," he sighed, wistfully.

The boss said Shlomo was recovering, "...almost ready to go logging again," which was good to hear. He mentioned the newspaper article and offered to send me a copy. I thanked the boss and wished him luck.

The Tribune showed up a few days later along with a half-dozen professional-looking *before* and *after* shots of a badly battered *Lorena* sleeping in the snow, then loaded on the trailer, sans tail boom. Up in the nose, Big Al's fancy sheet metal dual-battery box had stood up well, but everything around it sorta collapsed. The old gang was captured standing frozen as they surveyed the wreck, hands in pockets. *Lorena's* shattered main rotors hinted at the tremendous energy that had so easily destroyed them.

Curious as to why the slider failed, I waited a polite week or so and then started asking the usual questions. One mechanic I talked to (who probably wouldn't want me using his name) told me the slider had allegedly been purchased off the Internet, and may not have come with the proper airworthiness tags. Price may have been the issue, as it often is when a small business flirts with insolvency.

At any rate, it was allegedly *months* before the boss's insurance company paid the settlement on *Lorena*. Meanwhile, his dwindling crew limped along with the last Huey in the fleet, another Bell/Garlick UH-1H pseudo named *Blue Duck*.

I don't know for sure what the boss is up to lately, but I heard he was turning wrenches for the notorious logging pilot *Uncle Milty*—his partner from the old Husky logging days. They make quite a pair. Not many loggers outwork those two.

I often wonder about my old loggin crew—*The "A" Team*, we called ourselves. Darned good men, for the most part. Laid off again, eh boys? It's kinda like Jeffro told me down in Raton last April, his four girls clustered around the sofa: *"I liked Montana; I just couldn't eat it."*

Hear tell "Big Al" up and headed for Vegas. Lordy, there's a commute for you. I used to drive the back course to Missoula through Bishop-Tonopah back when we were still loggin' buddies. (Lordy, how things do come 'round, like them twirlin' rotors…)

Rumor Control reported that the bank and the boss agreed to park *Blue Duck*. She's allegedly sitting in a hangar now—somewhere in Montana—waiting for a wheelbarrow full of cash to arrive so the wind loggers can resume grapple logging…or go fight more of them stupid fires.

The boss may still have his parts shop in the Missoula area. Word is, *Lorena* has gone to pasture there—a grand hotel for the field mice—out in the tall grass and stinging nettles, near an old wire fence, sleeping soundly.

(I sure loved that old Huey.)

Section IX:
Old Friends, Pain, and Closure

In Memoriam

**This page is dedicated to my fellow logging pilots
who have paid the ultimate price for defying gravity.**

Rest in Peace:

Paul "Hollywood" Bryant" Earl Burlhanz * William "Bart" Colantuono
Joe Cook * L. Marshall Couvillier III * Robert S. "Bob" Davis
Kevin C. Doll * Craig Dunn * William S. "Bill" Fife
Griffin E. "Skip" Fisk * Mike Golden * Ken Graves
Loren L. Groetzke * "Rockin" Robin Kennedy * Roy D. "Dan" Kettle
Jack Wesley Klein * Jim Ladd * Thomas A. "Tom" Leitz
Hugh McKay * Donald J. "Don" Nepereny * Jack J. Ruby
Danny L. "Dog" Salin * Carson N. Snow III
William R. "Bill" Wehling * Kirk Zowasky

And still with us:
Wheelchair Pilot: Jay Worman

[My apologies to the families of any helicopter logging pilots I may have missed. Author]

Flash Sikorsky

*   a.k.a. William R. Wehling

Bill told me once over a *Cuba Libre*—poured with his favorite Captain Morgan's Rum—that it was his Region VI Forest Service Helitack crew who named him *Flash Sikorsky*, back 'round 1980 or so. (Being such a flamboyant personality, they couldn't just call him "*Bill!*")

He was piloting a Sikorsky-55T turbine conversion in a time that the formerly piston-powered four wheelers were fairly common on fires. Lots of room for passengers, shovels, and chainsaws in the hold, with the happy pilot tucked away above the engine. The S-55 was considered a fine machine; but even then, it was showing its age.

William R. Wehling, or "Bill" to his friends, stood a couple of inches taller than I. He was what I would call aristocrat material. Bill had an air about him, a way with words that attracted friends and helped pave many roads. Alas, two of them were roads he would wish he had never started down.

We first met on a frozen, windswept seismic job in the dead of winter near Kemmerer, Wyoming, in the late seventies. Both of us were flying for the same Utah-based helicopter outfit. Somewhere in my collection there's a thirty-year-old snapshot, the first I ever took of Flash.

When I chuckled and said, *"Smile, Bill,"* he was twenty feet away, relieving himself on the logo of the company's fuel truck. He seemed to have a bone of contention to pick with his employer, but I stayed out of it. Thereby, and through a grand sense of humor, we got along great together.

We were both brimming with stories to tell of our adventures, and *Flash* told his with a suave delivery and an authoritative flair. He had picked up a considerable medical education of sorts in over a year of hospitalization. His Latin was in good shape! Bill was admittedly charmed by my beautiful Spanish-speaking wife, Lourdes, and vice versa.

We almost never talked about Vietnam, but I remember him rattling off the names of cities around Southeast Asia I'd only heard about. He had visited or lived in more than a few of them; Vientiane, Laos among them. His knowledge of their cultures and political persuasions was impressive. Bill's manner and tone of delivery convinced the listener that he was hearing the naked truth, much in the way Walter Cronkite does it.

It was a couple of years later that I happened to share a motel room overnight with Flash Sikorsky. I don't remember where we were staying, but I recall I was watching the evening news when Bill warned me he was about to expose his *AK-47 wounds*. He was on his way to the shower.

(Warning me was the right thing to do!) Exceedingly few people endure what William R. Wehling went through and live to tell about it. Seeing the damage done to him firsthand reminded me how lucky I've been in war.

Bill served with the 128th AHC in Vietnam in 1970 and '71. I know virtually nothing about his tour of duty there, but I believe he completed his military obligation without earning a Purple Heart. He returned home like most of us, relatively in one piece.

It was sometime afterward that Bill went down one of those roads I was talking about earlier; he hired on with a new outfit out of Arizona. The Company had helicopters in use in war-torn Southeast Asia, and the money and machinery were said to be good.

They were hiring former Vietnam combat pilots to help fill in for the kind of work that might be performed by Air America in Cambodia and Laos. As the war ground on, Air America's role in the war became a political tempest; villages on the fringe began to fall to the enemy.

It was at this volatile juncture in the war that Bill signed on for what amounted to mercenary work. In Bill's mind, it must have sounded attractive over the phone. He hadn't been in-country long when he was called upon to fly some local officials around in a five-seat Bell 206 JetRanger. They wanted to check out a remote location *thought* to have been infiltrated by the North Vietnamese Army (NVA).

Arriving at the scene, Bill flew reconnaissance. At some point in the mission, he was called on to fly low and slow, checking out a trail or something in a clearing, when he saw a camouflaged NVA soldier—"*pith helmet and all*"—stand up in the waist-high grass not fifty feet off his nose. The soldier aimed an AK-47 assault rifle directly at him. The soldier had apparently been hiding and didn't have to be told that the helicopter was not on his side.

The NVA soldier fired the Kalashnikov with deadly precision. The chopper was a sitting duck.

Flash had no chest armor and took three rounds in the gut. Devastated by the gunfire, he somehow summoned every molecule of his being to bear the shock and pain, tearing away as low and as fast as he could fly as more weapons opened up in their wake. Splattered throughout with their pilot's flesh and blood, his passengers were rightfully horrified with this turn of events and pleaded with Bill to get them on the ground before he bled to death at the controls!

Bill's guardian angel might have missed his first opportunity, but he performed admirably thereafter. Bill was able to stay at the controls long enough to cross the river into Thailand, where he landed his panicky passengers safely. He was quickly carried to a nearby shelter. Someone ran to fetch the local medicine man. The sawbones came running with a big hypodermic needle and injected Bill with a load of morphine, and he passed out.

Following "a seemingly endless ordeal," Bill was evacuated to the Philippines. The doctors there had little personal experience with the degree of complicated surgical reconstruction necessary to repair Bill. It would take eight months (and some *experimental surgery*) before the remnants of his large and small intestines were reconnected and re-suspended.

Amazingly, Bill healed well enough to begin flying again a year or so later - with an FAA Class One flight physical!

I remember that Bill's first wife—a pretty blonde—had disturbing mental problems, by his vivid descriptions; a shocking revelation, but then, we were always frank with one another.

"She has been institutionalized," he sighed. The divorce came later, their dream derailed.

They had a daughter named Chevis whom he dearly loved and customized his work schedule around, in order to provide for her and their Michigan apartment. I never met Chevis in the twenty years I knew Bill, but he showed me billfold photos of her from time to time.

Bill and I shared our intimate thoughts about flying, the helicopter business, women, wine, *The Fabulous Furry Freak Brothers,*[125] and the meaning of life in general. When the seismic boom went bust, we went our separate ways. We made each other laugh, though, so there were still random phone calls to keep in touch, and the occasional letter.

Two years later, I was flying a desk as the Director of Operations for Western Helicopters in southern California. I had just finished talking to an unemployed Flash Sikorsky on the telephone. We didn't have a flying contract for Bill at the time, but the very next gentleman to call was *"looking for a good Hughes 500 pilot"* for an offshore job in Singapore!

I assured the entrepreneur at the other end of the line that Bill Wehling was the right man for the job, and I put them in contact with each other, no strings attached. Bill hired on for the assignment and was able to take his daughter with him. He told me years later "...that was probably the best job I ever had." It was nice to be able to make the match for an old friend.

When the overseas job played out some time later, Bill found his way home again and started working as an air ambulance pilot. He was finally able to put his hard-earned Airline Transport Rating and instrument ticket to good use, flying the latest Twin Dauphin helicopter for a hospital in

125 A popular underground comic book by cartoonist Gilbert Shelton.

Grand Rapids, Michigan.

Bill mailed us a fine letter soon after—brimming with humor, rhetorical prose, and acidic barbs for anyone in authority—along with a photo of his two-million-dollar helicopter sitting on an icy hospital helipad.

Turns out, Flash had had an emergency of his own a few months before, when his old machine gun wounds ruptured internally and touched off a deadly toxic-shock situation. Fortunately, he was in the hospital environment at the time and was quickly diagnosed and whisked into surgery.

When his recovery was complete, Bill returned to flight duty. Reading between the lines of his long letter, I got the impression Flash was growing tired of the city environment and yearned once again for a long-line job— and aerial adventure out west.

He told me later over another of his famous *Cuba Libres* that one of the doctors at the hospital had made him take "several" random piss tests after noting that Flash was an avid reader of *The Freak Brothers* comic books. He passed all his drug tests, of course—frustrating his detractor to no end.

Bill was a *straight agent* in those days; most commercial pilots were subject to random and post-accident urinalysis by then and he conducted himself in a responsible manner. That was the way Bill's mind worked—he would always be a gentleman, but he could go out of his way to get someone's goat, if they failed to treat *him* the same.

When yours truly decided to become a heli-logger in '93, Bill was coincidentally contacting the same potential employers I was, and darned if we didn't end up in Thorne Bay, Alaska, flying together early that summer. Our employer, however, had had his share of problems over the course of the past few months. There were deaths involved and we found ourselves filling vacancies in a forested island of anguish.

The Thorne Bay location included a *dry* logging camp, meaning no beer, no booze, etc. Somehow that rule was being overlooked—there *was* a State of Alaska Liquor Store two hundred feet across the lot, after all—but any drinking that went on in camp was done discreetly. That is, until the new chief logging pilot showed up.

The Chief had his little brown paper sack in one hand; despite himself, he wobbled when he walked. We knew from previous experience, inside that paper bag was his favorite alcohol mixture: half *Wild Turkey* and half *Peppermint Schnapps*. He must have started chuggin' early because it was only four in the afternoon and the *Chief* was already seven sheets to the wind.

The Chief was a shorter guy of medium build who fancied himself a "black belt karate expert," but lately he just drank like a fish. That very likely had something to do with having to help bury three of his fellow logging pilots; his predecessor among them. One month after the latest funeral, he was still dealing with the losses; the sobering reality that he worked in a dangerous occupation.

Yet here the man was flagrantly drunk, taking snorts from his plain paper bag in plain sight of our logging crew, as they climbed out of the Crummy. He cursed needlessly at one of my sober hookers passing by, figuring he needed to display some *sack*—seein' as how he was a *black belt*. "*Heads up, mother f'er!*" he growled.

When he and his paper sack finally plopped down on the edge of Bill's bunk—allegedly to lecture two former Vietnam combat pilots on the dangers of helicopter logging—the Chief's jaw hung slack and his eyes began twitching horizontally, no longer able to conduct his safety lecture or focus his pupils.

Bill and I exchanged glances, stood up, and announced, "Well, gotta run," and we left the Chief sitting there to figure it out for himself. Neither one of us had much patience for a mean-spirited drunk, *Chief* or no.

We saw little of the Chief over the next couple of days—thankfully. Bill and I started logging together in the Bell "Super 204" helicopter that the Company trained in, teaching ourselves how to haul big logs and clusters of logs efficiently, without scaring everyone—including ourselves—to death. We would trade seats during refueling, taking turns as pilot in command.

Eventually, the chief logging pilot returned, flying a mighty Bell 214B—the last of three that had started the logging operation. The other two were in the Company's "bone yard" in Ketchikan, dripping rain; broke beyond fixing.

"Who wants to go loggin'?!" the Chief barked in my direction, helmet in hand.

The Chief and I took off for the big island west of Ketchikan, a fairly short helicopter flight across some very cold, scary, deep water. I had flown with the Chief before and found him to be an adequate enough pilot, but a tough guy at heart and a humorless soul—something that makes flying a helicopter alongside of him a *job* instead of a pleasure. (Bill kept logging in the 204 and, for the first time in years, didn't have any complaints!)

At Bill's next *Cuba Libre* meeting in his bunkroom, we debated the merits of logging in the 214—with the Chief. Maybe it was better to continue "training" in the 204 single pilot and avoid the Chief problem altogether. If not, we'd have to rotate flying right seat with the Chief and get our fillings hammered. He was famous for ignoring the scale,[126] reverting back to the macho technique of flying logs that helped get the outfit into their current situation.

Things worked out okay for both of us, over time. The Chief left the 214 logging to us and went to flying Skycranes. I grew proficient in the 214B and—following the Alaska job—went around the Northwestern USA on private timber sales and fire salvage contracts. Bill also moved down to the Northwest and continued logging in the 204 on the same jobs with the 214, awaiting his opportunity to graduate to the Big Bell.

I finally got the opportunity to check Bill out in the 214B in January of '94 on a logging sale near Rimrock, Washington. Skip Fisk was flying a Skycrane off the same huge log-and-service landing, so we often had a daisy chain going, bringing in more timber in a day than I'd ever seen.

Bill had himself a serious girlfriend by then, a lovely (blond) college grad by the name of Cheryl Amos who enjoyed following Flash Sikorsky around the logging camps of the Northwest.

By that time I had added a thirty-two-foot motor home to my logging inventory. Like me, Bill was sick of giving his money to the motel clerks and eating at truck stops and cafés, so we worked out a deal to share the motor home. We designed the schedule to relieve each other every two weeks, turning over the keys along with a list of groceries on hand.

---

126 Aircraft scales advise the pilot of overweight loads, which should be bucked-up into reasonable weights.

Cheryl was a great homemaker. She brought her little white doggy *Shasta* along on road trips and usually had Flash's favorite dinner waiting when he poured out of the helicopter of an evening. The motor home had all the conveniences and plenty of room for two, plus Shasta.

This arrangement wouldn't last for long, because Cheryl was an ambitious lady. She had worked hard for her Masters in Hospital Administration and was examining employment opportunities on the west coast while Bill brought in the bacon.

Alas, we both saw the writing on the wall for our current employer. Things had been going badly for too long. There were many rumors of the Company's impending collapse. The ax finally fell in June of '94, with a short phone call from Chief Pilot Rick Leishman, who had hired me in '93. "Nobody has a job anymore," he would have me believe. Many never received their last month's paycheck or expenses.

What followed was a tumultuous time for over a dozen former logging pilots, mechanics, and their families. We found ourselves unemployed overnight and facing a long, hot, summer. We were unfortunately all out scrambling for work at the same time. I found it difficult to rope anything solid for about three months, and by then, Bill had gone one way and I the other.

Cheryl became Mrs. William R. Wehling in 1994. I got a formal wedding invitation, but the big affair was back East, and I was in debt, making up for lost time. Around then, Bill was working for a logging outfit out of Olympia, Washington. (The pilot was the ramrod for each heli-logging crew at that time, an excellent arrangement—once the pilot assembles a good crew.)

There was an opening on Bill's crew for a woods boss position one day, and the guy who dropped by to fill it just happened to have been the Project Manager (PM) for our old defunct 214 logging outfit. Bill didn't like the guy for personal reasons and said "No" when "Mike's" name came up. So Mike was sent packin' and Bill hired someone else.

In a regrettable example of *what-goes-around-comes-around*, a multi-ship heli-logging contract came up for the Olympia outfit a month or so later; the papers were already signed. As it turns out, Mike was the customer's new PM, and as such, he had the say-so of which pilots worked on his logging sale.

Bill and Cheryl were home on break when the fateful letter came in the mail. It was from his employer, letting him know that his services were no longer required! It must have been a shock to get his notice of termination that way. Not face to face, or—one would think—over the phone. Once all the facts were known, Bill would understand why.

In Bill's place, Mike hired me! Once I got the call to report for UH-1K model heli-logging, I was able to amicably sever my ties with my non-logging job in Boise. Yours truly jumped on the next airliner for Olympia, not knowing about Bill's untimely termination. Shoot, I figured maybe we'd be flying on the same contract again, just like old times!

When Bill began calling the usual West Coast operators for logging work, an outfit out of central California just happened to need a pilot for their UH-1B. (I had also put in an application there.) Bill had no way of knowing, but he sealed his fate when he took that job.

A little over a year into his new job, Bill and Cheryl settled into a new home in Marysville, California. Cheryl was working in her field of expertise at a nearby hospital, joining Bill on ferry flights in the helicopter whenever they could arrange it. Bill bought a new *Holiday Rambler* motor home and an Oldsmobile Bravada SUV to tow behind it, enjoying all the comforts of home while in the field.

Bill was logging away in N896W near Skykomish, Washington on August 27, 1997. His hookers reported afterward that Flash was having quite a tussle getting a stout two-log turn into the air. Just as I would have done it, he gathered the turn together for one last try and reared back to launch the load. Facing into the wind, Flash Sikorsky gave it the old heave-ho, then pulled aft cyclic to reef the stubborn logs into the air.

At this point in the maneuver, Bill's "thin-walled"[127] mast broke in two at the damper splines, just below the rotor head. The result of the fracture sent his forty-eight-foot rotor system streaking skyward, unfettered. The rest of the helicopter—with Bill strapped to his seat above his heavy turn

---

127 This was the last UH-1B to go logging using an old style, thin-walled mast as far as I know. I'm sorry, amigo. I doubt that your Guardian Angel knew that. He does now.

of logs – fell over two hundred feet, straight into the ground. There would be no suffering this time.

Flash had just finished up a logging sale in eastern Washington State a week before this tragic event. The happy couple had loaded up the Huey and enjoyed their last flight together to Skykomish. Cheryl took one last photo of *Flash Sikorsky*, waving and smiling happily for the camera as he flew west into the sunset—snowcapped mountains in the background. She mailed the photo to me with along with a brief note, following Bill's somber funeral. This is the last photo I took of the happy couple, posing together in front of the mighty Bell 214B.

Ode to Flash Sikorsky
William R. Wehling, R.I.P.

(To the Tune: "She Wore a Yellow Ribbon")

Flash Si-kor-sky
Was a chopper pilot!
A gray-haired combat vet'ran
Who ate his share of lead.

And if you asked him
Why the heck he ate it?
'Twas for old Richard Nixon
Who was far, far away!

(Chorus) (With feeling!)
Far away, far away,
'Twas for old Richard Milhous
Who was far, far away.

And on his head,
He wore a battered helmet.
He wore it in the Delta,
And 'round Anita Bay!

And if you asked him
Why the heck he wore it
'Twas for a friend who did not –
And is not here today!

(Second Chorus)
Far away! Far away!
'Twas for a friend who did not –
And is not here today!

The Captain's pals,
They don't deserve to know him.
They can't pick up his jockstrap,
Nor stand so tall as he!

But if you ask them
Why they love the **Captain**,
"Despite a belly full of lead
He flew his crew away!"

(Repeat Chorus)
Far away! Far away!
Despite a belly full of lead
He flew his crew away!

Flash Si-kor-sky
Was a logging pilot!
He pulled wood in Wenatchee,
And 'round Lake **Pend Oreille**!*

And if you asked him
Why the heck he pulled it,
'Twas for a straw-haired lady
Who was far, far away!

(Final Chorus: Sing like you've got a pair!)
Far away! Far away!
'Twas for a straw-haired lady
Who was far, far away!

* Pronounced "Pon-dur-A")

Philthy Phil

---

* *Perhaps the Best One-Eyed Helicopter Pilot in the World*

Kelly Cannon was the biggest, strongest man on his logging crew, but the task lying before him was more than he could handle. His one-eyed, three-hundred-pound logging pilot was passed out drunk in the narrow hallway of a cheap Montana motel that the crew occupied, and there was no waking him up. As usual, his left (glass) eye was looking off in the other direction—but Kelly was used to that.

"Philthy Phil" had relieved himself in his blue jeans, to boot. He had apparently been on his way to the head, and that is when he crumpled to the floor. His bloated self blocked the thoroughfare to the toilet, and he would have to be dealt with.

Kelly was the project manager, and I've never seen *him* anywhere even close to drunk. Trouble was, Kelly needed to go—but he couldn't get past Philthy. He couldn't leap over him, nor could he leave his pilot lying there, considering the shape he was in. Cannon summoned help, then stripped Phil of his soiled jeans, exposing his blubbery bod for all to see, but—at least—he had removed the evidence of his "accident" and likely saved him a rash. Kelly dispatched two of his hookers to help levitate Phil to his room and into his bunk.

Philthy and the boys had seen the writing on the wall early that cloudy morning. Thick, stationary snow clouds obscured their logging show in the nearby mountains. The forecast was redundant. Phil was known to head straight for the bar whenever the helicopter broke down or weather closed the logging strips.

It was barely nine o'clock in the morning in Bear Mouth—a small, old-time logging community out in the middle of nowhere. Seated at the tacky motel's bar, Philthy produced a brand-new sack of his favorite Crown Royal whiskey, just as his logging crew sauntered in from the cold. The *party* was on.

In due time, Philthy's fifth disappeared—consumed primarily by himself. There would be no logging the following day, neither—'cause Philthy was seriously under the weather. It wasn't the first time! You might call this Phil's *heavy drinking* phase.

Born March 17th, 1948 in Watertown, New York, Philip M. Rogers was the middle of three sons in a close family. Phil grew up to be a key player on the local high school's soccer team. His interest in flying led him to become an Army aviator. Warrant Officer Rogers served in Vietnam with the 128th Assault Helicopter Company in 1970 and '71 and earned several medals for his voluntary service.

I met Philthy four years later—in Oregon—where we were mutually employed by a fairly big outfit. Back then he was known simply as *Phil*, and he still had both of his keen eyes. He was a stout fellow of around one hundred and eighty pounds in those days, hardly any fat on the man. He frequently jogged after work to stay in shape, but didn't seem to relish the sweaty workouts.

Without a doubt, Phil was a hoot to be around—especially after the rotors were tied down for the day. He wasn't afraid to ask bold questions of complete strangers. His language probably earned him his handle; the man could dish it out like George Carlin. But he could be civil, too. He had an infectious giggle; one that would put a manic-depressive in a jolly mood. It was practically guaranteed that we would overstay our visit at the pub whenever Phil waltzed in.

Intelligent, flamboyant, free-spending, and irreverent, here was a chopper pilot the likes of which only Hollywood could produce. Phil had little interest in movie work, however. He was single, and an adventurer—more interested in flying helicopters around the globe and partying than hanging around a movie set.

The Company kept him busy, flying all over the Northwest. He was spraying in those days. They had him dispensing a chemical known as 2,4,5T[128] over federal and state forests that had been clear-cut. This is a routine but controversial treatment that speeds up the growth of young conifers by killing off the brush—which competes for sunlight and nutrients.

Spraying was a flying job that half of us rotor-heads loathed. But it seemed to suit Phil just fine, 'cause he got paid pretty good money to *yank and bank*—flying *low-level* all morning long—and he was usually back at the motel by noon, with plenty of time left to party.

Then came the seismic boom of the mid-seventies. A covey of us young bucks were sent to South America to wildcat for petroleum reserves. Phil was assigned to Bolivia—flying an SA-315B "Lama," and I wound up in the nearby jungles of Peru—flying Bell 205A-1s. It was great work for bachelors, but the risk was high—and before he made it home, Phil left part of himself in the jungle of northwestern Bolivia.

We got word of his crash through Company channels—there was good news with the bad. His Lama had flamed out with two Bolivian nationals on board over triple-canopy jungle. There was no place to autorotate to but into the top of a huge tree. Settling into its gigantic branches, the rotors struck several limbs and were beaten to pieces. The five-seat French helicopter teetered momentarily, then tipped over forward, slipping through the tree's loose grasp. The battered bird fell a terrifying distance straight down, and crashed hard near the tree's massive trunk.

Seated in the right-hand pilot's seat, Phil's head smashed into the instrument console, crushing his left eye socket and destroying the eye. Both of his passengers suffered painful injuries, but they were able to evacuate the ship and consider the serious pickle they were in. They would wait a long time for help.

No one at Base Camp knew exactly where they were, except that they had reported leaving a certain seismic line and station number. They weren't heard from after that. Search teams eventually gathered but the spotters never saw their damaged tree nor the three waving frantically under the

128   A powerful brush killer, very similar to Agent Orange.

super-thick foliage. Faced with a grim situation, the trio set out afoot for the nearest river—miles from the nearest settlement, Cobija.

Three days later, they were fortunate to meet some friendly natives boating on the river who took mercy upon them. A medicine man offered Phil a primitive jungle brew (banana liquor) to ease his pain. They were soon returned to their Base Camp, stunning their elated coworkers with the details of their harrowing exodus.

Phil was soon evacuated to the States for surgery and recuperation, during which time the French helicopter manufacturer's representatives were flown to the Bolivian jungle crash site in an attempt to determine the cause of his flameout.

(Phil told me later that he had *over* twenty gallons of Jet-A1 turbine fuel indicated when the flameout occurred—but the Aerospatiale team allegedly came back with a report of *fuel exhaustion*, which infuriated Mr. Rogers to no end. The Company appeared to support Phil's version—but there were rumors.)

Phil finished rehabilitation and eventually obtained a medical waiver from the FAA, demonstrating his ability to fly with one eye. That took some getting used to, he told me—but he was buoyed by the knowledge that there were some 1,500 licensed one-eyed pilots in the USA at the time.

Phil freely admitted that it took extra effort to scan for traffic, turning his head more to the left to protect his expanded *blind spot*. Worse—his depth perception was *nil*. We used to toss the Frisbee for hours in the warm summer days of southern Oregon. Phil urged me to sail it right at his head so he could adapt to his handicap. It would sometimes "blow (his) mind" and he'd freak out, ducking as the disc zipped over his head. Over time, Phil used his guts and intelligence to divide and conquer his doubts and disability.

The Company knew that Phil had no logging or long-line experience, but in a move he perceived was designed to weed him out, he was assigned to a logging crew. With a minimal amount of training, he was dispatched to pilot a small support helicopter, which required him to use a long wire rope to deploy logging chokers, as directed by the hookers working under a big Sikorsky. The odds were indeed against him.

But Phil took on the challenge, *blade-in-teeth*. He was determined to succeed in an assignment that is a challenge for a *non*-impaired pilot. Despite the odds, he became a capable hand with the long-line and remote hook. The ground crews loved his jovial personality, and Phil Rogers was back in demand!

The seismic boom came to the Northwestern USA soon after that, and new helicopter operators popped up practically overnight—up and down the Rocky Mountains. Chief pilots everywhere were scrambling to find long-line qualified chopper pilots, and for a change, they were offering good salaries and even bonus pay. A bevy of pilots up and pulled out of Oregon, and—in a matter of months—Phil and I ended up working for a bustling outfit in central Utah.

Life was good for a while. There was a per diem allowance adequate enough to live in a decent motel room, or—as Phil and I did—save up and buy a motor home (or trailer) and camp out near the roving seismic operation. Working in the snowy reaches of the Uintas and along Commissary Ridge put us in contact with scores of athletic young men and women—displaced *ski bums*—who retrained as *juggies;*[129] they loved to party, too!

In those days, drug testing was in its infancy and seldom ever applied. Marijuana use (after hours) was fairly commonplace—but cocaine was the party drug of choice—and it was no real secret when a *shipment* came to town.

The prevailing buzz in the Seventies was that coke was non-addictive, and I guess many believed the big lie. Bonus pay provided expendable income for "recreational use," so dealers supplied the juggies, juggies supplied their favorite pilots, and—vice versa.

Seismic crews worked hard for their money, freezing their butts off and worse—and the casual use of *blow* soon got out of hand. I recall looking over my left shoulder one morning after lifting off to the east. Three juggies in the rear seat of the Lama were lit up by a spectacular Grays River Range sunrise and grinning broadly as they snorted big, fat lines of coke from a small mirror via a rolled-up hundred-dollar bill. That shocked even me; I thought I'd seen just about everything.

There was one heck of a liability in having anything of that nature on board <u>an aircraft, but I</u> had just gotten married and my bonus money was going to

129 Juggies are also known as *Doodlebugs*. They hike several miles a day, packing and positioning sensitive seismic geo-phones for the recording of data.

help pay off some land in Oregon. They were the *customers*, after all—so I kept quiet, as did other seismic pilots in my peer group.

In due time, several of our juggies fell into the vicious loop of *working harder to earn more money, so they could buy more coke—so they could work harder.* Even the top jocks on the crew started dragging ass before midday, and more and more the guys I flew around were bleeding from the nose, ill-tempered, strung-out, and had a hard time keeping up with production.

It was a good time gone bad, and before long the "seismic shuffle" became more of a liability than an adventure. The newfangled eight-hook carrousels came out about that time, and suddenly seismic pilots were dependent on seeing tiny blue and red station markers for their drops of jugs or powder, instead of long-lining them to an old friend with a radio. I missed the camaraderie, joking on the radio, and the smiling faces.

Being slightly deficient in color-vision, I had a *heck* of a time seeing any markers that were not in the sunshine. I was suddenly costing the team some valuable flight time searching for the darned flags, and realized where this was all heading. Frustrated, I asked to be reassigned. Fortunately for me, I was diverted to construction work, which proved to be a lot of fun and a tremendous monkey off my back.

During all this, Phil and I crossed paths many times. He'd drop by our motel room in Alpine, Wyoming and watch the football playoffs with me while trying out his Spanish on Lourdes. When stumped for a word, we'd use a pass-around blackboard to draw a picture. My beautiful young Mexican wife found Phil to be "very charming"—when he wasn't plucking out his glass eye and playing with it. (Phil started out wearing an eye patch, but he said it made him "look like a villain," so he opted for a custom-made glass eye.)

Philthy particularly enjoyed the helicopter-related cartoons I whipped out, some of which were published in the Company's Safety Newsletter. Some never got published, like the new sketch I was working on: it depicted a bionic chopper pilot leaning against an ugly black barrel that was leaking toxic chemicals. The label on the barrel read "***1,2,3-UR-Dead***." In the background stood a heavily soiled spray ship, while the greedy pilot counted out his pay on the head of the barrel—a big wad of cash! I drew him with three eyes—amid a plethora of facial scars and an Elvis hairdo.

Lourdes, Phil, and his dog, Chether, in Alpine, WY

The idea behind the three-eyed bionic protagonist was that Phil had allegedly been in a midair collision with another legendary spray pilot—Mike Pond—and the ER surgeons only had enough good body parts to put *one* pilot back together. Out he walks months later as *Magic Mike Wand, the World's Only Three-Eyed Chopper Pilot.* Phil thought it was hilarious. He giggled like he'd gone crazy, and urged me to *"keep whippin' 'em out!"*

Shortly thereafter, Lourdes and I took off to my new assignment to the Grand Canyon,[130] and Phil—mutually disenchanted with "silly seismo"—took a *Flight for Life* job. We never crossed paths again after Wyoming, but kept loosely in touch by phone.

While Lourdes and I went on to settle in southern California, Phil stayed close to the Rockies flying air-medical, heli-ski contracts, heli-logging, and various construction jobs. While operating out of Summit County, Colorado, he met and fell in love with Kathryn J. Demboski. He and "Kit" were married in 1982. Residing in Frisco, Colorado until 1995, they found an ideal place in Westcliffe, just east of the dominating Sangre de Cristo Mountains.[131]

I am proud to report that Phil was very supportive during my trials over the terrible movie accident I was involved in. "F... those guys," referring to my co-defendants. *"You're the one that got f...'d!"* he would growl.

---

130 See *Wind Loggers:* "Rat Wars" and "Flying the Ultra-Ripe, Blue Plastic Outhouse!" for my Grand Canyon tales.

131 The author wishes to thank Kit Rogers, pilot Fred Cappo, and Carol at the *Wet Mountain Tribune* for their valuable assistance and hospitality in helping tell Phil's story.

Phil's last conversation with me was over a telephone line to let me know he thought a certain helicopter operator in our state was *screwing* their pilots and using military parts on standard category helicopters. *"Don't climb into one-a their f'ing helicopters, if you know what's good for you!"* Phil advised. (And I didn't!)

Philthy was a big fellow by then, owing in part to a big appetite, expensive whiskey, and a metabolic ailment that made him put on weight. One of our favorite mechanics, Scott Kimball, said he used to have to help Phil in and out of the pilot's seat of the Lama because of his bulk.

It was around this time that Phil adopted the naughty handle, "Philthy Phil, the One-Eyed Fat (guy)." Shortly thereafter he flew relief for my logging crew at Bear Mouth - and added another illustrious page to his ribald reputation.

The following year—with Kit's help, Phil brought his weight down through a rigorous protein shake diet and lots of exercise. By January of 1998, he was back in form—and nearing his 50th birthday.

One sunny February morning thereafter, Phil arose in a jubilant mood, stacked his favorite tunes into the CD player, and started dancing in the buff! Kit appraised his unusually good humor and joined in the fun. Instead of the usual pet project, he kicked back. After a great breakfast and relaxing around the house most of the day, Phil suggested, *"Let's go for a putt!"*

Phil had recently purchased a beautiful Harley Davidson for Kit and a hot Honda ST1100 motorcycle for himself. It was simply too fine of a day *not* to go for a *putt*—as he put it.

Although it was still officially winter and fairly cool in southern Colorado, the roads were clear of snow. Always ready for a good time, Kit got movin'. They bundled up in the mid-afternoon sunshine and motored off southbound out of Westcliffe on Highway 69, toward Gardner. After a thirty-four-mile drive, both were feeling liberated and revived by the exhilarating ride. It was about time to head home, though—the afternoon sun dipped toward the gorgeous snowcapped Sangre de Cristos. A chill was in the air.

Agreeing to backtrack on Highway 69 to Westcliffe, Phil chatted briefly with Kit as they rubbed their cheeks and fingers warm. He slyly suggested that she might have to speed up a bit if she wanted to keep up with him for the ride home—and off he went, northbound.

The ST1100 was a *crotch rocket,* quite capable of outrunning her Harley. Kit was accustomed to Phil's occasional *need for speed,* and was content to just keep him in sight. Within minutes, however, Phil was pulling away—racing the Honda's six-speed transmission through its gears on the scintillating two-laned asphalt ribbon that turned and twisted toward Westcliffe. Kit pushed her bike as hard as she felt was safe, but the big Harley didn't handle like his *café racer,* and she was beginning to shiver in the sixty-mile-an-hour draft.

The sun had slipped behind the mountains when Kit pulled into their driveway, her exposed flesh numb from the ride. But where was Phil? No Honda, their garage was locked and empty. Thinking he had pulled a trick on her, she considered backtracking to find the rascal. She waited a few minutes. Soon, her worst fears overwhelmed her, and she called the Colorado State Patrol.

As word spread of a missing motorcyclist, a pair of hikers from Wolf Springs Ranch came upon the scene of the accident. Phil lay motionless, his helmet strapped on tight, as usual. He came to rest close to his machine, which had settled in an upright position—destroyed—but still idling.

Phil left us that sixth day of February, flying off the highway on a right curve just past the thirty-eight-mile marker of Highway 69. One of the finest helicopter pilots and motorcycle riders alive, he left few clues as to what might have gone wrong on his swift ride with Fate. His Honda would have been impossible for Kit to see, beyond the fence and down in the hollow, as she took the fifty-five-mile-per-hour curve, unaware.

Six years went by before I made the trip to Westcliffe. I had left the commercial helicopter pilot business by then and decided to go see the road that claimed Phil for myself, perhaps come to an understanding how he had met his end. I called ahead to reunite with Kit, whom I hadn't seen since our Wyoming seismic days. Kit graciously rode out on her Harley to meet me at the scene of the accident. I was relieved that she volunteered to meet me there—and to field some questions that had to be tough for any widow to answer.

Kit introduced me to her new beau, a rugged professional guide and part-time cowboy who rode up on a Harley Davidson soft tail Classic. Afterward, we had some drinks at the tavern in Westcliffe where Kit works. She was kind enough to put me up that evening at her cozy two-story house that Phil found so comfortable. Several cats had the run of the place, and made me feel right at home. I slept great in the upstairs studio, tastefully decorated with Kit's inspiring American Indian art pieces.

The next morning I was off for Raton, New Mexico to see my old logging buddy Jeff Holder and his big family. On the way back, I purposefully diverted off the freeway north to take the scenic route up Highway 69 yet again. After sleeping on it, I was intent on studying the last mile or so of Phil's transcendental ride. How well did Phil know this road, I wondered?

Taking my Nikon out of the Eldorado, I took a series of overlapping photos—hoping to fathom somehow what had taken my friend so rudely. There was no traffic that sunny afternoon, giving me total freedom on where I stood to shoot the frames. Finally, I worked my way up to the curve.

Kit's marker—a small wooden cross—lay almost hidden in the spring grass. It had toppled over on the slope just beyond the pavement; not far from a guy-wire supporting the nearby wood utility pole. Phil may have struck the guy-wire on his way over the barbed-wire fence, Kit had mentioned to me the day before...in a whisper.

An educated relative went to the scene the day after the accident and talked with the patrolmen. He did the math on Phil's trajectory. The official conclusion was that the bike had been laid down some distance before it left the road, and that Phil's body had to be travelling seventy miles per hour to clear the fence. There were no fresh tire skid marks before the curve. And our pal had been separated from his glass eye in the process.

Did Phil experience a frozen, wide-open throttle, I had to ask myself—having crashed my Big Bear Scrambler in a motorcycle race with the same problem. A tiny, horizontal scratch in the carburetor's barrel slide is all it takes.

Had a deer dashed out suddenly from the roadside, causing Phil to lose control? Had he wiped out on a patch of grit left by road-sanding equipment? Did his good eye tear up in the blast of cold air—to the point that he couldn't see the curve ahead? What about the sun? It must have been setting almost directly in front of him, lined up going into the curve. Six minutes after 4 p.m., they concluded. Contributing factor?

These questions must have been mulled over and over by many others. As for me, I feel like I'm being pulled back to Wolf Springs. I want to erect an iron marker for Phil at the site, and set it in concrete. I am compelled to time the setting sun from the fateful curve, on the sixth of February. I'll probably have company. Perhaps it will put our minds to rest—perhaps not.

Some consolation I got from making the trip was knowing Phil didn't suffer that spirited day—and that he checked out doing what he loved. We should all be so fortunate.[132]

---

132 With Philthy Phil out of the game, cigar-champing Stu Taft has my vote as the greatest living one-eyed pilot.

On Losing Face

*   *Enter Jet-Dragster Slash Helicopter Pilot and My Pal, Mike Pond*

Michael—as his friends know him—had just purchased two surplus jet engines from a West Coast outfit. Parked next to the curb, he had both of them strapped down on a car trailer in front of my Rialto abode. He was about to head back to Cañon City, Colorado, where he would start building a racecar around one of the jets. He posed patiently while I took one last photo of his handsome mug. (**Click**.)

I got a funny feeling as I did so. It was like *déjà vu,* preserving Mike behind the wheel of his black Dodge Ram truck while his diesel engine grumbled.

It was a rare moment to have my old flying buddy back in my camera sights. A less sensitive person might have let the moment pass, but not *El Gringo Wingo from Chilpancingo.* I never would have met Lourdes were it not for Mike, dancing with her best friend back in Culiacán, Sinaloa. Yessir, it was in *interior* Mexico that Mike and I flew Bell 212's on one of those *low-profile* jobs the government isn't always happy to have aired out in short stories. We were soldiers of the War on Drugs.

Captain Pond was—in fact—eyewitness to my somewhat spectacular crash while slinging a 3,600-pound jet-fuel bladder (described earlier in *The Forbidden Fruit of Tierra Blanca*). It was an ugly thing to watch, I am sure Mike would agree. I lost face that day, if you're keeping score. But that's another story, and this one is about *Michael.*

Mike and I first worked together in the Amazon Flood Plain—specifically northeastern Peru back in '75, a wonderful assignment for a rookie like me. I remember the day he got off the Pilatus Porter floatplane at Puerto Amelia; Mike spied me languishing up in my "Torre de Paz" overlooking the big, wide Rio Huallaga.

After dropping his bags in the pilot's shack, Mike sauntered through the tall grass to check out my retreat. A big fellow—picture a six-foot-three *John Goodman* with a smaller waist—Captain Mike had a wool golf cap pulled down over his steely blue eyes and was soon standing at the base of the tower's ladder.

"You sure 'bout this?" he grumbled, giving the new, hand-wrought pole structure a couple of shakes.

"It's stronger than it looks, Mike," I assured him. "I'm still bracing it, though. Come on up!"

Mike's 230 pounds made my spindly perch tremble as he climbed up the notched-and-nailed rungs of the ladder—finally joining me on the small platform and bench seat, still under construction. Mike exchanged a cordial hello with me in his customary easy drawl—followed by *"how's-it-goin'"* and *"see you after you get this thing reinforced a bit."* And to this day, that's the closest I ever came to seeing Mr. Pond in the shadow of fear.

Born and raised in Crystal City, Texas, Cary Michael Pond was the son of a WWII P-38 pilot. As a youth, Mike enjoyed the sunny Tex-Mex coastal life until *Vietnam* became a *conflict*. Mike answered the call to duty. Serving in the Army Signal Corps until his chopper training dream-sheet was approved, Mike was soon in *the 'Nam* flying *slicks*.

The gunship platoon acquired Pond a month later, after Michael found out what it was like to bring a ship home full of holes. Fourteen hundred flight hours later they pinned Air Medal number thirty-five on the man's military blouse. He took his final month removed from flight duty—rightfully so. Last time I looked, it took twenty-five combat missions to acquire *one* Air Medal. That's what I'd call *exposure*.

Returning to civilian life was somewhat of a shock, any combat veteran can tell you. Mike found commercial flying jobs to be *few, scattered,* and *cheap*. Not afraid to learn a back-up trade, Mr. Pond found work as a diesel mechanic—postponing his flying ambitions while learning valuable mechanical skills. A year or so later, and several overhauls down the road, he was back under the twirling rotors.

Mike soon became one of the preferred spray pilots for a big outfit in Oregon where we both hired out as commercial helicopter jockeys. This was around 1974 or so. Taking a hiatus from spraying, someone rewarded his seniority with a ticket to the Peruvian operation. I was flying 205s there at the time.

Captain Pond was still there when the Hueys were sent home and a Sikorsky 61 took over the workload, moving H&P heli-drill rigs across the jungle, with all their trappings. Mike stayed on through monsoons and drought, and made a name for himself when it came to moving heli-rigs—*and* when it came time to *"suit up!"*

The naughty, off-duty aviator warrior custom—suiting up—allegedly started in Mike's old outfit in Vietnam. A strike outfit like that takes pride in the fact that everyone in the Unit fights together, everyone eats together, everyone drinks together, and by gosh, everyone **suits up** together!

One is sometimes required to *suit up* rather spontaneously, which makes it easy if you're already butt-naked: Take one white tee-shirt or vest (preferably your buddy's) and turn it upside down, the tag at six o'clock; next, step into the sleeve holes. If your thighs won't make it through the sleeve holes, cut or tear them until they will. (You *vest* wearers will appreciate having no clumsy sleeves to deal with.)

Grabbing one side of the shirt's bottom hemline (right or left, your choice) tear or cut a hole to thrust your mighty arm through so you can now wear your suit over one shoulder, toga style. Feel a breeze around the neck hole? Of course you do! Now you are fully suited up and may join in on the vicarious, manly art of beer drinking and discussions worthy of helicopter combat veterans, and their guests!

Which naturally provided many a jovial exchange of culture several years later, while the crew languished around their all-male jungle Porta-Camp—attired in their *suits*—in the dull tedium and sweltering heat found rampant in the jungles of the Amazon Basin. It was one of those *off days* where nobody went to Iquitos, nor fishin'—nor nothin' else.

How it happened that so many manly types were *suited up* for the arrival of a mysterious medium-sized helicopter one sunny Sunday morning is unclear. The approach into the prevailing winds at the *plataforma* brought the landing rotorcraft fairly close to the *new* Tower of Peace that everyone pitched in to build, fifty miles west-northwest of the original *Torre de Paz* in Puerto Amelia. The new tower was big enough to support a dozen grown men; standing open ranked; shoulders back; guts sucked in, and crisp, military salutes from every swinging individual.

The flight was what one might call a *junket*, whereas someone on board had the power to authorize what was otherwise a *joy ride* for his family, wives, girlfriends, or whatever. Such as this morning, when a ranking native engineer and his female entourage made a surprise *parts run* to the remote jungle rig, perhaps for a *cafécito* with the Americanos—if they were around. And yes, there they are—grinning broadly, as the Bell 205 whoppity-whops slowly by them on short-final approach to the heli-pad. *Mornin', Gaylord!* (Sure beats sprayin', eh Mike?)

Not long afterward Mike and I shipped out to that big spraying job down in Mexico. We shared rooms in Sinaloa for the most part, renewing our old roommate manners in short order. Captain Methane and Mike, the human-bagpipe-Pond. We improvised some amazing theatrical dialog and banal stunts for an audience of two—which drove our white-collar neighbors and the poor hacienda's hooch maids to distraction.

Mike moved around with all the grace of John Wayne, being wide at the shoulders and narrow near the belt buckle. I think he stayed as trim as he was by sticking to his one-meal-a-day dining habit. He'd go along when the guys wanted some breakfast or coffee; and he'd take the gang out for tacos and beans or *hamburgesas* for lunch; only a Coke or an *agua mineral* for Mike. But when it came to dinnertime, don't get in the man's way—especially if you are a thick, juicy steak! I've called him *Captain Carnivore* more than once. Once he is fed, I've discovered—he usually goes dancing!

After ridding Mexico of a few million thriving opium poppy and marijuana plants, I'd seen enough chromed, camouflaged, and nickel-plated gun barrels pointed in my direction and decided to cash in; get safely back on home to my cabin—leaving lovely Lourdes behind. Mike showed no such hesitation to re-up—staying on for another six-month tour, and adding hundreds more *plantillos* to his already impressive coup count.

Mike found his way to Denver eventually, changing horses to the Aerospatiale 316B, a bloated air ambulance version of the Lama, with three wheels—and ideally suited for the high-altitude work around his new home state. Mike stayed on in the Denver area for years, airlifting hundreds of injured Coloradans to trauma centers and rescuing those who dared challenge some of the tallest peaks in America. If there was a better mountain helicopter pilot around, I fergit his name.

In the background all this time was the fact that Mike had a thing for fast automobiles. While we suited up in Peru, a tricked-out Honda Z600 coupe sat in his garage near Redding. (I honestly don't know how he got in and out of the speedy little box.) When we languished in Mexico, a sleek black *Pantera* with a big block Ford V-8 was waiting impatiently for his heavy foot to return home. But once he relocated to Colorado, Mike's taste in fast machinery took on a new dimension: *Jet power!*

The drag strip attracted Mike in mid-life, getting his high *g-load* kicks at two hundred and fifty miles per hour. The venerable J-34 power plant in his Dodge Dakota race replica was something Mike became an expert on, eventually earning a jet-engine mechanic rating certified by the NHRA.[133]

133 National Hot Rod Association

The J-34 kicks out 3,400 pounds of thrust and—on a good day—will propel a bullet-shaped racecar upward to two hundred and eighty miles per hour in the quarter-mile. Mild-mannered, soft-spoken Michael just couldn't get enough! Starting out as an exhibition jet-car, Mike's dragster enjoyed a multi-strip popularity and was instrumental in attracting other drivers.

The lure for any bona fide adrenaline junkie was obvious, especially if you did the numbers. Top fuel dragsters are the biggest attraction at drag strips around the USA, but are very expensive machines that require a highly trained, dedicated three or four man crew, which burns a ton of their sponsor's money to stay among the top in competition.

Mike—on the other hand—could buy a J-34 and install it in a hand-wrought chassis for a fraction of the cost. He could drive and maintain the thing himself, and it would run almost as fast as the top fuelers. "If you hit three hundred, the track's computer is programmed to display a blank screen, 'cause the big guys don't want some *cheap charlie* stealing their thunder. It took some high-dollar semi-trailers to bring their show to town." Mike explained the politics and pecking order to me. After all, their heavily sponsored machinery was hand-built, technically more complicated, and blew up frequently.

During the summers, Captain Pond operated a helicopter sightseeing service near the Royal Gorge in southern Colorado. Starting out with an MD500, Mike's little operation grew to a Bell seven-seat LongRanger, which you'd have to be blind to miss, parked at his roadside helipad near the east entrance to the Royal Gorge Bridge. Mike and the river rafters who worked the canyon's whitewater trade promoted each other, and set up package deals for their thrill-seeking clients.

Whenever time allowed, Captain Pond would race his Dodge Dakota at nearby Pueblo, Denver, or wherever there were paying exhibition jet-car drivers to blaze down the drag strip.

The May-through-September tourist season brought thousands of sightseers to Cañon City, and Mike became famous for giving a helicopter ride like no other. While they saw a lot of international tourists come through town, word among the locals was this: if you want a helicopter ride to remember, buckle up tight and go fly the Royal Gorge with Captain Mike Pond!

Racing became a big deal with Mike, as did travel. While sightseeing in Moscow, the captain was introduced to a beautiful young Russian lady by way of a blind date. Love blossomed! Nadya came blessed with a daughter, and it was their good fortune to return to the USA some time later as a family!

It was in March of '99 that soon-to-be-married Mike Pond paid Lourdes and me an overnight visit on his way to the coast to buy those jet engines I referred to earlier. Mike was building up a '55 Chevy jet-car for a friend to own and operate. He had selected a Rolls-Royce 202 jet engine to power the new car. Twenty-five hundred pounds of thrust would compete nicely with the J-34's 3,400, by virtue of its compactness and lighter weight. "A bullet on wheels," as Mike put it.

The car was ready to test run by June of 2000, and Mike had access to the Pueblo Drag Strip. This was the long awaited day, finally testing his virgin race car/engine combination. It was an "off" day at the track, so there were few people on the grounds that day—just Mike's girls and the essential track crew.

Mike fueled his new machine with Jet-A out of his black Dodge *Dually* support-rig. He only needed half a tank for the preliminary run—about twenty gallons. Suiting up in his regulation fire-resistant race suit, Mike squeezed the familiar crash helmet onto his curly head and fastened the chinstrap.

Like any prudent test pilot, Mike planned to do only *half-a-burn*; that is, throttle up with brakes engaged for the abrupt takeoff; *full* throttle until halfway down the track, then throttle *off*. The car had never zipped down a track before, so it was prudent of Mike to test the hot water with his big toe before taking the plunge.

It wouldn't have looked that way to Nadya and Natalia—and a few horrorstruck race fans who witnessed Captain Mike Pond's spectacular blastoff and crash during that ill-fated run. There was no video of the crash, and Mike's memory of the event is gone. All we have been able to learn about it is, the engine's burn lasted beyond the halfway mark and the racecar went out of control. A stuck throttle linkage, a gust of wind—who knows?

The smashed chassis of the '55 Chevy replica came to rest far down the quarter-mile track, inverted. Some fellow with a fire extinguisher belatedly appeared on the scene as everyone ran to help. One witness thought the well-meaning firefighter spent more time trying to put the car out than aiming the stream on the flaming driver. After such an awful crash, it might have appeared to the fireman that the driver's time had come—he was controlling the collateral damage as best he could.

But that wouldn't be like the Mike Pond I know to check out so rudely! Although the force of the crash knocked his helmet off his head and fractured some bones—he was still with us. Knocked unconscious, Mike dozed with his gloved hands gripping the flaming steering wheel while jet fuel—in the tank upended directly above him—dripped steadily onto his face—which was on fire.

Mike's guardian angel was *slow*, but Captain Pond would live to fly again.

There are third-degree burns, pilgrim—and then there's *fourth*-degree burns. The latter is down to the bone. Mike had plenty of both. It would be four months before our famous patient was brought gently out of a medically induced slumber. The doctors had worked miracles while the captain was out, setting bones, grafting skin, and surgically removing what wouldn't heal.

Mike was burned over sixty percent of his upper body. Nadya and Natalia had been in the USA only one year, and now *this* happened to their beloved Michael. For months they were at his hospital bedside, cradling his heavily bandaged head in their arms. Whispering in Russian, they would say to him, "Sleep now, Michael, but come back to us."

Michael would end up losing his nose and most of both ears. He lost half of both little fingers, and some of both eyelids. The moustache is gone; he no longer has to shave! He has some scattered hairs on his head, just enough to annoy his barber now and then. Wearing mirrored sunglasses, you couldn't recognize those familiar blue eyes and you would have no clue *who* you were looking at. Other than he was around six foot three, and two hundred and fifty pounds. A badly burned citizen smiling right back at you.

An old Reeder Air pilot friend from years back, Gordon Knight came to the Pond's rescue by taking over the flying for Royal Gorge Helicopter Tours. While Mike recuperated, Gordon held off the financial pressure and kept the tourists happy.[134] An appreciative Michael told me later, "Gordon Knight saved my bacon!"

ﻥﻥﻥ

Wind Loggers was in its *proof* stage (April, 2005) when I finally was able to drive to Cañon City, Colorado to see my old poppy-spraying pal. Lourdes and I refinanced our home in Rialto and used some of the cash to self-publish my book. We also bought a pre-owned white, long-bed Ford F150 pickup for our high school honor graduate son, Jon Alan.

Jon was about to pack his bags for USC[135] to become a filmmaker. I had just enough cash left over to purchase the '90 Eldorado, make the trip to Philthy Phil's old place, then over to Mike's, who lived not far away. These two pilots had earned a place in my next book, and I was determined to do the necessary research.

Turning my back on a flying career to become a writer was tough on our income but essential for my health. The Veterans Administration had diagnosed me with hypertension, high cholesterol, arthritis, and most significantly, the familiar PTSD that kept coming back to infuriate me. Writing was part of the therapy, my counselors kept telling me.

My VA prescriptions were supposed to help with stress and anger, but I only noticed the meds when I forgot to take them: I'd soon get the awkward sensation of walking around underwater. My old herbal remedy worked better, frankly, and its only side effect was a case of the munchies. It will be a cold day in hell when the federal government hands out *weed* at a VA Hospital.

I had my share of problems, but there was little time to feel sorry for myself. Lourdes was in far worse shape. Three weeks after my run-in with the power line, my love came down with a serious immune system disorder. She hemorrhaged and found herself in the Redlands Community Hospital's Intensive Care Unit (ICU), fighting for her life. Thank God I wasn't on the road when that happened.

---

134 Sadly, Gordon Knight was killed piloting a Lama, fighting a fire in Colorado, August of 2002.

135 The University of Southern California in Los Angeles.

Lourdes was in the ICU a total of three times from 2004 to 2008. We faced a battery of the same health-history questions each time we checked in the Emergency Room, so I keep a printout of relative information in my wallet. Lourdes has had thirteen operations since we were married. She has endured so much since our 1977 wedding in Reno, and delivered three children, poor woman. So, while she was healthy, this brief Colorado trip would involve some expeditious research—then the Cadillac was headed back home to baby.

Mike had to have seen the shock in my expression when we were finally reunited. A little over two years had passed since I took his memorable photo in Rialto. Racing, fire, wear and tear had taken their toll, and here we were once again, standing three feet apart. The guy in the photo was the Mike of Old. The big man in front of me had Mike's friendly eyes and voice, and an unfamiliar face. This was the *New Mike*.

It was a joy to give Mike Pond a big hug; he is not unlike a big cuddly teddy bear. Natalia was monitoring us while doing her science homework behind the counter. Appropriately, she was assembling a four-atom methane molecule out of shish-kebab sticks and Styrofoam balls. "Coincidental?" I asked a grinning Mike.

Before he could respond, the wind blew in and around us as the heavy door to Mike's Royal Gorge Helicopter business flew open. Mike turned aside to make room for two middle-aged female customer/tourists, climbing the wood-beam steps up into the foyer.

Natalia was a dashing young lady of fourteen. Her blue eyes lit up as she book-marked her chemistry text and smiled, beaming like a blond Russian poster child. She spoke first, welcoming the ladies while reciting the short list of helicopter tours available from memory. Her accent was charming.

"*Plostic or cosh?*" she added, finishing off her sales pitch.

By this time, Mike had maneuvered his way around behind his pretty stepdaughter, and he was wearing his sinister mirror-shades. Facing his would-be passengers, there was an eerie silence as the ladies realized, *The guy who looks like* Freddie—*is our pilot!*

The ladies did a double-take, scanning back and forth between smiling Natalia (still waiting patiently for an answer) and the menacing Captain Pond. Behind him, the captain's untied helicopter appeared through the open east doorway, impatiently pawing the earth. The windsock snapped and popped in the brisk afternoon breeze. A half-mile away, the yawning abyss beckoned.

(The lady tourists stare questioningly at each other—a last-minute gut-check to see if one or the other has inexplicably gone chicken!)

"Sounds great!" one of the ladies finally blurted out, handing over her American-in-Distress Card. "We'll take the *deluxe* tour!"

It dawned on me after a parade of tourists came and went that day that this sort of thing happened hundreds of times every summer, and *man*, it's great theater! Natalia sets 'em up, Mike stares 'em down and takes their dough. Off they go, and minutes later, he brings 'em back alive. Alive—but *changed*.

❧❧❧❧

The two lady tourists drive away limp, giggling like children as they reenact their awesome helicopter ride with replayed **"waaaaahs"** and **"shrrriiieeeks!"**

As Mike would tell you, "Yeah, we get that a lot." Telltale stains on the passengers' seat cushions were testimony to those who were so thrilled. Nobody gives a chopper ride like my buddy Mike!

What about his close call with death, you ask? What did my fast flyin' friend have to say about that, and his new face? "Goes with the territory," he calmly drawled. "Goes with the territory."

Pedo Heights

---

*   *A remote, rustic cabin in the Oregon woods.*

Looking back, sixty-odd times around that hot old star we circle, flying was hardly ever about the money. For me, it was more often about the *adventure*. Floating over the razor-like spine of the High Sierra, flittering slowly by the sacred pinnacles of Monument Valley, parked on a grassy Alaskan mountaintop overlooking Glacier Bay, or weaving a snakelike path between monstrous Peruvian thunderstorms with a low fuel light—*that's* what I call earning a paycheck!

A couple of years before I met lovely Lourdes, I built a tiny cabin on ten acres of heavily timbered land in southwestern Oregon. There was no road the last two hundred feet to my humble abode. The rare visitor had to leave his/her rig behind and hike the hilly trail—if they knew where to look.

Totaling less than two hundred square feet, my cabin with a loft was more a playhouse than not. Tall, fragrant cedar and pine trees all around, a splendid *baño primitivo*[136] downwind a-ways.

Eloquently carved on the sturdy front door of the cabin were the words *Pedo Heights*. They were patiently chiseled into the Douglas fir planks by Steve Mankle, one of my live-in smoke jumper pals. Pinto beans with

---

136 Outhouse

white onion garnish were a staple on the menu around the Heights, so the name fit.

Situated on a hogback ridge overlooking the West Fork of Oregon's Illinois River, with three cats and three dogs, it was a wonderful retreat. No jangling telephones, no plumbing problems, no Jerry Springer, no utility poles (no utility bills), and a year-round swimming hole.

Another of my Siskiyou smoke jumper friends, "Trooper Tom," paid me a surprise visit late one afternoon. Tom was the young owner-builder of several large, classic, hand-wrought log homes in the area, so I was a little embarrassed when he stepped inside my doorway for the first time.

Trooper's cabins were spacious and in demand. They had most of the modern conveniences, and money rolled in every month from the renters. I had heard all kinds of praises about his latest, a three-story affair of around 3,500 square feet, built straddling a creek! Notching thousands of big logs into position, Tom has killed more chainsaws than a busload of loggers.

My simple structure was quite modest in comparison. As I began to show Tom around, the kittens came to play and the magic of Pedo Heights came upon us. We found some shade to catch the show and waxed philosophical. Pulling a couple of ice-cold Henry's out of the bucket, Tom handed me one and we kicked back. Before long, he loosened up and began to recant highlights from his trip around the world. He had begun his epic voyage a teenager, with all of nineteen cents in his pocket.

Tom learned a ton of things on his epic voyage, and as he reminisced, some of his revelations about money surfaced. In the warm glow of the afternoon sun, I felt I was on the same wavelength with Trooper and found myself interjecting a quote from another wise man:

"True happiness comes from within," I pontificated.

We savored a golden moment as the river gurgled by and a couple of tiny turtledoves cooed from the interior of a blackberry thicket, yonder. After a pregnant pause, Tom spoke again. *"Mighty profound thinkin' for an Okie,"* he added with a grin.

Trooper could see the level of my contentment; the love I had put into the cabin's small details, building the whole thing without nails. Except for several hundred cedar shake shingles, of course.

As the autumn sun began to set behind Lone Mountain, we leisurely hiked down the trail toward Tom's truck. My three scrappy kittens raced ahead, clawing up and down the trees along the path. Tumbling over each other in the golden oak leaves, they had us in stitches.

As Tom opened the rusty door of his pickup, I was shocked to hear the legendary former Marine captain admit,

"Dorce, I wish I had what you've got here."

I stood there speechless, my outstretched fingers blocking the sun's horizontal rays. Tom's battered rig rattled slowly down the hill over the rough jeep trail called Arrowhead Road. Trooper left me feeling like I might just be the luckiest guy on Planet Earth. I've learned that's one of many things smoke jumpers do for their fellow firefighters.

The End

About the Editor

Editor Steve Owen first met Dorcey Wingo in the early '60s at Las Cruces High School, New Mexico, and was awed by his performances – musical, artistic, and otherwise. Steve is a Vietnam veteran who served at Qui Nhon and Phu Bai. Steve has spent more than 20 years in mining and civil engineering around the world, plus 10 years of research project work for the Arizona Department of Transportation.

CPSIA information can be obtained
at www.ICGtesting.com
Printed in the USA
LVOW09s0717040218
565231LV00001B/1/P

9 781432 748289